12th International Workshop on Tree Adjoining Grammars and Related Formalisms 2016 (TAG+12)

Dusseldorf, Germany
29 June – 1 July 2016

ISBN: 978-1-5108-2683-0

The 12th International Workshop on Tree Adjoining Grammars and Related Formalisms (TAG+12)

June 29 - July 1, 2016
Heinrich Heine University
Düsseldorf, Germany

Sponsored by

DFG Deutsche
Forschungsgemeinschaft

SFB 991

HEINRICH HEINE
UNIVERSITÄT DÜSSELDORF

Preface

Welcome to TAG+12, the 12th International Workshop on TAG and related formalisms!

The TAG+ workshop series was inaugurated in 1990 at Dagstuhl, and this year, the 12th workshop returns to Germany for the third time, to the Heinrich Heine University Düsseldorf. We received 18 submissions and accepted 12, forming what we believe is an outstanding program spanning the areas of formal language theory, theoretical syntax and semantics, discourse, and statistical grammar induction and grammar development.

ChungHye Han (Simon Fraser University) and Daniel Bauer and Owen Rambow (Columbia University) will provide tutorials on synchronous TAG semantics and graph grammars, respectively. Marco Kuhlmann and Stephen Clark will deliver keynote talks, both combining ideas from the TAG and CCG literature – Kuhlmann on the formal relationship between CCGs and TAGs, Clark on neural models for CCG supertagging and parsing.

This year seemed to us to be a time of transition, both in natural language processing as well as in the tree adjoining grammars community. As such, we have selected tutorials and invited talks that emphasize the related formalisms, while maintaining the connection to TAG. We also thought that it would be productive to set aside blocks of time for discussion using the *Open Space* format. We look forward to these discussions and hope that they will help set a course for future research directions.

We would like to express our heartfelt gratitude to everyone who helped make TAG+12 happen. We were supported by a wonderful program committee, who helped put together an excellent program. We are also deeply grateful to the local organizers, chaired by Laura Kallmeyer, who were a joy to work with, and who were sure have put together a flawlessly organized conference. This TAG+ workshop is supported by the German Science Foundation (DFG) funded CRC 991 and DFG-funded project "BeyondCFG".

Finally we are happy to announce that primarily through the efforts of the TAG+12 publications chair, Wolfgang Maier, nearly all of the proceedings of past TAG/TAG+ workshops are being made freely available online in the ACL Anthology (`aclweb.org/anthology`).

We wish you an enjoyable conference!

David Chiang and Alexander Koller
TAG+12 Program Chairs

Program chairs:

David Chiang, University of Notre Dame (USA)
Alexander Koller, University of Potsdam (Germany)

Invited Speakers:

Stephen Clark, University of Cambridge (UK)
Marco Kuhlmann, Linköping University (Sweden)

Tutorial Speakers:

Chung-Hye Han, Simon Fraser University (Canada)
Daniel Bauer, Columbia University (USA)

Program committee:

Anne Abeillé, University Paris VII (France)
Srinivas Bangalore, Interactions Labs (USA)
Daniel Bauer, Columbia University (USA)
Tilman Becker, DFKI (Germany)
Rajesh Bhatt, University of Massachusetts (USA)
David Chiang, University of Notre Dame (USA)
Stephen Clark, University of Cambridge (UK)
Vera Demberg, Saarland University (UK)
Frank Drewes, Ume University (Sweden)
Robert Frank, Yale University (USA)
Claire Gardent, CNRS/LORIA, Nancy (France)
Daniel Gildea, University of Rochester (USA)
Chung-Hye Han, Simon Fraser University (Canada)
Liang Huang, Oregon State University (USA)
Aravind Joshi, University of Pennsylvania (USA)
Laura Kallmeyer, University of Düsseldorf (Germany)
Makoto Kanazawa, National Institute of Informatics (Japan)
Alexander Koller, Universität Potsdam (Germany)
Marco Kuhlmann, Linköping University (Sweden)
Adam Lopez, University of Edinburgh (UK)
Andreas Maletti, University of Stuttgart (Germany)
Yusuke Miyao, National Institute of Informatics (Japan)
Mark-Jan Nederhof, University of St. Andrews (UK)
Owen Rambow, Columbia University (USA)

Maribel Romero, University of Konstanz (Germany)
Sylvain Salvati, INRIA Bordeaux Sud-Ouest (France)
Anoop Sarkar, Simon Fraser University (Canada)
Tatjana Scheffler, University of Potsdam (Germany)
William Schuler, Ohio State University (USA)
Mark Steedman, University of Edinburgh (UK)
Matthew Stone, Rutgers University (UK)
Heiko Vogler, TU Dresden (Germany)
Bonnie Webber, University of Edinburgh (UK)
Luke Zettlemoyer, University of Washington (USA)

Local committee:

Laura Kallmeyer (chair)
Kata Balogh
Alexander Diez
Timm Lichte
Wolfgang Maier
Rainer Osswald
Simon Petitjean
Younes Samih
Christian Wurm

Table of Contents

Conference Program

Wednesday, June 29, 2016

9:00–9:10   *Opening* (ULB Düsseldorf 24.41)

9:10–10:35   **Tutorial** (ULB Düsseldorf 24.41)
Synchronizing Structure and Meaning in Tree Adjoining Grammars
Chung-Hye Han

10:35–11:05   *Break*

11:05–12:30   **Tutorial** (ULB Düsseldorf 24.41)
Beyond Strings and Trees Hyperedge Replacement Grammars for Syntax and Semantics
Daniel Bauer

12:30–14:00   *Lunch*

14:00–15:00   *Open Space setup (ULB Düsseldorf 24.41)*

15:00–16:00   *Open Space session 1 (26.21.01.32, 26.21.01.33, 26.21.01.34)*

16:00–17:00   *Open Space session 2 (26.21.01.32, 26.21.01.33, 26.21.01.34)*

Thursday, June 30, 2016

9:00–10:30   **Invited Talk** (ULB Düsseldorf 24.41)
Distant Cousins. The equivalence of TAG and CCG revisited
Marco Kuhlmann

10:30–11:00   *Break*

11:00–12:30   **Session: Syntax/Semantics** (ULB Düsseldorf 24.41)

11:00–11:30   *Modelling the ziji Blocking Effect and Constraining Bound Variable Derivations in MCTAG with Delayed Locality*
Dennis Ryan Storoshenko

11:30–12:00   *Parasitic Gaps and the Heterogeneity of Dependency Formation in STAG*
Dennis Ryan Storoshenko and Robert Frank

12:00–12:30   *Hyperedge Replacement and Nonprojective Dependency Structures*
Daniel Bauer and Owen Rambow

12:30–14:00   *Lunch*

14:00–15:00   **Session: Discourse** (ULB Düsseldorf 24.41)

14:00–14:30   *Interfacing Sentential and Discourse TAG-based Grammars*
Laurence Danlos, Aleksandre Maskharashvili and Sylvain Pogodalla

14:30–15:00   *Modelling Discourse in STAG: Subordinate Conjunctions and Attributing Phrases*
Timothée Bernard and Laurence Danlos

15:00–15:30   *Break*

15:30–17:00   *Open Space regrouping (ULB Düsseldorf 24.41)*

15:30–17:00   *Open Space session 3 (23.21.U1.91, 23.21.U1.93)*

17:00–18:00   *Break*

18:00–20:00   *Sightseeing tour*

20:00   *Dinner*

Friday, July 1, 2016

9:00–10:30   **Invited Talk** (ULB Düsseldorf 24.41)
Neural Models for CCG Parsing and Supertagging
Stephen Clark

10:30–11:00   *Break*

11:00–12:30   **Session: Grammar Induction and Parsing** (ULB Düsseldorf 24.41)

11:00–11:30   *Node-Based Induction of Tree-Substitution Grammars*
Rose Sloan

11:30–12:00   *Revisiting Supertagging and Parsing: How to Use Supertags in Transition-Based Parsing*
Wonchang Chung, Siddhesh Suhas Mhatre, Alexis Nasr, Owen Rambow and Srinivas Bangalore

12:00–12:30   *An Alternate View on Strong Lexicalization in TAG*
Aniello De Santo, Alëna Aksënova and Thomas Graf

12:30–14:00   *Lunch*

14:00–15:00   **Session: Grammar Development** (ULB Düsseldorf 24.41)

14:00–14:30   *ArabTAG: from a Handcrafted to a Semiautomatically Generated TAG*
Chérifa Ben Khelil, Denys Duchier, Yannick Parmentier, Chiraz Ben Othmane Zribi and Fériel Ben Fraj

14:30–15:00   *Argument linking in LTAG: A constraint based implementation with XMG*
Laura Kallmeyer, Timm Lichte, Rainer Osswald and Simon Petitjean

15:00–15:30   *Break*

15:30–16:30   **Session: Syntax** (ULB Düsseldorf 24.41)

15:30–16:00   *Coordination in Minimalist Grammars: Excorporation and Across the Board (Head) Movement*
John Torr and Edward Stabler

16:00–16:30   *Verbal fields in Hungarian simple sentences and infinitival clausal complements*
Kata Balogh

16:30   *Closing*

Coordination in Minimalist Grammars: Excorporation and Across the Board (Head) Movement

John Torr
School of Informatics
University of Edinburgh
11 Crichton Street, Edinburgh, UK
john.torr@cantab.net

Edward P. Stabler
Nuance Communications
1198 E Arques Ave
Sunnyvale, CA 94085
stabler@ucla.edu

Abstract

This paper describes how coordination has been integrated into a broad coverage statistical Minimalist Grammar parser currently under development, and presents a unified analysis for a number of coordinate (and related) constructions sometimes considered problematic for transformational syntax; these include across-the-board (ATB) head and phrasal movements, argument cluster coordination, right node raising and parasitic gaps. To accommodate all these structures, a number of novel extensions are introduced into the formalism, including a mechanism for *excorporation* which enables ATB head movement; this supplements a variant of Kobele's (2008) mechanism for ATB phrasal movement. The weak expressive power of the formalism is shown to be unaffected by these extensions.

1 Introduction and Background

This paper documents the core mechanisms that have been implemented within *MGParse*, a broad coverage (Extended Directional) Minimalist Grammar (MG) parser currently being developed at the University of Edinburgh[1]. Minimalist Grammars (Stabler, 1997) are formally a kind of highly succinct and lexicalized Multiple Context Free Grammar (Seki et al. 1991), and constitute a mildly context sensitive interpretation of many aspects of Chomsky's (1995) Minimalist Program. The mechanisms presented below enable MGParse to generate structures for a range of coordination (and related) phenomena sometimes considered problematic for movement-based approaches to syntax. For example, Gazdar et

al. (1985) state that "transformational grammar has never been able to capture a unitary notion of coordination, for reasons that were endemic to the framework." Considered particularly troublesome are constructions which involve movement to a single position of two or more constituents which do not stand in a c-command[2] relation with one another, as shown in schematic form in fig 1.

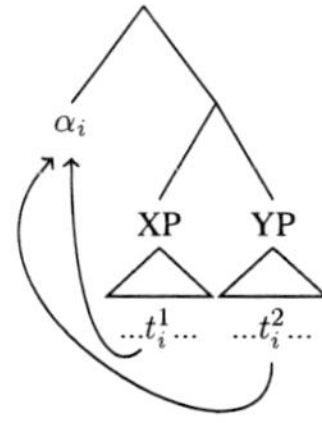

Figure 1: Across-the-board Movement Schema

Examples of constructions arguably involving this configuration are given below[3]:

1. I know who$_i$ [$_{TP}$ Jack likes t$_i$] and [$_{TP}$ Mary hates t$_i$].   (ATB Phrasal Movement)

2. Who$_i$ does$_j$ [$_{TP}$ Jack t$_j$ like t$_i$] and [$_{TP}$ Mary t$_j$ hate t$_i$]?   (ATB Head and Phrasal Movement)

3. [$_{TP}$ [$_{TP}$ Jack likes t$_i$] and [$_{TP}$ Mary hates t$_i$], [Pete's sister]$_i$].   (Right Node Raising)

4. He [$_{vP}$ gave$_i$ [$_{VP}$ Pete t$_i$ a book] and [$_{VP}$ Mary t$_i$ a flower]].   (Argument Cluster Coordination)

One approach to ATB phenomena has been to introduce a mechanism of *sideward movement* (Nunes (1995), (2001), (2004)) into the grammar.

---

[1]MGParse extends Harkema's (2001) CKY variant.

[2]A node c-commands its sister and its sister's descendants.

[3]We adopt the Verb Phrase Internal Subject Hypothesis (Koopman and Sportiche, 1991), according to which AGENTs are generated in the verb phrase before moving to their surface subject position. We also adopt the Movement Theory of Control (Hornstein (2001)), which avoids the need for additional meaning postulates to derive indices on PRO, which is now simply treated as a trace of A-movement.

Proceedings of the 12th International Workshop on Tree Adjoining Grammars and Related Formalisms (TAG+12), pages 1–17,
Düsseldorf, Germany, June 29 - July 1, 2016.

This operation moves elements cyclically between trees before those trees are merged together into a single structure. For example, in fig 1, α could first move sidewards from t^2 to t^1 prior to the merger of XP with YP, before undergoing standard (upward) movement to its final surface position.

Two further constructions that have been argued to involve sideward movements, and hence the configuration in fig 1, are adjunct control and parasitic gap structures, as in 5 and 6.

5. $[_{TP}$ He$_i$ $[_{vP}$ $[_{vP}$ t$_i$ filed the paper] $[_{PP}$ without $[_{vP}$ t$_i$ reading it]]]]. (Adjunct Control)

6. [Which paper]$_i$ did $[_{TP}$ he$_j$ $[_{vP}$ $[_{vP}$ t$_j$ file t$_i$] $[_{PP}$ without $[_{vP}$ t$_j$ reading t$_i$]]]]? (Parasitic Gap)

Under certain assumptions, both 5 and 6 feature movement out of an adjunct in apparent violation of Huang's (1982) *Condition on Extraction Domains* (CED). However, if these movements occur prior to adjunction[4] taking place, i.e. before the adjunct PP actually becomes an adjunct, then arguably CED is never violated. Stabler (2006) shows how sideward movement can be incorporated into MGs to accommodate just such an analysis of adjunct control. Unfortunately, this formulation of sideward movement is severely restricted to moving just a single element as an integral part of adjunction. As a result, it cannot accommodate example 6 which involves *two* elements moving out of the adjunct.

Kobele (2008) introduces an approach to leftward ATB phrasal movement for MGs which can accommodate these cases by 'unifying' any identical movers inside the dependent and main clause structures. However, Kobele does not extend his analysis to examples arguably involving ATB head movement (2 and 4) or Right Node Raising (RNR) (3). Moreover, as things stand, this system also appears to overgenerate 7 below, which features illicit ATB leftward phrasal movement from two different structural case positions.

7. *I know who$_i$ $[_{TP}$ Jack likes t$_i$] and $[_{TP}$ t$_i$ hates Mary].

To accommodate such examples, we will augment Kobele's system with mechanisms for rightward movement, case valuation and excorpora-

tion[5]. Excorporation is argued to exist for example in Roberts (2010) in the context of a discussion of Romance clitics such as the French object pronoun 'l' in *je l'ai vu* (*I have seen him/her*). Clitics are interesting because they behave like heads in being affixal and adjoining to other heads, but they are also capable of moving over much greater distances than typical heads and in this sense behave more like phrases. Here, for instance, the clitic has moved from the object position, past its governing verb, and adjoined to the auxiliary. This, Roberts argues, is achieved via excorporation, which here we will extend to cases of ATB head movement.

The rest of the paper is arranged as follows: section 2 introduces the MG formalism together with some extensions; next, section 3 provides a general framework for coordination; section 4 then presents the analysis of ATB phenomena; finally, section 5 concludes the paper.

2 Minimalist Grammars

2.1 Introduction to MGs

Minimalist Grammars (Stabler, 1997) are a derivational, lexicalized and feature-driven formalism. Structures are built bottom up using the two operations of binary merge and unary move, which each check and delete features on lexical items and derived constituents, while reordering and concatenating strings. Each partially built structure is represented in the collapsed tree format of Stabler (2001a) and Harkema (2001), in which the actual geometry of derived phrase structure is largely discarded[6] and only the strings/spans and features of the head and any moving elements are retained. For instance, consider the collapsed tree representation for the vP *Jack helped who* in which *who* and *Jack* will later move to check -wh and -case respectively:

[[cause] *help* : +case v, *who* : -wh, *Jack* : -case]

Each collapsed tree, or *expression*, is composed of between 1 and $k + 1$ *chains*, where k is the size

---

[4]Here and throughout, *adjunction* refers to the merger of an adjunct dependent with a main structure and should not be confused with the operation by that name used in Tree Adjoining Grammar.

[5]Two further important differences between Kobele's framework and ours are: 1. We do not adopt a GPSG-style slash-feature mechanism; and 2. We do not handle control into complements via ATB movement (this is reserved for control into adjuncts); instead, we allow selectee x features (see section 2.2) to persist as licensees after initial selection and to check further selector =x/x= features (now also control licensors) via standard movement; for complement control, the base position of the controller therefore always c-commands the base position of the controllee in our system.

[6]The full derived phrase structure tree, with indices, is deterministically recoverable from the derivation tree.

of the set of licensee features[7]. The first chain of the expression (here, [cause] *help* : +case v) is the head of the expression, while any other chains are movers (their ordering being irrelevant). Each chain is in turn composed of a string and a feature sequence. Moving chains are kept separate only until their syntactic features have all been checked and deleted, at which time their strings are concatenated with the head chain's string and they cease to exist. Importantly, the collapsed tree representation entails that MGs as defined above are type-driven as opposed to structure-driven: all of the information that is input to the rules is contained within the category labels themselves. As well as affording MGs some important computational advantages (the set of MG derivation trees is a regular set), this fact will be crucial in the account of coordination that follows.

2.2 A simple Directional MG

A Directional Minimalist Grammar (DMG)[8] is defined as a quadruple (V, Cat, Lex, F) s.t.[9]:

1. $V = P \cup I$ is a finite set of non-syntactic features (P = phonetic features, I = semantic features).

2. $Cat = selectees \cup selectors \cup licensees \cup licensors$ is a finite set of syntactic features, s.t. for each feature $x \in selectees$ there are features $(=x, x=) \in selectors$, and for each feature $-y \in licensees$ there is a feature $+y \in licensors$.

3. Lex is a finite set of axioms (lexical items) over $V \cup Cat$, with the Cat features on each simplex tree strictly ordered from left to right.

4. F is a set consisting of the structure building functions $MERGE$ and $MOVE$ (the deductive rules of inference), defined as the union of their respective sub-functions, given in figures 2 and 3, where expressions are contained within square brackets, chains are separated by commas, $\alpha_1, ..., \alpha_k$ is a (possibly empty) set of moving chains, δ and γ are feature sequence suffix variables, with $|\delta| \geq 1$ and $|\gamma| \geq 0$, s and t are string variables, and string/feature separators indicate whether a chain represents an unmerged lexical head (::) or a derived element (:), or can be either (;).

$$\frac{[s::x= \gamma] \quad [t\,;\,x,\ \alpha_1, ..., \alpha_k]}{[st:\gamma,\ \alpha_1, ..., \alpha_k]}(merge1(comp))$$

$$\frac{[t\,;\,x,\ \alpha_1, ..., \alpha_k] \quad [s::\,=x\ \gamma]}{[ts:\gamma,\ \alpha_1, ..., \alpha_k]}(merge2(comp))$$

$$\frac{[t\,;\,x] \quad [s:\,=x\ \gamma,\ \alpha_1, ..., \alpha_k]}{[ts:\gamma,\ \alpha_1, ..., \alpha_k]}(merge3(spec))$$

$$\frac{[s::x= \gamma] \quad [t\,;\,x\ \delta,\ \alpha_1, ..., \alpha_k]}{[s:\gamma,\ t:\delta,\ \alpha_1, ..., \alpha_k]}(merge4(comp))$$

$$\frac{[t\,;\,x\ \delta,\ \alpha_1, ..., \alpha_k] \quad [s::\,=x\ \gamma]}{[s:\gamma,\ t:\delta,\ \alpha_1, ..., \alpha_k]}(merge5(comp))$$

$$\frac{[t\,;\,x\ \delta] \quad [s:\,=x\ \gamma,\ \alpha_1, ..., \alpha_k]}{[s:\gamma,\ t:\delta,\ \alpha_1, ..., \alpha_k]}(merge6(spec))$$

Figure 2: Sub-functions of MERGE

$$\frac{[s:+f\ \gamma,\ \alpha_1, ..., \alpha_{i-1},\ t:-f,\ \alpha_{i+1}, ..., \alpha_k]}{[ts:\gamma,\ \alpha_1, ..., \alpha_{i-1}, \alpha_{i+1}, ..., \alpha_k]}(move1)$$

$$\frac{[s:+f\ \gamma,\ \alpha_1, ..., \alpha_{i-1},\ t:-f\ \delta,\ \alpha_{i+1}, ..., \alpha_k]}{[s:\gamma,\ \alpha_1, ..., \alpha_{i-1},\ t:\delta,\ \alpha_{i+1}, ..., \alpha_k]}(move2)$$

Figure 3: Sub-functions of MOVE

For a given Minimalist Grammar $G = Lex$, the language $L(G)$ is the closure of Lex under the structure building functions $\{MERGE, MOVE\}$ in accordance with the Shortest Move Constraint:

The Shortest Move Constraint (SMC): no expression may contain two chains with precisely the same initial feature.

Notice that only where a selector is a head word/morpheme (and so consequently contains no movers) can its selectee contain movers. This encodes the specifier part of CED, according to which only complements ($\approx$objects) allow extraction of their contents, not specifiers ($\approx$subjects) (or adjuncts[10]). A complement is formally defined as the first argument dependent to be merged

---

[7]Licensee features are located on moving elements. In LCFRS terminology, $k + 1$ = the *fan-out* of the grammar.

[8]Directional MGs are MGs in which the directionality of selection is determined by a feature on the selecting head, rather than by the complement vs. adjunct/specifier status of the dependent. Following Ernst (2002), and contra Kayne's (1994) LCA, we therefore allow both leftward *and* rightward complements and adjuncts, as well as rightward movement to adjoined positions. There is good evidence for the non-existence of rightward specifiers, however (perhaps for processing reasons), such as the lack of reverse V2 languages and the extreme marginality of OS languages; these are therefore currently disallowed by MGParse. Note that Directional MGs are similar to Categorial Grammars up to movement.

[9]In order to unify the notation for merge and move, we adopt the convention that all diacritics appear on the side of the Part of Speech (PoS) symbol on which selection occurs; hence x= indicates rightward selection, =x leftward selection.

[10]Adjuncts are discussed in section 2.3.1.

[*who* :: d -wh]   [[pres] :: v= +case t]
[*Jack* :: d -case]   [[int] :: t= +wh c]
[*likes* :: d= =d v]

Table 1: A DMG lexicon

with a head; all subsequently merged arguments are specifiers. With the simple lexicon in table 1, this grammar will generate the derivation tree in fig 4 for the embedded clause *who Jack likes*[11].

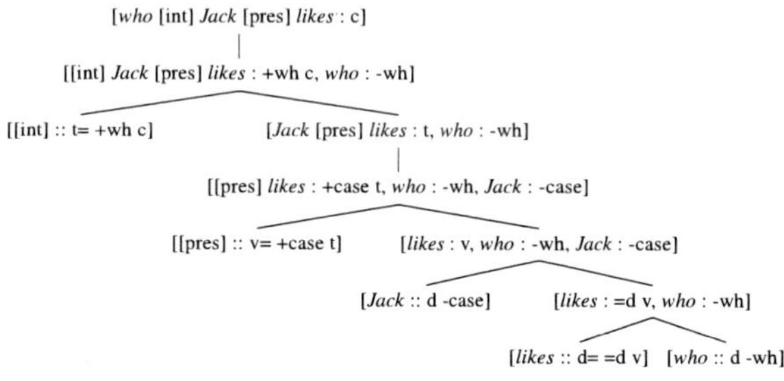

Figure 4: DMG Derivation tree for *who Jack likes*

2.3 Extending a Directional MG

MGParse incorporates a number of extensions to the simple DMG presented above which are discussed briefly below. We will refer to a DMG which includes these and the mechanisms to be introduced in sections 3 and 4 as an Extended Directional Minimalist Grammar (EDMG).

2.3.1 Adjunction

Linguists have proposed that in addition to complements and specifiers, a third type of *adjunct* dependent can be distinguished. Adjuncts are usually (though not exclusively) semantically adverbial, and include adverbs themselves as well as modificational PPs and (at least some) relative clauses. They also display the following properties: they are usually optional, iterative, type-preserving and opaque to extraction (CED). MG-Parse incorporates the approach to leftward adjunction of Frey and Gärtner (F&G) (2002) and extends it with rightward adjunction. F&G introduce a new category into the lexicon, which we will refer to here as an *adjunctizer*. Adjunctizers select other categories which are then effectively transformed into adjuncts; they can be null or overt. Below are the categories for two adjunc-

---

[11]Head strings enclosed in square brackets indicate silent morphemes; t = *tense*; c = *complementizer*.

tizers which map clauses (CPs) and PPs respectively into rightward adjuncts that adjoin to VPs.

[*because* :: c= ≈v]   [[adjunctizer] :: p= ≈v]

We must also add the ADJOIN rules in fig 5 to the grammar to accommodate the new ≈x/x≈ adjunction selector features. Notice that these rules involve *asymmetric* checking in contrast to the earlier MERGE rules: only the selector feature, not the selectee feature, is deleted; this captures the optional, iterative and type-preserving properties of adjunction. Note also that this time the head features of the mother derive from the selectee not the selector, making the selectee the head. Consequently, only the selectee may contain movers, thereby observing CED.

$$\frac{[t\,;\,x\approx]\quad[s\,;\,x\,\gamma,\,\alpha_1,\,...,\,\alpha_k]}{[ts\colon x\,\gamma,\,\alpha_1,\,...,\,\alpha_k]}(adjoin1)$$

$$\frac{[s\,;\,x\,\gamma,\,\alpha_1,\,...,\,\alpha_k]\quad[t\,;\,\approx\!x]}{[st\colon x\,\gamma,\,\alpha_1,\,...,\,\alpha_k]}(adjoin2)$$

$$\frac{[t\,;\,x\approx\,\delta]\quad[s\,;\,x\,\gamma,\,\alpha_1,\,...,\,\alpha_k]}{[s\colon x\,\gamma,\,t\colon\delta,\,\alpha_1,\,...,\,\alpha_k]}(adjoin3)$$

$$\frac{[s\,;\,x\,\gamma,\,\alpha_1,\,...,\,\alpha_k]\quad[t\,;\,\approx\!x\,\delta]}{[s\colon x\,\gamma,\,t\colon\delta,\,\alpha_1,\,...,\,\alpha_k]}(adjoin4)$$

Figure 5: Sub-functions of ADJOIN

2.3.2 Rightward Movement

Rightward movement was at one time the standard tool in analyses of constructions such as heavy NP shift and extraposition, but the rise in popularity of Kayne's (1994) Linear Correspondence Axiom resulted in its almost total abandonment in Minimalism[12]. However, abandoning rightward movement often necessitates using additional silent heads and elaborate sequences of multiple (remnant) leftward movements for what is intuitively a single weight-theoretic requirement: that a heavy constituent appear sentence-finally. We therefore retain rightward movement (of phonetic features only) to adjoined positions. To do this we adapt F&G's (2002) approach to German leftward scrambling, which makes use of a ~x scrambling licensee, and introduce the rightward movement licensee x~. Selectee x features will now serve a second purpose as licensors for rightward movement. The R_MOVE rule is given in fig 6.

---

[12]Ernst 2002 is a notable exception.

$$\frac{[s:x\,\gamma,\ \alpha_1, ..., \alpha_{i-1},\ t:x{\sim},\ \alpha_{i+1}, ..., \alpha_k]}{[st:x\,\gamma,\ \alpha_1, ..., \alpha_{i-1}, \alpha_{i+1}, ..., \alpha_k]}$$

Figure 6: R_MOVE

$x{\sim}$ features enter the derivation on null *extraposer* heads which map items into rightward-moving versions of themselves. For example, the category for an extraposer causing a DP to move rightward and adjoin to the closest dominating TP is: [[extraposer] :: d= +case d -case t$\sim$][13].

Note that we can obtain a *Right Roof Constraint*[14] (RRC) (Ross, 1967) preventing rightward movement from crossing (non-small, non-defective[15]) clause boundaries by assuming that $x{\sim}$ features cannot persist, i.e. they always delete immediately upon being checked.

2.3.3 Head Movement

MGParse incorporates Stabler's (2001b) head movement rules. Head movement is a highly local operation that causes the head of a selector's complement to adjoin to the head of the selector as an integral part of MERGE, the vanilla case being subject-auxiliary inversion in English main clause questions. Stabler's key insight is that the lexical head string of an expression must be kept separate from its left and right dependent strings until that expression has itself been merged/adjoined as a dependent, in case the head has to move. We therefore introduce new feature diacritics $>$ and $<$ to indicate head movement with adjunction onto either the left or the right of a governing head. Fig 7 gives the MERGE rules for rightward selection with leftward adjoining head movement.

$$\frac{[(e,s_h,e)::\,{>}x{=}\ \gamma]\quad [(t_l,t_h,t_r)\,;x,\ \alpha_1, ..., \alpha_k]}{[(e,t_hs_h,t_lt_r):\gamma,\ \alpha_1, ..., \alpha_k]}(merge\_hm1)$$

$$\frac{[(e,s_h,e)::\,{>}x{=}\ \gamma]\quad [(t_l,t_h,t_r)\,;x\,\delta,\ \alpha_1, ..., \alpha_k]}{[(e,t_hs_h,e):\gamma,\ (t_lt_r):\delta,\ \alpha_1, ..., \alpha_k]}(merge\_hm2)$$

Figure 7: MERGE_HM functions for rightward selection with leftward adjoining head movement

2.3.4 Covert Movement

MGParse includes covert movement rules to accommodate a range of phenomena including apparent long-distance agreement[16], case checking of prepositional objects and Quantifier Raising in a strictly monotonic/type-driven system. We follow Stabler (1997) in treating covert movement as moving just syntactic (and semantic) features, not phonetic features (cf. Chomsky's (1995) Move-F). The applicability of overt vs. covert movement is determined by the licensor feature: +f licenses covert movement and +F overt movement. Merge rules are added to the grammar splitting an expression into its syntactic and phonetic parts. For example, merge4 and merge5 have the corresponding *phonetic merge* rules in fig 8 which fuse the selectee's string to the selector's head chain but keep the selectee's syntactic features separate.

$$\frac{[s::x{=}\ \gamma]\quad [t\,;x\,\delta,\ \alpha_1, ..., \alpha_k]}{[st:\gamma,\ e:\delta,\ \alpha_1, ..., \alpha_k]}(p\_merge1(comp))$$

$$\frac{[t\,;x\,\delta,\ \alpha_1, ..., \alpha_k]\quad [s::\,{=}x\,\gamma]}{[ts:\gamma,\ e:\delta,\ \alpha_1, ..., \alpha_k]}(p\_merge2(comp))$$

Figure 8: Two sub-functions of P_MERGE

The moving chains now contain no phonetic material, and so their movements will not be visible in the string, but may have an impact on the semantics. Note that since it is licensors, not licensees, which determine whether movement is overt or covert, both MERGE and P_MERGE options initially have to be pursued by the system.

3   Coordination

MGParse's EDMG adopts the binary Xbar theoretic view of coordinate structures[17] proposed most recently by Zhang (2010), in which the coordinator (Coord) is the head, its complement is the rightmost conjunct and all leftward conjuncts are in (multiple) specifier positions. Zhang also assumes that Coord heads inherit the PoS category[18] of their (leftmost) conjuncts, which here we will simply precompile into the lexicon.

We take coordination to be a 'recursive transitive closure over same types' (Partee and Rooth,

---

[13]Note the simulation of feature percolation without actual percolation here. This is desirable since Kobele (2005) shows that genuine feature percolation results in Type 0 MGs. This mechanism is also used by MGParse to achieve pied-piping, e.g., of *to* by *whom* in *to whom did you complain?*

[14]Whether the RRC actually exists has been contested (see e.g. Gazdar (1981)). However, for the purposes of practical parsing, this constraint significantly improves efficiency and hence is currently adopted by MGParse.

[15]Defective clauses are bare TPs lacking a CP layer (standardly assumed to exist in ECM and raising structures).

[16]Note that Chomsky's (2000) long-distance Agree operation is non-monotonic and structure-driven rather than type-driven, hence incompatible here.

[17]See Appendix C for a discussion of the problem posed by lexical X^0 head coordination for Xbar theoretic accounts.

[18]Selectee x features indicate PoS category in MGs.

1983), where 'type' here refers to the cluster of syntactic features on the entire expression (though see Appendix B), not just the PoS/selectee feature of its head chain. The abstract feature sequence schema for all coordinators is: $x = =\bar{x} \; x$[19]. This is similar to the Combinatory Categorial Grammar (CCG) (Steedman, 2000) approach to coordination, except that here it is not formally treated as involving adjunction, and full type uniformity is not enforced by the selector features alone, but instead falls out from the interaction of two constraints on rules: CED, and the Coordinate Structure Constraint (CSC) (Ross, 1967) (see Appendix B on the like-types constraint)[20].

One problem for the analysis so far if we assume that all D elements carry -case is that this needs to be checked for all DP conjuncts. We cannot achieve this by adding covert +case features to the Coord head because this would require the use of potentially infinite sequences of the form $(=d +case)^+$ to ensure that all specifier conjuncts can check case without triggering SMC. To solve this problem, we exploit a null prepositional dative head, independently used by MGParse to avoid SMC violations in *promise*-type subject control structures[21]. This head has the category [[dat] :: d= +case p], which covertly[22] checks the -case feature of its DP complement; the resulting PP is then selected by a P-selecting Coord with PoS category D (i.e. with a d selectee feature).

Notice that this implies that coordinators are able to inherit the PoS category of their complement's complement (D), rather than that of the complement (P) itself. Again, we simply pre-compile this into the lexicon, permitting coordinate schemas of the form $[x^T = =\bar{x}^T \; y]$ where the PoS category of the coordinator differs from that of its conjuncts. Since we do not formally treat coordination as adjunction, sacrificing this aspect of type-preservation becomes possible[23]. Interestingly, this move may not be entirely ad hoc: arguably, *Jack and me went home* is more natural than the prescriptively 'correct' *Jack and I went home*, as evidenced by the fact that *I and Jack went home* seems awkward, whereas *me and Jack went home* is informal but perfectly fine. This is explained if nominal conjuncts in English are in fact PPs with null dative case-checking P heads.

A further problem for the analysis of coordination so far is that there exist structures which do not appear to adhere to the like-types restriction on conjuncts, such as 8 below.

8. Jack is [$_{VP}$ working] and [$_{PP}$ in the garden].

9. *Jack [$_{VP}$ works] and [$_{PP}$ in the garden].

As 9 indicates, coordination of a VP with a PP is generally not permitted, and yet in 8 it is allowed. It is in fact a general feature of the verb *be* that its complement can be a coordinate phrase with apparently unlike conjuncts. However, somewhat tellingly, only predicative categories can be coordinated following *be*. For instance, while *Jack is happy and in the garden* is fine, **Jack is happily and in the garden* is ungrammatical because *happily* is adverbial rather than predicative. In fact, only VPs, PPs, AdjPs and DPs can be coordinated in this way. One approach pursued in the literature (e.g. Jacobson (1987)) is therefore to assume that the expressions entering into such coordinate structures are in fact of the same super Prd category. We implement this here by adding the null *predicatizers* in table 2 to our lexicon[24].

[[prd] :: d= +case =d prd]	[[prd] :: >v= =d prd]
[[prd] :: p= =d prd]	[[prd] :: adj= =d prd]

Table 2: Predicatizers

These are essentially unary functions which map expressions of a given PoS category into expressions with the Prd PoS category[25]. We can

---

[19]The overline is a diacritic enabling =x selector features to optionally persist after checking to generate structures such as *Jack, Pete and Mary*. Note that examples with multiple conjuncts such as *Jack and Pete and Mary* are also generated: CoordP with D conjuncts is in reality just DP, hence it can be selected as the complement of a higher D-selecting Coord head.

[20]Unlike in CCG, selector features in MGs are never complex, i.e. we cannot define an abstract coordinator category equivalent to $(X\backslash X)/X$ and then reify it as, e.g., $((S/NP)\backslash(S/NP))/(S/NP)$ where both conjuncts are specified as being clauses containing object holes/traces; all we can specify is that both conjuncts are clauses (i.e. that they have a c selectee as their first feature), using the sequence: $c = =\bar{c} \; c$. We can, however, ensure that a pair of MG expressions entering into a binary merge rule have identical sets of moving chains (see section 4.1 on ATB); this, together with CED and CSC as constraints on the form of MERGE rules, derives the like-types constraint on conjuncts (see Appendix B).

[21]This implements an analysis in Boeckx et al. (2010).

[22]All prepositions are assumed here to trigger *covert* movement of their objects to spec-P to check case, since overt movement would yield postpositions (this only really matters for overt prepositions of course).

[23]We must, however, impose heavy restrictions in the lexicon to rule out many unwanted cases here.

[24]Observe that each [prd] element base generates the DP subject as its specifier.

[25]A similar approach incorporating null adverbializing

then simply coordinate the resulting PrdPs in the usual manner[26].

4 ATB Head and Phrasal Movement

4.1 ATB Phrasal Movement

Consider deriving just the embedded clause from example 1, given as 10 below.

10. who_i $[_{TP}$ Jack likes $t_i]$ and $[_{TP}$ Mary hates $t_i]$.

In terms of the schema in fig 1, *who* corresponds to α_i and the two TP conjuncts to XP and YP. Recall that our problem here is to derive the fact that the two traces have only one overt antecedent and yet neither c-commands the other. Adapting an approach in Kobele (2008), we can accomplish this as follows: first we construct each TP conjunct (cf. fig 4 up to the first unary branching node). This yields the following two expressions:

[*Jack*, [pres], *likes* : t, *who* : -wh]

[*Mary*, [pres], *hates* : t, *who* : -wh]

Next, we merge the right conjunct *Mary hates who* as the complement of the conjunction [*and* :: t= =t̄ t], which after feature deletion yields:

[*and, Mary* [pres] *hates* : =t̄ t, *who* : -wh]

This is where things become interesting. Notice that when the conjunction head merged with its complement, the mover inside the complement was transferred into the resulting expression. If this were to also happen when we merged the specifier, the result would be an SMC violation as we would now have two elements in the same tree whose first feature was -wh. Moreover, transferring a mover out of a specifier is in any case impossible with the rules as currently formulated in accordance with CED. To solve this, we will bleed both SMC and CED by allowing the system to simply drop[27] any mover inside any dependent if that mover's features exactly match those of a mover already inside the governing structure. Dropping the occurrence of *who* from the left conjunct and merging the latter into the main structure

will then yield the following TP coordinate phrase, containing only one occurrence of *who*[28]:

[*Jack* [pres] *likes, and, Mary* [pres] *hates* : t, *who* : -wh]

We can now merge this expression with a null interrogative [[int] :: t= +WH c]] head and move *who* to spec-CP in the usual manner. The updated MERGE rules for specifiers are shown in fig 9[29] (along with the updated version of adjoin2, adj_atb1, which derives 5 and 6 - the derivation for 6 is given in Appendix A) where the string (α^s) and syntactic (α^f) parts of the α chains have been separated and identity is enforced only on syntactic features. This is because the same language is generated whether or not we stipulate string identity[30], but not doing so results in a standard MCFG rule and therefore the proof of MCFG-equivalence[31]. Note that by combining mrg_atb1 with the rightward movement mechanism introduced in section 2.3.2, we are also able to generate the RNR in 3 as rightward ATB movement (though see section 4.3 for an alternative analysis).

$$\frac{[l:x,\ \alpha_1^f, ..., \alpha_l^f(\alpha_1^{s\prime}, ..., \alpha_l^{s\prime})]\quad [s: =x\,\gamma,\ \alpha_1^f, ..., \alpha_k^f(\alpha_1^s, ..., \alpha_k^s)]}{[ts:\gamma,\ \alpha_1^f, ..., \alpha_k^f(\alpha_1^s, ..., \alpha_k^s)]} \quad (mrg\_atb1)$$

$$\frac{[t:x\,\delta,\ \alpha_1^f, ..., \alpha_l^f(\alpha_1^{s\prime}, ..., \alpha_l^{s\prime})]\quad [s: =x\,\gamma,\ \alpha_1^f, ..., \alpha_k^f(\alpha_1^s, ..., \alpha_k^s)]}{[s:\gamma,\ t:\delta,\ \alpha_1^f, ..., \alpha_k^f(\alpha_1^s, ..., \alpha_k^s)]} \quad (mrg\_atb2)$$

$$\frac{[s:x\,\gamma,\ \alpha_1^f, ..., \alpha_k^f(\alpha_1^s, ..., \alpha_k^s)]\quad [t: \approx x,\ \alpha_1^f, ..., \alpha_l^f(\alpha_1^{s\prime}, ..., \alpha_l^{s\prime})]}{[st: x\,\gamma,\ \alpha_1^f, ..., \alpha_k^f(\alpha_1^s, ..., \alpha_k^s)]} \quad (adj\_atb1)$$

$$\frac{[s:x\,\gamma,\ \alpha_1^f, ..., \alpha_k^f(\alpha_1^s, ..., \alpha_k^s)]\quad [t: \approx x\,\delta,\ \alpha_1^f, ..., \alpha_l^f(\alpha_1^{s\prime}, ..., \alpha_l^{s\prime})]}{[s: x\,\gamma,\ t:\delta,\ \alpha_1^f, ..., \alpha_k^f(\alpha_1^s, ..., \alpha_k^s)]} \quad (adj\_atb2)$$

Figure 9: Left merge and right adjoin ATB rules

Note that for coordination, we enforce $l = k$ whereas for all other cases $l \leq k$. This ensures

---

[adv] heads, e.g. with category [p= adv], accommodates coordination of unlike modifiers in MGParse: *Jack works happily and with great speed.*

[26] A reviewer notes that an alternative analysis treats unlike coordination as ATB head movement, e.g. of *be* out of multiple remnant coordinated verb phrases which it heads. This is straightforwardly implementable using the mechanism for ATB head movement introduced in section 4.2.

[27] Alternatively, we can see this as the unification of two *sets* of feature sequences, with sets only admitting single instances of their members.

[28] Note that although we drop an occurrence of *who* in the syntax, the fact that in the semantics its trace must be co-indexed with the other trace (and the antecedent) is deterministically recoverable from the derivation tree.

[29] A variant of mrg_atb1 allows =x̄ to persist and generate, e.g., *who does Jack like, Mary hate and Pete despise?*

[30] For practical purposes, however, we allow MGParse to also enforce string identity, since otherwise many partial parses are generated in which a moving substring in the dependent is dropped which does not phonetically match some moving substring in the main structure, and such a strategy can clearly never result in the recognition of a sentence.

[31] If we view the syntactic part of the head chain plus the α^fs as a single atomic category symbol, then all we are saying in effect here is that combining a category of type A with a category of type B results in a category of type C, which is no different from any other MCFG rule. Seki et al.'s (1991) lemma 2.2 shows that banning variables that become erased during a derivation has no effect on expressive power.

that the like-types constraint (see Appendix B) applies only to coordination and not, for instance, to parasitic gaps such as *which celebrity did pictures of disgrace?* or 6 above, where we only require the α^fs in the specifier or adjunct to be a (possibly empty) subset of those in the main structure. That parasitic gaps are not subject to precisely the same constraints as coordination structures is evident from the fact that it is possible to fill a parasitic gap, leaving just the trace in the main clause, as in *which paper did Jack file without reading its title*, whereas we cannot extract from one conjunct but not the others (**who does Jack like and Mary hate Pete*) (part 2 of CSC)[32]; we assume that both parasitic gaps and ATB-coordinate structures involve the ATB-dropping mechanism, but differ in that only coordination is subject to a like-types constraint owing to its semantics.

Finally, recall that example 7 featured illicit coordination of two conjuncts containing traces in different structural case positions. To disallow these structures, we adopt Kobele's (2008) Earley-style dotted feature mechanism so that features remain visible after they are 'deleted'. Additionally, we assume that -case features are valued as acc., nom., gen. etc., when checked. This will then distinguish the two movers in 7 and prevent ATB-drop from applying[33]. To implement this, licensee and licensor features will be split into attribute/value pairs: e.g., -f represents an unvalued licensee feature, while -f^v is the valued equivalent (e.g. -case^{nom}). We then reformulate our rules using this new notation. Fig 10 gives the reformulated version of move-2, showing both the valuation and dotted feature mechanisms, where β and ζ are feature sequence prefix variables. To avoid clutter, for the rest of the discussion we will omit this valuation notation from any rules.

$$\frac{[s:\beta \cdot +f^v\ \gamma,\ \alpha_1, ..., \alpha_{i-1},\ t:\zeta \cdot -f\ \delta,\ \alpha_{i+1}, ..., \alpha_k]}{[s:\beta +f^v \cdot \gamma,\ \alpha_1, ..., \alpha_{i-1},\ t:\zeta -f^v \cdot \delta,\ \alpha_{i+1}, ..., \alpha_k]} (move2')$$

Figure 10: Move-2 with valuation and dotted feature mechanisms

4.2 ATB Head Movement

We still need to derive 2 and 4, both of which by hypothesis involve ATB head movement: T-to-C in 2 and V-to-v in 4. Note that the head movement rules presented in section 2.3.3 are insufficient here because there the moving head fused immediately with the head it adjoined to, making head movement a highly local operation. In general, this appears descriptively correct since heads cannot usually skip other heads (**Have you would helped?*) (cf. Travis' (1984) *Head Movement Constraint*). There are, however, certain arguable exceptions to this constraint, such as clitic climbing in Romance and the ATB head movement in 2 and 4. Consider again example 2, repeated below with the CoordP (in reality a TP) now shown.

2. Who$_j$ does$_i$ [$_{CoordP}$ [$_{TP}$ Jack t$_i$ like t$_j$] [$_{Coord}$ and] [$_{TP}$ Mary t$_i$ hate t$_j$]]?

The derivation for this sentence initially proceeds precisely as in section 4.1 (except that T is now overt). However, when the conjunction head merges with its right TP conjunct, the T head (*does*) of that conjunct will become fused either with its dependents as before or with the Coord head, rendering it inaccessible to C. The situation for the left conjunct is even worse as our rules do not allow for head movement out of specifiers (which would violate CED). Our solution is to extend the grammar with a mechanism for excorporation which allows the head of a complement to move successive cyclically through the governing head rather than incorporating with it (see fig 11).

To implement excorporation, we add a new diacritic ^ to the selector which once again causes the complement's head to move (we also add conjunctions with the feature sequence: ^x= ^=x̄ x). This time, however, the raising head will become

---

[32]We must also ensure that for conjunct (but not other) specifiers, only mrg_atb1 can apply, i.e. |δ| = 0, and similarly for the comp merge rules in fig 2 if the complement is a conjunct. These restrictions capture the fact that while ATB extraction of the identical contents of conjuncts is possible, extraction of conjuncts themselves is not (**who$_i$ does mary like t$_i$ and t$_i$, *who$_i$ does Mary like Pete and t$_i$*) (part 1 of CSC). We achieve these restrictions via the use of a diacritic on coordinator projections. For example, instead of :: and : coordinator projections are marked by ⁛ and ⁚ separators. We can then formulate coordination-specific MERGE rules to ban moving complement and specifier conjuncts.

[33]Gazdar (1981) notes that if either gap is in an embedded clause, it no longer matters if the traces have different structural cases (*I know a man who Mary likes and hopes will win*). MGParse also correctly generates these constructions by assuming that the valuations of case are only temporary, and that as soon as an item moves to a higher landing site it reverts to (checked but unvalued) -case. This, combined with the standard assumption of successive cyclic wh-movement via intermediate spec-CPs (implemented with 'suicidal' licensors (+F$_?$) on intermediate C heads which attract but do not check licensees and which self-delete if they themselves are unchecked), yields the correct result, assuming that -f matches -f^v for ATB-drop. Evidence that case valuation is indeed temporary is provided by the following contrast: **the man whom likes Mary* vs. *the man whom Pete said likes Mary.*

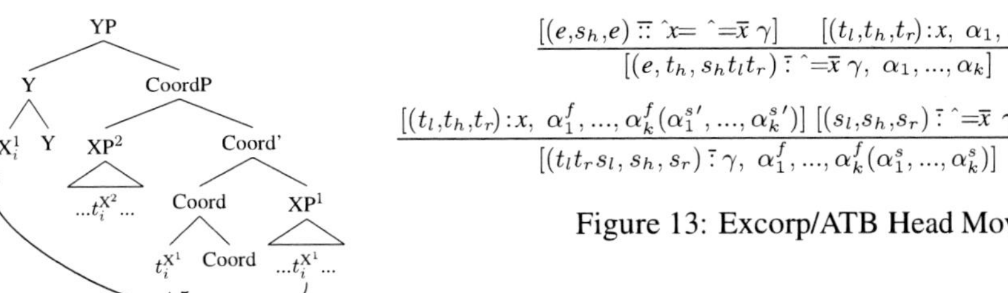

$$\frac{[(e,s_h,e) :: \hat{x}= \hat{}=\bar{x}\ \gamma] \quad [(t_l,t_h,t_r):x,\ \alpha_1,...,\alpha_k]}{[(e,t_h,s_h t_l t_r) : \hat{}=\bar{x}\ \gamma,\ \alpha_1,...,\alpha_k]}\ (mrg\_excorp)$$

$$\frac{[(t_l,t_h,t_r):x,\ \alpha_1^f,...,\alpha_k^f(\alpha_1^{s\prime},...,\alpha_k^{s\prime})]\ [(s_l,s_h,s_r): \hat{}=\bar{x}\ \gamma,\alpha_1^f,...,\alpha_k^f(\alpha_1^s,...,\alpha_k^s)]}{[(t_l t_r s_l, s_h, s_r):\gamma,\ \alpha_1^f,...,\alpha_k^f(\alpha_1^s,...,\alpha_k^s)]}\quad (mrg\_hm\_atb)$$

Figure 13: Excorp/ATB Head Movement Rules

sented in section 2.3.2 could generate RNR structures. However, rightward movement analyses of RNR are not without theoretical problems (see, e.g., Abels (2004) and Gazdar (1981)). For example, it is well known that RNR is always order-preserving, that it does not exhibit many island effects, and that the shared material (which has a focused interpretation) cannot survive VP ellipsis in the rightmost conjunct with which it appears to associate despite also scoping over all traces.

Fortunately, an alternative ATB strategy is available, under which the mover inside the rightmost conjunct undergoes *covert* leftward focus movement (to spec-CP where it c-commands and scopes over all the traces), while the movers inside the other conjuncts begin to undergo *overt* focus movement. Then, when ATB-drop of these overt movers occurs, once again only the string of the mover belonging to the rightmost conjunct remains, though this time in its base position (see Appendix A for derivations and full discussion).

This analysis is closer to the *external remerge* or ellipsis proposals in the linguistic Minimalist literature (e.g. de Vries (2009), Abels (2004)) and can better account for all of the aforementioned properties of RNR[37]. All that is needed is to relax the parser's constraint on string identity (fn.30) slightly, so that the empty string of a covert mover does not trigger a mismatch with the strings of overt movers for the purposes of ATB-drop.

5 Conclusion

We have presented the core mechanisms of MGParse and shown how coordination can be incorporated into an EDMG that uses relatively few (currently around 45) MCFG-equivalent rules to assign expressive structural descriptions to a wide range of construction types. While many open questions remain (gapping was not addressed, for instance), this is an important step towards our goal of constructing of a practical MG parser with both broad and deep coverage.

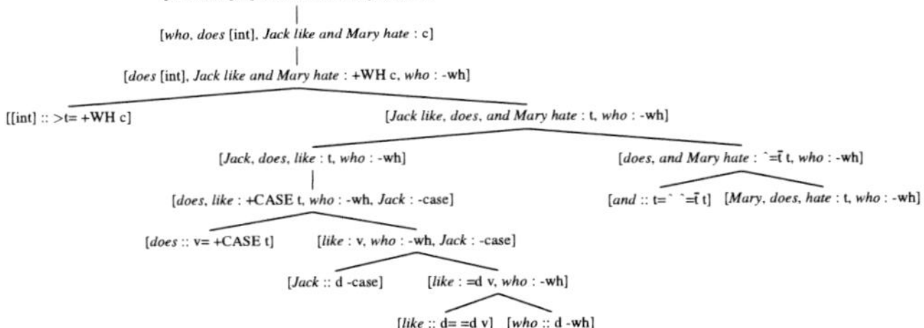

the new head of the selecting phrase, with the old head being fused onto the remnant complement string. This sets the stage for the new head to subsequently raise further, leading to successive cyclic head movement. The heads of any specifier conjuncts will simply be dropped[34], just as their α chains are dropped for ATB phrasal movement. The two rules are given in fig 13[35]. The first involves the complement case, hence the selector cannot yet contain any α movers. The second rule shows the specifier case, and is rather like the specifier rule for ATB phrasal movement in that it involves dropping any α chains in the selectee under feature identity with those in the selector. This time, however, the excorporation diacritic on the selector causes the head string of the selectee also to be dropped. Again only feature identity is required, hence the rule is MCFG-equivalent. The derivation for example 2 is given in fig 12 (only the leftmost conjunct's derivation is given in full)[36].

Figure 12: *who does Jack like and Mary hate*

4.3 Right Node Raising

In section 4.1, we stated that the ATB mechanism combined with the rightward movement rules pre-

---

[34] Again, co-indices on all head traces are deterministically recoverable from the derivation tree.

[35] Again, an additional rule is need to allow $=\bar{x}$ to persist.

[36] Note that the final step in this derivation is a unary rule fusing together the three string parts of a head chain iff it is the only chain in the expression and it has just one feature and that feature is a c (equivalent to reaching the S node).

---

[37] Covert movement has been observed to escape certain island effects (see, e.g., Richards (2000)).

9

Acknowledgments

A very big thank you to Mark Steedman for many hours of inspiring and insightful discussions on the topics contained in this paper. We would also like to thank the three anonymous reviewers for their comments and suggestions, several of which have been incorporated into the final paper. This work was funded by the Engineering and Physical Sciences Research Council (EPSRC).

References

Anne Abeille. 2006. In defense of lexical coordination. *Empirical Issues in Syntax and Semantics 6*, pages 7–36.

Klaus Abels. 2004. Right node raising: Ellipsis or across the board movement. *Proceedings of NELS*, 34.

Cedric Boeckx, Norbert Hornstein, and Jairo Nunes. 2010. *Control as Movement*. Cambridge University Press, Cambridge, UK.

Robert Borsley. 2005. Against conjp. *Lingua*, 115:461–482.

Noam Chomsky. 1995. *The Minimalist Program*. MIT Press, Cambridge, Massachusetts.

Noam Chomsky. 2000. Minimalist inquiries: The framework. In Roger Martin, David Michaels, and Juan Uriagereka, editors, *Step by Step: Essays in Minimalist Syntax in Honor of Howard Lasnik*, pages 89–155. MIT Press, Cambridge, MA.

Mark de Vries. 2009. On Multidominance and Linearization. *Biolinguistics*, 3.4:344–403.

Lisa deMena Travis. 1984. *Parameters and Effects of Word Order Variation*. Ph.D. thesis, MIT, Cambridge, Massachusetts.

Thomas Ernst. 2002. *The Syntax of Adjuncts*. Cambridge University Press, Cambridge, UK.

Werner Frey and Hans-Martin Gärtner. 2002. On the treatment of scrambling and adjunction in minimalist grammars. In Gerhard Jäger, Paola Monachesi, Gerald Penn, and Shuly Wintner, editors, *Proceedings of Formal Grammar*, pages 41–52.

Gerald Gazdar, Ewan H. Klein, Geoffrey K. Pullum, and Ivan A. Sag. 1985. *Generalized Phrase Structure Grammar*. Harvard University Press, Cambridge, Massachusetts.

Gerald Gazdar. 1981. Unbounded dependencies and coordinate structure. *Linguistic Inquiry*, 12:155–184.

Hendrik Harkema. 2001. *Parsing Minimalist Languages*. Ph.D. thesis, UCLA, Los Angeles, California.

Norbert Hornstein. 2001. *Move! A Minimalist Theory of Construal*. Blackwell Publishing.

C.-T. James Huang. 1982. *Logical relations in Chinese and the theory of grammar*. Ph.D. thesis, MIT, Cambridge, Massachusetts.

Pauline Jacobson. 1987. Review of gerald gazdar, ewan klein, geoffrey k. pullum, and ivan a. sag. generalized phrase structure grammar. *Linguistics and Philosophy*, 10:389–426.

Richard S. Kayne. 1994. *The Antisymmetry of Syntax, Linguistic Inquiry Monograph Twenty-Five*. MIT Press, Cambridge, Massachusetts.

Gregory M. Kobele. 2005. Features moving madly: A formal perspective on feature percolation in the minimalist program. *Research on Language and Computation*, 3(4):391–410.

Gregory M. Kobele. 2008. Across-the-board extraction in minimalist grammars. In *Proceedings of the Ninth International Workshop on Tree Adjoining Grammar and Related Formalisms (TAG+9)*, pages 113–128.

Hilda Koopman and Dominique Sportiche. 1991. The position of subjects. *Lingua*, 85(2-3):211–258.

Jairo Nunes. 1995. *The Copy Theory of Movement and Linearisation of Chains in the Minimalist Program*. Ph.D. thesis, University of Maryland, College Park.

Jairo Nunes. 2001. Sideward movement. *Linguistic Inquiry*, 32:303–344.

Jairo Nunes. 2004. *Linearization of Chains and Sideward Movement*. MIT Press, Cambridge, Massachusetts.

Barbara Partee and Mats Rooth. 1983. Generalized conjunction and type ambiguity. In *Meaning, Use, and Interpretation of Language*. Berlin: de Gruyter.

Norvin Richards. 2000. An island effect in japanese. *Journal of East Asian Linguistics*, 9:187285.

Ian Roberts. 2010. *Agreement and Head Movement: Clitics, Incorporation and Defective Goals, Linguistic Inquiry Monograph 59*. MIT Press, Cambridge, Massachusetts.

John Robert Ross. 1967. *Constraints on variables in syntax*. Ph.D. thesis, MIT, Cambridge, Massachusetts.

Hiroyuki Seki, Takashi Matsumura, Mamoru Fujii, and Tadao Kasami. 1991. On multiple context free grammars. *Theoretical Computer Science*, 88:191–229.

Edward Stabler. 1997. Derivational minimalism. In Christian Retoré, editor, *Logical Aspects of Computational Linguistics (LACL'96)*, volume 1328 of *Lecture Notes in Computer Science*, pages 68–95, New York. Springer.

Edward P. Stabler. 2001a. Minimalist grammars and recognition. In Christian Rohrer, Antje Rossdeutscher, and Hans Kamp, editors, *Linguistic Form and its Computation*. CSLI Publications, Stanford, California.

Edward P. Stabler. 2001b. Recognizing head movement. In P. De Groote, G. Morrill, and C. Retoré, editors, *Logical Aspects of Computational Linguistics: 4th International Conference, LACL 2001, Le Croisic, France, June 27-29, 2001, Proceedings.*, volume 4, pages 245–260.

Edward P Stabler. 2006. Sidewards without copying. In *Proceedings of the 11th Conference on Formal Grammar*, pages 133–146.

Mark Steedman. 2000. *The Syntactic Process*. MIT Press, Cambridge, Massachusetts.

Niina Ning Zhang. 2010. *Coordination in Syntax, Cambridge Studies in Linguistics Series 123*. Cambridge University Press, Cambridge, UK.

Appendix

A Right Node Raising and Parasitic Gap Derivations

Figures 14-16 give the derivations for the RNR example 3 and parasitic gap example 6 from the text. Here, as in the text, we have made certain simplifications, for example by removing -case features from objects (checked by big V in MGParse) and ignoring the little v causative head. Example 3 has two alternative derivations, corresponding to the rightward movement and leftward focus movement approaches discussed in sections 4.1 and 4.3. The rightward movement analysis works in precisely the same way as the leftward phrasal ATB mechanism discussed in section 4.1, except that now all the movers involved are undergoing rightward instead of leftward movement.

In the alternative focus movement analysis, the mover from the rightmost conjunct undergoes covert leftward focus movement to spec-CP, leaving behind its phonetic material inside the rightmost conjunct. Simultaneously, the movers inside the leftmost conjuncts begin to undergo overt leftward focus movement, but (both their syntactic and phonetic components) are dropped under

identity with the covert mover when those conjuncts are merged with the main structure - recall that for ATB, MGParse enforces string identity, in addition to syntactic identity, as doing so improves efficiency (see fn.30) without affecting weak generative capacity; however, we must relax the string identity requirement here slightly so that the empty string in the main structure (which originated in the complement conjunct) will not cause a mismatch for ATB-drop when compared with the overt strings in the specifier conjuncts.

Thus in the final structure, the silent syntactic/semantic component of the mover from the rightmost conjunct c-commands and therefore scopes over all the traces, while its phonetic component (and semantic trace) remains inside the rightmost conjunct and would therefore be deleted were VP ellipsis to occur. Instead of the rightward movement-based bracketing given in 3, then, the focus-based RNR analysis assigns this sentence the following structure (outline font indicates a silent, covertly moved constituent):

$$[_{CP} \text{ [Pete's sister]}_i \text{ } [_{TP} \text{ } [_{TP} \text{ Jack likes } t_i] \text{ and } [_{TP} \text{ Mary hates [Pete's sister]}_i]]].$$

Notice that if we reversed the situation here so that it was the movers inside the *specifier* conjuncts which underwent covert movement while the mover from the complement underwent overt movement, then simply dropping the covert moving chains via ATB would overgenerate sentences like *Pete's sister, Jack likes Pete's sister and Mary hates. We must therefore constrain the application of ATB-drop so that it cannot apply to covertly moving elements.

One way to do this is to allow the ATB rules to make reference to the empty vs. non-empty status of the string itself, and indeed this is precisely how MGParse operates. Grammatical rules do not usually make reference to string information, however, and in order to prove the MCFG-equivalence of our EDMG it is useful to show that we could encode this information in the category system itself. This can straightforwardly be done by marking the chain type of the covert mover in the output of the phonetic merge rules with a diacritic indicating its covert status. The ATB rules could then be reformulated so as to only apply to movers without this diacritic. This would clearly lead to a doubling of certain rules, but since the increase is finite, expressive power would be unaffected.

At present, MGParse uses the rightward movement approach to RNR because allowing covert focus movement into the system introduces lots of ambiguity which severely impacts on the parser's efficiency. We are, however, currently investigating ways to restrict the application of covert focus movement, perhaps using statistics. Note that both of the approaches to RNR described here are capable of deriving sentences which feature both RNR *and* overt leftward ATB, such as *The policeman to whom I offered, and may give, a flower* (Steedman, 2000).

Finally, note that the adjunct control example 5 from the text is derived in a very similar way to the parasitic gap construction in fig 17, except that now it is only the subject which moves and hence undergoes ATB. The argument cluster coordination in example 4 from the text is derived along the lines of example 2 and is left as an exercise (hint: little v is required); precisely the same mechanism can accommodate cases of argument-adjunct cluster coordination, as in *I saw Harry yesterday and Peter today*.

B Enforcing the like-types constraint on conjuncts

In section 3 (paragraph 2 and fn.20) we stated that full type uniformity between conjuncts could not be enforced by the selector features in an MG, unlike in a CCG where such features can be complex and specify, for instance, that all conjuncts must be clauses/verb phrases with object holes. We also noted that in our EDMG, the like-types constraint falls out instead from the interaction of the two main constraints on rule formation that we have adopted (CED and CSC), together with the ATB mechanisms presented in section 4. In this section, we would like to elaborate on these remarks.

First, we will define more precisely what we mean by 'type' here. Recall that MG expressions are composed of a head chain and up to k moving chains. Each chain is in turn composed of a string element and a feature sequence. Consider again the example from section 2.1, repeated below:

[[cause] *help* : +CASE v, *who* : -wh, *Jack* : -case]

There are two senses of 'type' to be defined here. First, we will define an 'expression type' as all and only the syntactic components of the entire expression, with all non-initial features replaced by feature suffix (and, if we were to include the dotted feature mechanism, prefix) variables. The expression type of our example is thus as follows, where the ordering of the non-head chains is irrelevant:

[+CASE γ, -wh, -case]

In addition to the type of the entire expression, each chain can be viewed as having its own individual 'chain type', which is its (fully reified) feature sequence. For instance, the type of the head chain in our example is: +CASE v. The question to be addressed is how we can ensure that in our EDMG, coordination applies to two or more conjuncts with the same expression types *and* the same chain types (i.e. the features in the suffix and prefix variables matter).

Leaving aside the question of how to enforce identity between the head chains of the conjuncts for a moment, consider how we ensure that all conjuncts have identical sets of moving chain types. Recall that CED prohibits rules enabling extraction from within specifiers and that in section 4.1 we proposed a way to bleed this constraint by allowing movers inside a dependent structure to be dropped under identity with movers inside the governing structure. Recall further that for coordination, we stated that the rules must be formulated in such a way as to ensure that the number of movers inside the dependent is the same as the number of movers inside the main structure (coordinator projections being identified by :: and :). This enforces part 2 of CSC, which states that it is not possible to extract the contents of any conjunct (even the complement conjunct), with one exception to this being cases of ATB movement.

Now, when the complement conjunct is merged with the Coord head, any movers which that conjunct contains will be transferred into the resulting expression. Subsequently, as additional (specifier) conjuncts are merged into the main structure, their sets of moving chains will be compared with the set of moving chains which originated inside the complement conjunct and either be dropped if they exactly match this set or lead to a doomed derivation if they do not (because no rule will ever allow them to escape the specifier conjunct). This ensures that all conjuncts must have identical sets of moving chain types.

The situation with the head chains is different: because the head chain of the complement conjunct cannot contain any licensee features (no conjuncts may move - part 1 of CSC), as soon as it is merged with the coordinator it will cease to exist (though its string will be fused with the coordinator's string). Therefore, it will be unavailable for comparison with the head chain of any incoming specifier conjuncts. How can we overcome this problem?

First, observe that the syntactic feature sequences in MGs have a tripartite structure composed of requirements (=selectors+licensors), the selectee (PoS category) feature, and the licensee features. These three parts are strictly ordered from left to right; that is, an element must have all its argument positions fully saturated before it can be selected as the argument of a higher head in accordance with Xbar theory (unlike in CCG, where unsaturated elements can be selected), and only after it is selected can it undergo movement.

Now consider how we enforce the like-types constraint between the head chains of conjuncts. The selectee/PoS category feature is straightforwardly matched by the constraint on the lexicon that all coordinators must follow the general schema: $x= =\overline{x}\ x$ (or in certain special cases perhaps $x= =\overline{x}\ y$), where both rightward and leftward selector features must have the same PoS category. As noted in Steedman (2000), this (and the like-types constraint more generally) derives from the semantics of coordination, which is a 'recursive transitive closure over same types' (Partee and Rooth, 1983). The licensee features, meanwhile, are trivially matched by the fact that they are disallowed on all conjunct heads owing to part 1 of CSC: no conjuncts may move.

What of the requirement features? Interestingly, there is no way in our current rule system to ensure that the selector and licensor features of each of the conjuncts' head chains match. Thus we predict that the like-types constraint on conjuncts is not absolute: conjuncts may have different types, but only with respect to the selector and licensor features on their head chains.

There is some evidence that this may be correct. For instance, it is possible to coordinate a yes-no interrogative with an interrogative featuring wh-movement, as in *Pete asked* [*who had been at the party*] *and* [*whether Jack had seen Mary*]. Assuming *whether* to be an interrogative complementizer, only the (silent) complementizer head in the first embedded clause will contain a +WH feature triggering movement. Thus the requirements of the two C heads would seem to differ here, suggesting that we have a genuine case of coordination of (partially) unlike-types. Another example would be the coordination of a ditransitive with an intransitive VP (*Jack remained and gave Mary his ticket*).

Of course, there are other ways to derive such sentences, for instance by assuming for our first example that an additional projection layer (perhaps ForceP) exists above the phrase hosting the wh-element (perhaps FocusP) and that it is actually ForcePs which are coordinated here. Nevertheless, the data at the very least does not appear to conflict with the approach to the like-types constraint on conjuncts described here.

C On the coordination of lexical X^0 heads

Xbar theory requires all complements and specifiers to be fully saturated, maximal XP projections. As pointed out in Borsley (2005), this poses a serious challenge to the Xbar theoretic view of coordinate structures, given that the coordination of unsaturated X^0 lexical heads is apparently also possible, as in *Hobbs* [*criticized and insulted*] *his boss*. In an attempt to rescue Xbar theory here, Kayne (1994) proposes that lexical coordination is only apparent, arguing that such examples feature ellipsis within the left XP conjunct. However, as Borsley notes, there are other cases which do not appear amenable to this analysis. For example, *Hobbs whistled and hummed similar tunes* clearly does not mean the same thing as *Hobbs whistled similar tunes and hummed similar tunes*.

Another strategy sometimes pursued here is to assume that apparent lexical head coordination is actually an instance of RNR (this is in fact how the Penn Treebank analyses such constructions). However, as discussed in Abeille (2006), RNR and lexical head coordination have rather different prosodic and semantic properties, meaning that this analysis too faces problems. We will therefore take X^0 coordination at face value, and in this section propose a solution within the EDMG formalism that makes crucial use of the dotted feature mechanism introduced in section 4.1 (and adopted from Kobele (2008)).

Within MGs, the Xbar theoretic requirement that all arguments be maximal XP projections is encoded by the fact that all requirement features (=selectors+licensors) must precede all selectee (and licensee) features. That is, a given head must have all its requirements checked and deleted before itself being selected as a dependent. In other words, taking β to be requirements, and γ to be licensees, the only abstract head chain type which can be selected is the following, where the dot immediately precedes the selectee feature:

$$[\beta \cdot x\,\gamma]$$

Assuming β to be non-empty, on standard assumptions the above category could only have been derived via the application of MERGE and perhaps also MOVE operations. However, formally, nothing prevents us from allowing this category type to appear directly on X^0 heads, or from defining a unary function which 'type-saturates' unsaturated X^0 heads. Such items would not truly be saturated semantically, of course, but this is fine provided they can only be selected for by a coordinator with a matching set of requirement (and licensee) features; the matching requirement features on the coordinator projection can then subsequently satisfy the semantic requirements of all its X^0 conjuncts in one fell swoop.

The rules for type-saturation and coordination of complement and (multiple) specifier X^0 conjuncts are given in fig 14, where the asterisk is equivalent to the dot, except that it uniquely identifies the type-saturated heads so that they are only ever selected for by coordinators. As noted in fn.32, an overline on the feature separators ($\overline{::}$ $\overline{:}$) indicates a coordinator projection.

head would be lost following the type-saturation operation, as the β requirements would simply be deleted. However, we would then have no way to ensure that we were only coordinating heads of the same valency.

$$\frac{[s :: \cdot\,\beta\,x\,\gamma]}{[s :: \beta * x\,\gamma]}\;(\text{type-saturation})$$

$$\frac{[s\,\overline{::}\cdot\;\; x{=}\;{=}\bar{x}\,\beta\,x\,\gamma]\;[t :: \beta * x\,\gamma]}{[st\,\overline{:}\;\; x{=}\cdot\;{=}\bar{x}\,\beta\,x\,\gamma]}\;(\text{h\_coord1(comp)})$$

$$\frac{[t :: \beta * x\,\gamma]\;[s\,\overline{:}\,x{=}\cdot\;{=}\bar{x}\,\beta\,x\,\gamma]}{[ts\,\overline{:}\;\; x{=}\;{=}\bar{x}\cdot\,\beta\,x\,\gamma]}\;(\text{h\_coord2(spec)})$$

$$\frac{[t :: \beta * x\,\gamma]\;[s\,\overline{:}\,x{=}\cdot\;{=}\bar{x}\,\beta\,x\,\gamma]}{[ts\,\overline{:}\;\; x{=}\cdot\;{=}\bar{x}\,\beta\,x\,\gamma]}\;(\text{h\_coord3(spec)})$$

Figure 14: Lexical head type-saturation and coordination rules

Clearly this approach is very close to the CCG analysis of lexical head coordination, except that in CCG coordinated heads are formally as well as (at the point of coordination) semantically unsaturated. Notice too that without the dotted feature mechanism, the subcategorization frame of a

Figure 15: Rightward movement analysis: *Jack likes and Mary hates Pete's sister*

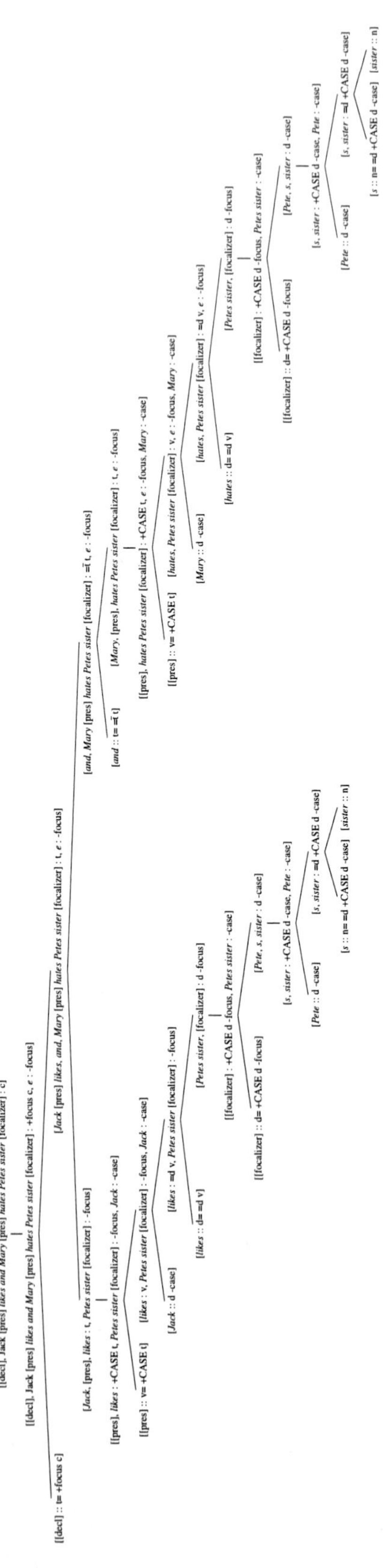

Figure 16: Focus movement analysis: *Jack likes and Mary hates Pete's sister*

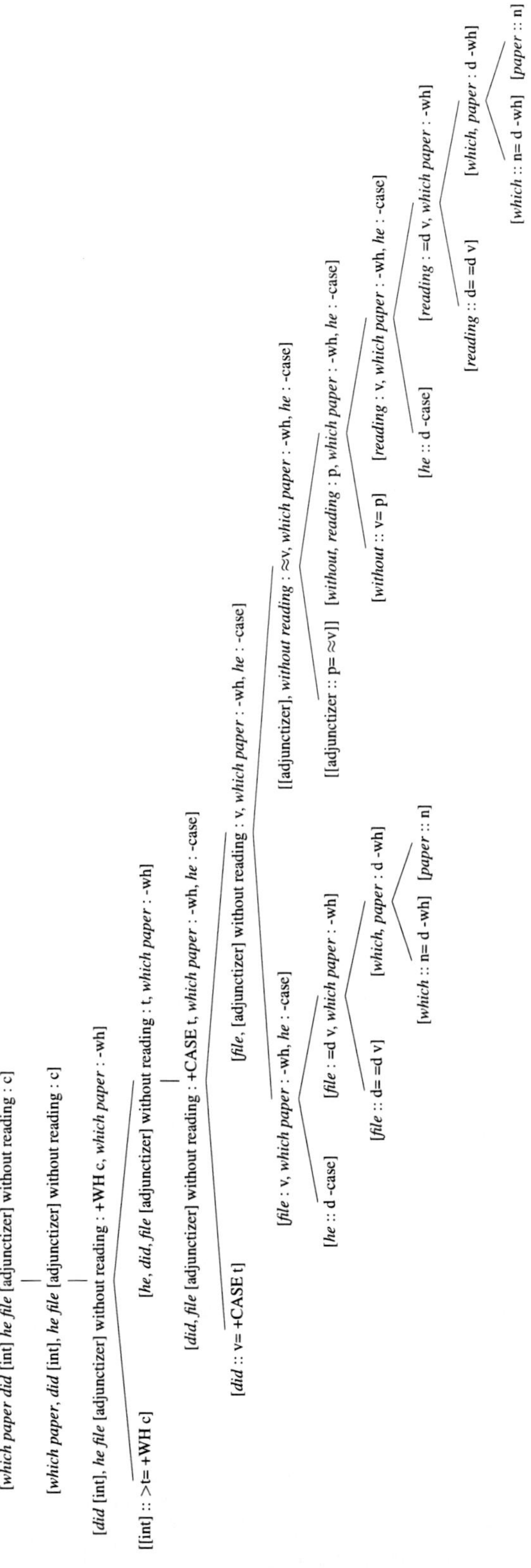

Figure 17: *Which paper did he file without reading*

17

ArabTAG: from a Handcrafted to a Semi-automatically Generated TAG

Chérifa Ben Khelil[1,2] Denys Duchier[1] Yannick Parmentier[1] Chiraz Zribi[2] Fériel Ben Fraj[2]
(1) LIFO - Université d'Orléans, France
`firstname.lastname@univ-orleans.fr`
(2) RIADI - ENSI, Université La Manouba, Tunisia

Abstract

In this paper, we present the redesign of an existing TAG for Arabic using a description language (so-called metagrammatical language). The use of such a language makes it easier for the linguist to share information among grammatical structures while ensuring a high degree of modularity within the target grammar. Additionally, this redesign benefits from a grammar testing environment which is used to check both grammar coverage and overgeneration.

1 Introduction

Precision grammars provide fine-grained descriptions of languages, which are beneficial for many NLP applications such as Dialog systems, Question-Answering systems, Automatic Summarization systems, etc. Still the development of such language resources is limited for it comes at a high cost. For instance, the development of the first large-coverage TAG for French took more than 10 person-years (Abeillé et al., 1999). In this context, many efforts have been put into semiautomatic grammar production, either in a dataoriented fashion (that is, by acquiring grammar rules from annotated corpora), or in a knowledgebased fashion (that is, by using description languages to capture generalizations among grammar rules).

A particularly interesting feature of the latter is that it offers a relatively good control on the grammar being produced. This allows among others to extend the produced grammar with various levels of description such as morphology or semantics (see e.g. (Duchier et al., 2012) or (Gardent, 2008)).

In this paper, we are interested in applying such grammar production techniques to the description of Arabic. Arabic is a challenging language when it comes to grammar production for it exhibits specific features such as (i) a relatively free word order, combined with (ii) a rich morphology, and (iii) the omission of diacritics (vowels) in written texts. These features motivates the use of highly-expressive description languages. In this work, we use the XMG description language (Crabbé et al., 2013) to describe in an expressive and yet concise way the syntax of Arabic. This description is based on an existing handcrafted Tree-Adjoining Grammar for Arabic named ArabTAG (Ben Fraj, 2011), which serves as a model for the current development.

The paper is organized as follows. In Section 2, we present the grammatical resource, namely ArabTAG, this work is based on. We particularly comment on the ArabTAG grammar coverage, its design choices and limitations. In Section 3, we present the XMG description language, together with recent advances in its implementation. These advances include a new level of modularity brought by the possibility to dynamically define the description language needed by the linguist in a given context and to *compile the compiler* for this description language.[1] In Section 4, we present a concise description of the syntax of Arabic using XMG. In particular, we show how to deal with the free word order of this language. We also present a testing environment which was designed to facilitate grammar development. In Section 5, we compare our approach with related work. Finally in Section 6, we con-

---

[1]As such, XMG2 can be seen as a meta interpreter which takes as an input a compiler specification and produces as an output a compiler for a description language. The latter is used by linguists to describe grammatical resources, as explained later in this paper.

Proceedings of the 12th International Workshop on Tree Adjoining Grammars and Related Formalisms (TAG+12), pages 18–26,
Düsseldorf, Germany, June 29 - July 1, 2016.

clude and present some short-term perspectives of development of the grammar (including morphological and semantic information).

2 ArabTAG: a Tree-Adjoining Grammar for Arabic

As mentioned above, Arabic language combines complex linguistic phenomena that make its processing particularly ambiguous. Let us recall briefly what these are:

- The diversity of lexical and grammatical interpretation of an Arabic word. This ambiguity is due to the absence of vocalic signs, which is frequent in modern Arabic.

- The order of the sentence's constituents in Arabic language is free. For a verbal sentence composed of **Verb**, **Subject** and **Object**, we can have three combinations (VSO, VOS, SVO) that are all syntactically correct.

- The phenomenon of agglutination: in order to have more complex forms, clitics can tie up with words. Thus, a sentence can correspond to just one agglutinative form as in the example فأسقيناكموه (which is the longest word in Quran) :

(1)   ف   أسقي نا كم و ه
it to you we gave-to-drink and
'and we gave it to you to drink'

It is composed of a conjunction, verb, subject and two objects which are all enclosed in the same textual form.

- The recursive structures whose length is not limited:[2]

(2)   الذي لم ينقطع طوال الليل
the-night during stop not that
أيقظته بنباحها
with-their-barking aroused-that-him
الكلاب هي التي
those are the-dogs
'the dogs are those that aroused him with their barking that does not stop during the night'

---

[2]This example is taken from (Ben Fraj, 2010).

Digital resources (grammars and treebanks) which can be used for parsing Arabic texts are scarce. In this context, let us describe a semi-lexicalized Arabic Tree-Adjoining Grammar called ArabTAG (Ben Fraj, 2010).

ArabTAG has been developed at RIADI Laboratory, National School of Computer Sciences, University of La Manouba, Tunisia. It includes a set of elementary trees representing the basic syntactic structures of Arabic. The construction of these structures was based on school grammar books and books of Arabic grammar such as (Kouloughli, 1992). To enhance interoperability between tools and resources, all these structures were encoded in XML.

ArabTAG has been used to build a treebank for Arabic. More precisely, ArabTAG's elementary trees served as representative structures to annotate syntactically a corpus. The resulting treebank consists of 950 sentences (5000 words) annotated with their corresponding TAG derivation trees.

2.1 ArabTAG and lexicalization

ArabTAG is semi-lexicalized since it contains trees where all nodes are labelled with nonterminal symbols (that is, syntactic categories). More precisely, ArabTAG contains two sets of elementary trees: lexicalized trees (that is, having at least one lexical item as a leaf node) and patterns trees. The choice of the semi-lexicalized TAG variant was made in order to reduce the important number of possible syntactic structures. The lexicalized trees are reserved to prepositions, modifiers, conjunctions, demonstratives, etc. On the other hand, the patterns trees represent verbs, nouns, adjectives or any kind of phrases.[3] These elementary trees are enriched by different information organized in feature structures.

2.2 ArabTAG coverage

To represent Arabic basic structures, ArabTAG contains 24 lexicalized elementary trees and 241 pattern-based elementary trees. Lexicalized trees correspond to the particles as the prepositions, conjunctions, interrogatives, etc.

These trees correspond to the simple syntactic structures of the Arabic sentences (nominal and verbal), all classes of phrasal structures (NP (Nominal Phrase), PP (Prepositional

---

[3]Concretely, this means that ArabTAG is largely made of tree schemata (unanchored lexicalized TAG trees) like XTAG (XTAG Research Group, 2001).

Phrase)) as well as the different sub-classes of the phrasal structures (Adjectival NP, Complement NP, Propositional NP). Moreover, ArabTAG presents different kinds of sentences: active, passive, interrogative, complex sentences. In addition, it covers elliptical, anaphoric and subordinate structures. It takes into account the change of the order of the sentence's components and the agglutinative forms. The current version of this grammar has some limitations that can be summarized as follows:

- The syntactic structures enriched with supplements (circumstantial complements of time, place, etc.) are not described.

- The representation of forms of agglutination is not well reflected in ArabTAG. These forms should be extended to improve the coverage of the grammar.

- ArabTAG emphasizes syntactic relations without regard to semantic information. However, syntactic interpretation cannot be complete if it does not involve semantic information.

- ArabTAG consists of a flat set of elementary trees (that is, without any structure sharing). In particular, it is not organized in a hierarchical way.

Therefore we propose a new version ArabTAG V2 that takes into account the aspects mentioned above. This new version is being enhanced with a new organization (using a description language to specify elementary trees) and new unification criteria (both at the syntactic and semantic-syntactic levels). Coverage is also being extended by adding elementary trees for the representation of additional complements. Finally, as will be shown in Section 4, we are currently in the process of structuring the grammar into a hierarchical organization.

3   XMG2: a new Generation of Description Languages

As mentioned above, a common strategy to semi-automatically produce precision grammars is to use a description language. Such a language permits the linguist to formally specify the structures of a target grammar. When this language comes with an implementation (that is, a compiler), the grammar specification (so-called *metagrammar*) can be compiled into an actual electronic grammar.

Designing and implementing description languages for grammar specification is a field which has been quite active over the past decades, seminal work includes languages such as PATRII (Shieber et al., 1983), DATR (Evans and Gazdar, 1996), LexOrg (Xia, 2001), DyALog (Villemonte De La Clergerie, 2010), or more recently XMG (Crabbé et al., 2013). These languages differ among others, in the way variables are handled (local versus global scopes) and how structure sharing is represented (inheritance versus transformations). Here, we propose to use XMG to describe Arabic for it exhibits particularly pertinent features :

- it is highly expressive, which makes it possible to define highly factorized grammar descriptions (in our case, this will be used to deal with semi-free word order) ;

- it is particularly adapted to the description of tree grammars (it has been used to develop several electronic TAG grammars for e.g. French, English, German, Vietnamese, Korean) ;

- it is highly extensible (as will be described in this Section, it can be *configured* to describe various levels of language, such as semantics or morphology) ;

- it is open-source and actively developed.

The first version of XMG was based on the following two main concepts:[4]

1. elementary trees are made of common reusable tree fragments, which can be combined conjunctively or disjunctively ;

2. each of these fragments can be (i) specified using a tree description logic such as the one defined by Rogers and Vijay-Shanker (1994) and (ii) encapsulated within *classes*.

On top of these, XMG includes a facility to define other types of reusable information (so-called *dimensions*), which can be used to extend tree fragments with e.g. semantic formulas.

---

[4] A detailed introduction to XMG can be found in (Crabbé et al., 2013).

An important limitation of XMG was the limited number of dimensions it can handle, namely syntax (tree fragments), semantics (predicate logic formulas) and syntax-semantic interface (attribute-value matrices). In order to make it possible for the linguist to describe several levels of language (whatever their number is), and to combine various data structures (not only tree fragments or predicate logic formulas), XMG was extended[5] as described in the following subsections.

3.1 Describing description languages

In order to allow for the description of an unlimited number of dimensions, XMG should include a support for user-defined dimensions. This involves (i) being able to formally define the description language for this dimension and (ii) being able to interpret formulas of this language to output valid linguistic structures.

To do this, XMG2 extends XMG by including a *meta* metagrammar compiler (Petitjean, 2014).[6] More concretely, the modular architecture of XMG2 makes it possible for contributors to develop so-called *language bricks*. A brick is the formal definition of a description language (that is, the CFG underlying this language) together with the implementation of the interpretation procedure for (abstract syntax trees of) formulas of this language. The meta metagrammar compiler can then compile *on-demand* sets of language bricks, which can then be used together to describe various levels of linguistic structures. In other words, the metagrammar compiler is now compiled from language bricks (hence the arbitrary number of dimensions).

As an illustration, let us consider the following bricks which are used to describe TAG grammars.[7]

Language brick for combining descriptions:

$$
\begin{array}{rcl}
Desc & ::= & Stmt \\
 & | & Stmt \wedge Desc \\
 & | & Stmt \vee Desc
\end{array}
$$

Basically descriptions are made of statements which can be combined either conjunctively or disjunctively.

Language brick for describing tree fragments:

$$
\begin{array}{rcl}
Stmt & ::= & \mathbf{node}\ id \\
 & | & \mathbf{node}\ id\ AVM \\
 & | & id \lhd id \qquad | \quad id \lhd^{+} id \\
 & | & id \prec id \qquad | \quad id \prec^{+} id
\end{array}
$$

Tree fragments are described using a tree description logic based on dominance (written $\lhd$) and precedence (written $\prec$) relations between node variables (identifiers).[8]

Language brick for describing Attribute-Value Matrices (AVMs):

$$
\begin{array}{rcl}
AVM & ::= & [Feats] \\
Feats & ::= & Feat \\
 & | & Feat, Feats \\
Feat & ::= & id = Value
\end{array}
$$

AVMs are sets of pairs (written *Feats* here). Each pair associates a feature (i.e. an identifier) with a value.

The interpretation of descriptions based on these bricks requires (i) unification (for interpreting AVMs and node or feature variable unification) and (ii) tree description solving. Hence the contributor has to write the Prolog code which performs these treatments.[9]

3.2 Assembling description languages

From the library of language bricks available within XMG2, metagrammar designers can load the necessary bricks to describe their target formalism. This is done by declaring within a YAML file, which bricks are to be loaded.

For instance, in order to describe TAG grammars using the above-mentioned bricks, one would have to write the following YAML file:

```
mg:
  _Stmt: control
control:
  _Stmt: dim_syn
dim_syn:
  tag: "syn"
  _Stmt: syn
syn:
  _AVM: avm
avm:
  _Expr: feats
feats:
  _Value: value
```

---

[5] And at the same time re-implemented in Prolog for the previous version of XMG was coded in the Oz Programming Language, which is no longer maintained.

[6] See https://launchpad.net/xmg-ng.

[7] For a detailed introduction to the description of TAG grammars with XMG2, see (Petitjean, 2014).

[8] The $^{+}$ refers to the relation's transitive closure.

[9] As described in (Petitjean, 2014), the contributor actually has to provide a repository where each compilation step is specified in Prolog.

Such a specification indicates that a metagrammar (mg) uses statements of type `control` (that is, which make use of our language brick for combining descriptions). This `control` brick itself uses statements of type `dim_syn`. Formulas of this type are declared using the keyword `"syn"` and contain statements of type `syn`. This brick `syn` itself uses externally defined AVMs. AVMs are made of features whose expressions are values. Again, note that this example is simplified, for instance nodes here are only decorated with AVMs, while in XMG2, they are also decorated with properties such as marks (e.g. $\downarrow$ for substitution) or colors (to guide node identification when solving tree descriptions).

3.3 Using assembled languages to describe natural language

Once the metagrammar language is fully specified and the compiler for this language compiled, the metagrammar designer can write the description of the target linguistic resource. In our case, such a resource is a TAG grammar. It is described as (conjunctive and disjunctive) combinations of tree fragments. Such fragments are defined as formulas of a tree description logic based on dominance and precedence relations between node variables.

For instance the following tree fragment:

$$S_{[cat=s]}$$
$$N \qquad SV_{[cat=sv]}$$

would be represented in an XMG2 metagrammatical description as follows:

$$\textbf{node } S \; [cat=s]$$
$$\wedge \textbf{ node } N \; [cat=n]$$
$$\wedge \textbf{ node } SV \; [cat=sv]$$
$$\wedge s \vartriangleleft n \; \wedge \; s \vartriangleleft sv \; \wedge \; n \prec sv$$

Note that, like in XMG, tree fragments in XMG2 are encapsulated within classes. A class corresponds to the association of a description (i.e., a combination of statements) with a name (making it possible to reuse a given description in various contexts). Unification variables (used to refer either to a node, a feature, or a value) are declared within classes (and their scope is by default limited to the class). When classes are combined, variables denoting the same information need to be explicitly unified (using the operator $=$). While providing the user with flexibility (variable names

can be freely used without any risk of conflict), this local scope and explicit unification hampers grammar design as shown by Crabbé *et al.* (2013). So XMG2 comes with an alternative handling of unification which was already present in XMG, namely *node coloring*. Each node of the meta-grammatical description can be colored in either black, white or red. A black node is a *resource* and can be unified with 0 or more white nodes; a white node is a *need* and must be unified with a black node; a red node is saturated and cannot be unified with any other node. Since metagrammar compilation solves descriptions in order to compute minimal tree models, variable denoting nodes are implicitly unified due to dominance constraints but also the above-mentioned color constraints. Colors are an elegant way to restrict and guide the ways in which variables can be unified, and so in which tree fragments can be combined.

In the next section, we will see how such a modular and expressive description language is being used to (re)describe the syntax of Arabic.

4 ArabTAG Revisited using XMG2

In this section, we aim to illustrate the flavor of the new formulation of ArabTAG by focusing on the modelization of simple verb subcategorization frames for matrix clauses. In order to make this presentation more easily accessible, we use a combination of logical and graphical notation rather than XMG's concrete syntax.

4.1 Describing verbal predicates in Arabic with XMG2

In an Arabic matrix clause, the verb and its arguments can mostly be freely reordered.[10] Since ArabTAG made the choice of flat trees for verbal constituents, the TAG grammar must supply initial trees for all possible permutations of the arguments. Thanks to the tree description based approach of XMG, this is easily achieved simply by not stipulating any precedence constraint among these arguments.

EpineVerbe(C) is an abstraction that contributes a fragment of tree description for the verbal spine of a matrix clause. Since adverbs can be freely interspersed between arguments, we need to provide appropriate adjunction points for them. AG

---

[10]Words are usually represented in Arabic in a VSO order, still alternative orders may be used as well with morphological constraints on the verb. See e.g. (El Kassas and Kahane, 2004).

is an adjunction point allowing an adverb at the front of the clause. AD is an adjunction point for inserting an adverb after the verb (or after an argument as we will see later). Nodes here are colored (represented by B, W and R for black, white and red respectively). EpineVerbe is parameterized by a color C as depicted below:[11]

$$\text{EpineVerbe}(C) \longrightarrow$$
$$\text{SV}^{C}\,[\texttt{cat=sv}]$$
$$|$$
$$\text{AG}^{C}\,[\texttt{cat=advg}]$$
$$|$$
$$\text{AD}^{C}\,[\texttt{cat=advd}]$$
$$|$$
$$\text{V}^{C}_{\diamond}\,[\texttt{cat=v}]$$

MatrixClause contributes the actual verb spine (which can be seen as a resource) and therefore instantiates EpineVerbe with the color black:

$$\text{MatrixClause} \longrightarrow \text{EpineVerbe}(\text{B})$$

EpineArg is an abstraction used for attaching to the verbal spine a tree description for an argument (seen as a need).

$$\text{EpineArg} \longrightarrow$$
$$[\text{AG}] \Leftarrow \text{EpineVerbe}(\text{w})$$
$$\wedge\ \text{AD}^{\text{R}}\,[\texttt{cat=advd}] \wedge \text{AG} \vartriangleleft \text{AD}$$

It instantiates EpineVerbe with the color white, thus forcing it to unify with the actual verb spine. $[\text{AG}] \Leftarrow \text{EpineVerbe}(\text{W})$ additionally imports into the current scope the variable AG provided by EpineVerbe, and attaches a new AD adjunction node for optional insertion of an adverb after the argument. Note that $\text{AG} \vartriangleleft \text{AD}$ only specifies that AG immediately dominates AD, but introduces no precedence constraint.

SujetCanon instantiates EpineArg and attaches an SN substitution node below the argument AD supplied by EpineArg:

$$\text{SujetCanon} \longrightarrow$$
$$[\text{AD}] \Leftarrow \text{EpineArg}()$$
$$\wedge\ \text{SN}^{\text{R}}_{\downarrow}\,[\texttt{cat=sn,cas=nom}]$$
$$\wedge\ \text{AD} \vartriangleleft \text{SN}$$

A direct object normally appears after the verb. If it appears before the verb, then it gives rise to a cleft-construction and requires an object-clitic marker on the verb (boolean feature `oclit`):

$$\text{ObjetCanonSN} \longrightarrow$$
$$[\text{AD, V}] \Leftarrow \text{EpineArg}()$$
$$\wedge\ \text{SN}^{\text{R}}_{\downarrow}\,[\texttt{cat=sn,\ cas=acc}]$$
$$\wedge\ \text{AD} \vartriangleleft \text{SN}$$
$$\wedge\ ((\text{V}\,[\texttt{oclit=-}] \wedge \text{V} \prec^{+} \text{SN}) \vee$$
$$(\text{V}\,[\texttt{oclit=+}] \wedge \text{SN} \prec^{+} \text{V}))$$

The direct object can also be just a clitic:

$$\text{ObjetCanonClit} \longrightarrow$$
$$[\text{V}] \Leftarrow \text{EpineVerbe}(\text{w})$$
$$\wedge\ \text{V}\,[\texttt{oclit=+}]$$

$$\text{ObjetCanon} \longrightarrow \text{ObjetCanonSN} \vee$$
$$\text{ObjetCanonClit}$$

The indirect object requires a particle PV (stipulated by the verb) that is realized either as a separate preposition or as a morphological affix on the noun.

$$\text{ObjetIndCanon} \longrightarrow$$
$$[\text{AD, V}] \Leftarrow \text{EpineArg}()$$
$$\wedge\qquad \text{SP}^{\text{B}}\,[\texttt{cat=sp}]$$
$$\overline{\qquad\qquad}$$
$$\text{P}^{\text{R}}_{\diamond}\qquad \text{SN}^{\text{R}}_{\downarrow}\,[\texttt{cat=sn,\ cas=gen}]$$
$$\wedge\ \text{AD} \vartriangleleft \text{SP} \wedge \text{V}\,[\texttt{p=PV}]$$
$$\wedge\ ((\text{P}\,[\texttt{phon=}\varepsilon] \wedge \text{SN}\,[\texttt{p=PV}]) \vee$$
$$(\text{P}\,[\texttt{phon=PV}] \wedge \text{SN}\,[\texttt{p=}\varepsilon]))$$

Finally the 3 basic verb families can be obtained as follows:

$$\text{Intransitive} \longrightarrow \text{MatrixClause} \wedge \text{SujetCanon}$$
$$\text{Transitive} \longrightarrow \text{Intransitive} \wedge \text{ObjetCanon}$$
$$\text{DiTransitive} \longrightarrow \text{Transitive} \wedge \text{ObjetIndCanon}$$

We saw that using a metagrammatical language based on (i) combinations of reusable tree fragments together with (ii) a tree description logic allowing for expressing (underspecified) dominance and precedence relations between nodes, makes it possible to describe the syntax of verbal predicates in Arabic in a concise and modular way. This metagrammatical description relies on linguistic motivations (e.g., alternative realizations of grammatical functions, valence, etc.), and can be easily extended by just adding missing tree fragments and combination rules (in this sense, the metagrammatical language is monotonic, since no fragment deletion needs to be expressed, only alternatives).

Note that this metagrammatical description language was already available within XMG. The benefit of using XMG2 will come shortly once the metagrammar will be extended with additional information such as morphological descriptions (see *infra*). Indeed, XMG2 will be needed to assemble a metagrammatical language that does not only permit the linguist to describe syntactic trees but other levels of description (e.g. morphological structures), which could be *connected* with each other (via shared unification variables).

4.2 Current state of ArabTAGv2

As mentioned above, the work presented here is based on an existing TAG for Arabic (Arab-TAGv1), which is handcrafted (the linguist uses a specific tool to describe elementary trees, this tool performs additional consistency checks during grammar development and also some predictions on the structures being described). Arab-TAGv1 contains 380 elementary trees, and was developed in the context of (Ben Fraj, 2010). 83% out of these 380 trees (that is, 315 trees) represent verbal predicates.

Our work is still in its early stage. The redesign of ArabTAG using a metagrammar started 4 months ago in the context of a PhD co-supervision. So far, we generated 114 trees from a description made of 30 classes (that is, 30 tree fragments or combination rules). The metagrammar is about 600 lines long. We focused on verbal predicates and are now working on nominal phrases. We aim at out-performing the coverage of ArabTAGv1 within a couple of years, while extending it with morphological and semantic information (which impact syntax, e.g. word order or agreements).

Arabic exhibits challenging properties including its rich morphology (making use, among others, of agglutination). We plan to integrate a morphological dimension in our metagrammatical description following seminal work by Duchier *et al.* (2012). The idea is to generate inflected forms from a morphological meta-description. This meta-description uses a two-layer representation. First a constraint-based description of morphological information (represented as ordered and potentially empty fields) is defined. Then, surface transformations (e.g. related to agglutination) are captured by means of postprocessings (in our case rewriting rules). The metagrammar compiler for this morphological meta-description is compiled from the selection of adequate description languages from XMG2's library of language bricks.

4.3 About metagrammar development

While designing ArabTAG with XMG2, we set up a development environment in order to check grammar coverage (in particular aiming at re-

ducing both under and over-generation).[12] More concretely, together with the metagrammar which actually consists of tree templates, we are also designing proof-of-concept syntactic and morphological lexicons for Arabic, following the 3-layer lexicon architecture (tree templates, lemmas, words) of the XTAG project (2001). Each new syntactic phenomena included in ArabTAG leads to the extension of a test corpus gathering both grammatical and ungrammatical sentences (associated with the number of expected parses). The TuLiPA parser (Parmentier et al., 2008) is then run on the test corpus to check the quality of the grammar, producing logs which can help metagrammar designer to fix potential bugs in the metagrammatical description. An extract of these logs is given in Fig. 1, and an example of derived tree in Fig. 2.[13]

```
Axiom:   sv
Anchoring failed on tree
Interrogative_2--متى for lexical item
متى
Grammar anchoring time:   0.023071728
sec.
@@##Tree combinations before classical
polarity filtering :   16
@@##Tree combinations after classical
polarity filtering :   2
Grammar conversion time:   0.051578702
sec.
Parsing time:   0.044386232 sec.
Sentence "إلى متى نامَ عليٌ" parsed.
Forest extraction time:   0.003370246
sec.
Number of derivation trees 1
Parses available (in XML) in
corpus0.xml.
XML production time:   0.418911166 sec.
Total parsing time for sentence
"إلى متى نامَ عليٌ" :   0.541318074 sec.
```

Figure 1: Log file produced during the development of ArabTAG (extract)

5 Related Work

To our knowledge, there are very few TAG-based descriptions of Arabic, the main attempt at such a description being work by Habash and Rambow (2004), where a tree-adjoining grammar was extracted from an Arabic Treebank (namely the Penn

---

[12]This development environment consists of Python scripts.

[13]Note that the sentence is displayed in the discourse direction (e.g., from left to right), a post-processing could be applied to display the syntactic tree using the sentence direction (e.g., from right to left).

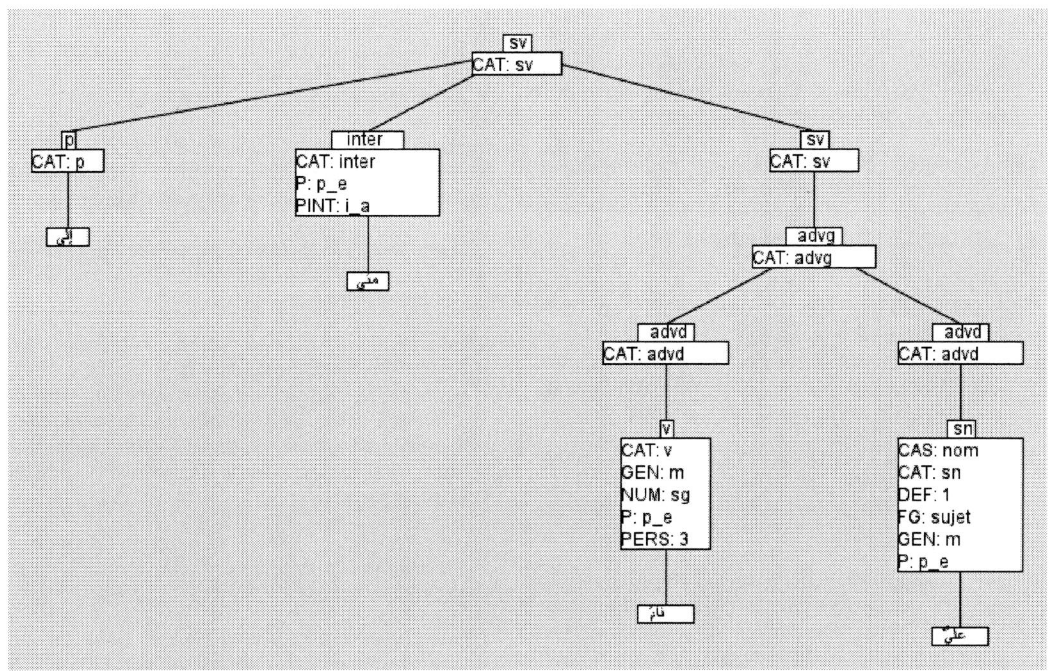

Figure 2: Derived tree for the sentence إلى متى نامَ عليّ ('*until when did Ali fall asleep ?*')

Arabic TreeBank – PATB). The corpus they used is the Part 1 v 2.0 of PATB (Maamouri et al., 2003; Maamouri and Bies, 2004). This extraction involved a reinterpretation of the corpus in dependency structures. The number of elementary trees generated was very high but they did not necessarily offer a good syntactic coverage. In fact, during the process, the authors were able to extract structures with varying positions of the sentence's component (grammatical functions). The resulting combinations are VSO, SVO and OVS. However they could not obtain the VOS combination. This failure is due to the absence of such structures in the corpus used for extraction. Furthermore, the resource is redundant because the researchers manipulated textual forms and not parts-of-speech. As acknowledged by the authors, this extraction was not optimal (grammar cleaning was needed). This somehow advocates for the conjoint use of description languages (that is, not only automatic extraction) to control the output grammar structures.

6 Conclusion and Future Work

In this paper, we showed how to produce a core TAG for Arabic by using the XMG2 system (Petitjean, 2014). First, a modular metagrammatical language for TAG is described by assembling language bricks and the corresponding metagrammar compiler automatically built using the XMG2 system. Then, this metagrammatical language is used to describe TAG trees.

This metagrammatical description benefits from XMG2's high expressivity (e.g. parameterized reusable tree fragments, node identification by means of colors). In particular, we showed how to describe in a relatively concise and yet easily extensible way, simple verbal subcategorization frames in Arabic. Such a description uses a verbal spine containing adjunction points to deal with the various constituent orders in Arabic.

While this work is still in progress, we are considering several extensions of this approach besides improving ArabTAG's coverage. Namely, we plan to integrate morphological and semantic dimensions to ArabTAG borrowing ideas from (Petitjean et al., 2015).

Acknowledgments

We are grateful to Simon Petitjean and three anonymous reviewers for useful comments on this work. This work was partially funded by LIFO.

References

Anne Abeillé, Marie Candito, and Alexandra Kinyon. 1999. FTAG: current status and parsing scheme. In *Proceedings of Vextal-99*, Venice, Italy.

Fériel Ben Fraj. 2010. *Un analyseur syntaxique pour les textes en langue arabe à base d'un apprentissage à partir des patrons d'arbres syntaxiques*. Ph.D. thesis, ENSI La Manouba, Tunisia.

Fériel Ben Fraj. 2011. Construction d'une grammaire d'arbres adjoints pour la langue arabe. In *Actes de la 18e conférence sur le Traitement Automatique des Langues Naturelles*, Montpellier, France, June. Association pour le Traitement Automatique des Langues.

Benoît Crabbé, Denys Duchier, Claire Gardent, Joseph Le Roux, and Yannick Parmentier. 2013. XMG : eXtensible MetaGrammar. *Computational Linguistics*, 39(3):591–629.

Denys Duchier, Brunelle Magnana Ekoukou, Yannick Parmentier, Simon Petitjean, and Emmanuel Schang. 2012. Describing Morphologically-rich Languages using Metagrammars: a Look at Verbs in Ikota. In *Workshop on "Language technology for normalisation of less-resourced languages", 8th SALTMIL Workshop on Minority Languages and the 4th workshop on African Language Technology*, pages 55–60, Istanbul, Turkey.

Dina El Kassas and Sylvain Kahane. 2004. Modélisation de l'ordre des mots en arabe standard. In *Atelier sur le traitement de la langue arabe, JEP-TALN 2004*, page 6. Modélisation de l'ordre des mots en arabe standard. Journées déroulées du 19 au 23 avril à Fès (Maroc).

Roger Evans and Gerald Gazdar. 1996. DATR: A language for lexical knowledge representation. *Computational Linguistics*, 22(2):167–216.

Claire Gardent. 2008. Integrating a unification-based semantics in a large scale Lexicalised Tree Adjoininig Grammar for French. In *Proceedings of the 22nd International Conference on Computational Linguistics (COLING'08)*, pages 249–256, Manchester, UK.

Nizar Habash and Owen Rambow. 2004. Extracting a tree adjoining grammar from the penn arabic treebank. *Proceedings of Traitement Automatique du Langage Naturel (TALN-04)*, pages 277–284.

Djamel Kouloughli. 1992. *La grammaire Arabe pour tous*. Press Pocket.

Mohamed Maamouri and Ann Bies. 2004. Developing an arabic treebank: Methods, guidelines, procedures, and tools. In Ali Farghaly and Karine Megerdoomian, editors, *COLING 2004 Computational Approaches to Arabic Script-based Languages*, pages 2–9, Geneva, Switzerland, August 28th. COLING.

Mohamed Maamouri, Ann Bies, Hubert Jin, and Tim Buckwalter. 2003. Arabic treebank: Part 1 v 2.0. LDC Catalog No.: LDC2003T06, ISBN: 1-58563-261-9, ISLRN: 333-321-196-670-5.

Yannick Parmentier, Laura Kallmeyer, Timm Lichte, Wolfgang Maier, and Johannes Dellert. 2008. TuLiPA: A Syntax-Semantics Parsing Environment for Mildly Context-Sensitive Formalisms. In *9th International Workshop on Tree-Adjoining Grammar and Related Formalisms (TAG+9)*, pages 121–128, Tübingen, Germany.

Simon Petitjean, Younes Samih, and Timm Lichte. 2015. Une métagrammaire de l'interface morphosémantique dans les verbes en arabe. In *Actes de la 22e conférence sur le Traitement Automatique des Langues Naturelles*, pages 473–479, Caen, France, June. Association pour le Traitement Automatique des Langues.

Simon Petitjean. 2014. *Génération Modulaire de Grammaires Formelles*. Ph.D. thesis, Université d'Orléans, France.

James Rogers and K. Vijay-Shanker. 1994. Obtaining trees from their descriptions: An application to tree-adjoining grammars. *Computational Intelligence*, 10:401–421.

Stuart M. Shieber, Hans Uszkoreit, Fernando Pereira, Jane Robinson, and Mabry Tyson. 1983. The formalism and implementation of PATR-II. In Barbara J. Grosz and Mark Stickel, editors, *Research on Interactive Acquisition and Use of Knowledge*, techreport 4, pages 39–79. SRI International, Menlo Park, CA, November. Final report for SRI Project 1894.

Éric Villemonte De La Clergerie. 2010. Building factorized TAGs with meta-grammars. In *The 10th International Conference on Tree Adjoining Grammars and Related Formalisms - TAG+10*, pages 111–118, New Haven, CO, United States, June.

Fei Xia. 2001. *Automatic Grammar Generation from two Different Perspectives*. Ph.D. thesis, University of Pennsylvania.

XTAG Research Group. 2001. A Lexicalized Tree Adjoining Grammar for English. Technical Report IRCS-01-03, IRCS, University of Pennsylvania.

Interfacing Sentential and Discourse TAG-based Grammars

Laurence Danlos
Université Paris Diderot
ALPAGE
INRIA Paris–Rocquencourt
Institut Universitaire de France
Paris, F-75005, France
laurence.danlos@inria.fr

Aleksandre Maskharashvili
INRIA, Villers-lès-Nancy, F-54600, France
Université de Lorraine, CNRS
LORIA, UMR 7503
Vandœuvre-lès-Nancy, F-54500, France
aleksandre.maskharashvili@inria.fr

Sylvain Pogodalla

sylvain.pogodalla@inria.fr

Abstract

Tree-Adjoining Grammars (TAG) have been used both for syntactic parsing, with sentential grammars, and for discourse parsing, with discourse grammars. But the modeling of discourse connectives (coordinate conjunctions, subordinate conjunctions, adverbs, etc.) in TAG-based formalisms for discourse differ from their modeling in sentential grammars. Because of this mismatch, an intermediate, not TAG-related, processing step is required between the sentential and the discourse processes, both in parsing and in generation. We present a method to smoothly interface sentential and discourse TAG grammars, without using such an intermediate processing step. This method is based on Abstract Categorial Grammars (ACG) and relies on the modularity of the latter. It also provides the possibility, as in D-STAG, to build discourse structures that are direct acyclic graphs (DAG) and not only trees. All the examples may be run and tested with the appropriate software.

1 Introduction

It is usually assumed that the internal structure of a text, typically characterized by discourse or rhetorical relations, plays an important role in its overall interpretation. Building this structure may resort to different techniques such as segmenting the discourse into elementary discourse units and then relating them with appropriate relations (Marcu, 2000; Soricut and Marcu, 2003). Other techniques use discourse grammars, and a particular trend relies on tree grammars (Polanyi and van den Berg, 1996; Gardent, 1997; Schilder, 1997). This trend has been further developed by integrating the modeling of both clausal syntax and semantics, and discourse syntax and semantics within the framework of Tree-Adjoining Grammar (TAG, Joshi et al. (1975); Joshi and Schabes (1997)). This gave rise to the TAG for Discourse (D-LTAG) formalism (Webber and Joshi, 1998; Forbes et al., 2003; Webber, 2004; Forbes-Riley et al., 2006), and to the Discourse Synchronous TAG (D-STAG) formalism (Danlos, 2009; Danlos, 2011). The latter derives semantic interpretation using Synchronous Tree-Adjoining Grammars (STAG, Shieber and Schabes (1990); Nesson and Shieber (2006); Shieber (2006)).

While one may think that using similar frameworks for both levels should help to interface them, it is not as smooth as one can expect. Indeed, a shared feature of D-LTAG and D-STAG is that grammatical parsing and discourse parsing are performed at two different stages. Moreover, the result of the first stage requires additional, not TAG-related, processing before being able to enter the second stage. This intermediary step consists in *discourse relation extraction* in D-LTAG and in *dicourse normalization* in D-STAG.

The reason for this intermediary step relates to the mismatch between the syntactic properties and the discourse properties of discourse markers. For instance, at the syntactical level, sentences as in (1) are well-formed.

(1)   a.   Then, John went to Paris.

       b.   John then went to Paris.

The discourse marker *then*, an adverb, is considered as a modifier, either of the whole clause in (1a) or of the verb phrase (1b). In TAG, they are represented as *auxiliary trees* with S or VP root nodes (XTAG Research Group, 2001; Abeillé, 2002). Using the elementary trees of Figure 1, Figure 2 (Figure 4, resp.) shows the TAG analysis of (1a) (of (1b), resp.).

Proceedings of the 12th International Workshop on Tree Adjoining Grammars and Related Formalisms (TAG+12), pages 27–37,
Düsseldorf, Germany, June 29 - July 1, 2016.

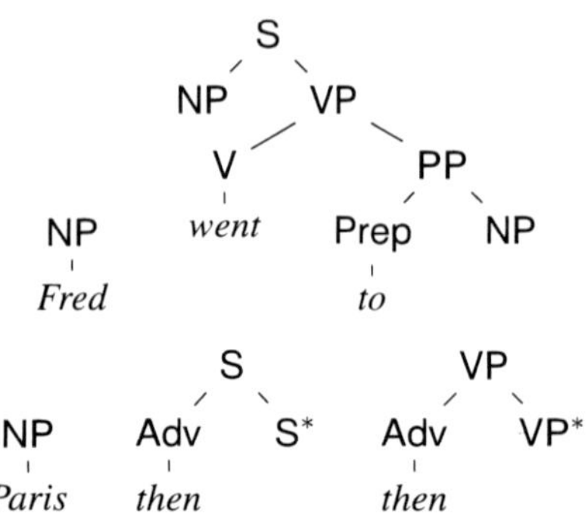

Figure 1: Elementary trees of a toy TAG grammar

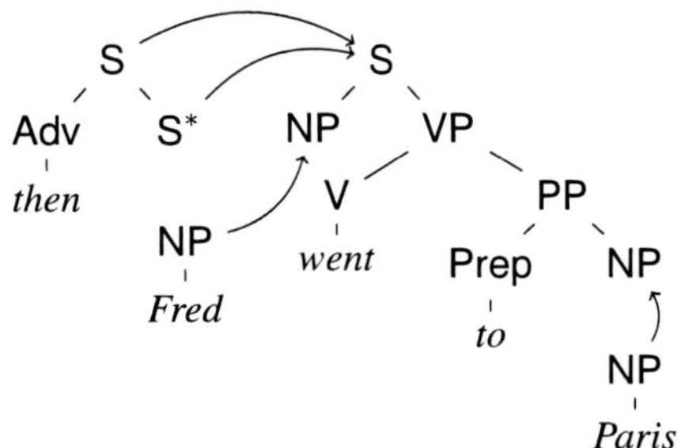

Figure 2: TAG analysis of (1a)

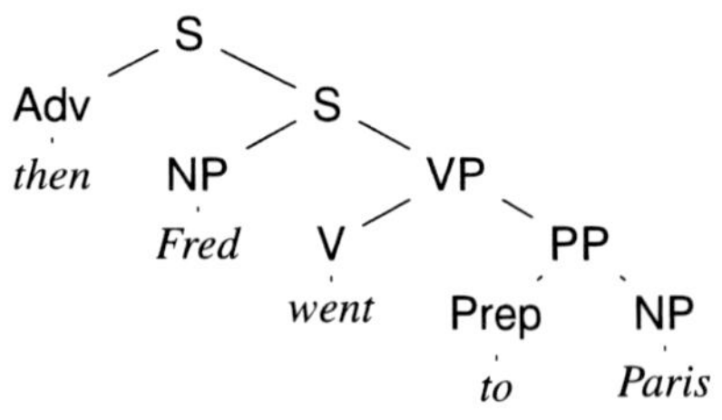

Figure 3: Derived tree for (1a)

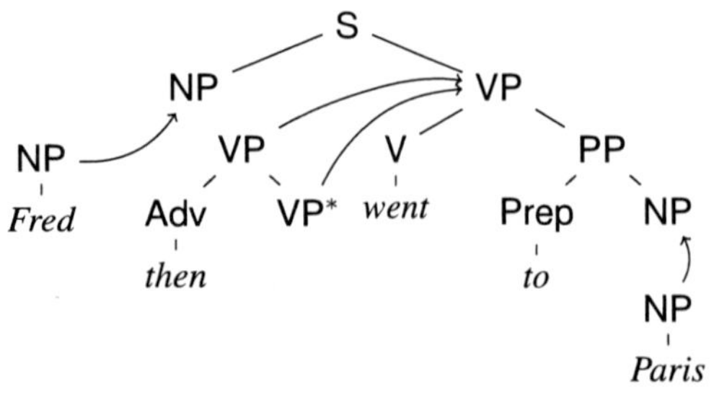

Figure 4: TAG analysis of (1b)

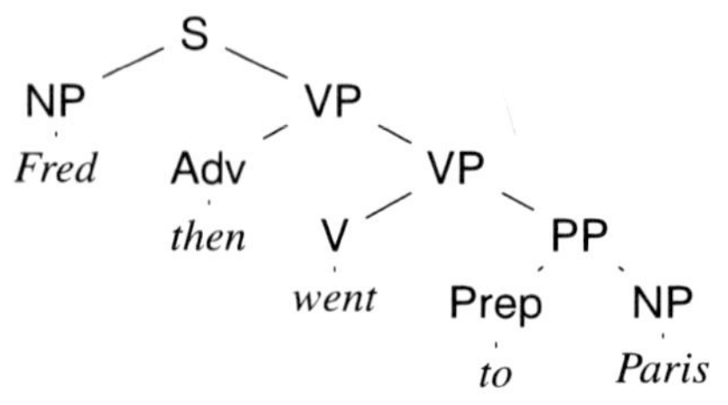

Figure 5: Derived tree for (1b)

At the discourse level, it is difficult to interpret these sentences without referring to preceding sentences. The discourse relation (e.g., Narration) has two arguments: the discourse unit consisting of the clause in which the discourse cue appears (the *host* clause), and some other discourse unit (it can be a complex one). D-LTAG and D-STAG propose different models of such adverbials, in particular in the way the first argument is provided. But in both accounts, adverbials are fronted (see Figure 6(c) and Figure 9(a)). Hence sentences with medial adverbials such as (1b) are excluded without the intermediary step of discourse relation extraction.

A similar mismatch occurs with subordinate conjunctions. In a typical TAG analysis, they are modeled with auxiliary trees because they modify the matrix clause and are not part of its predicate-argument structure.[1] In D-LTAG, however, they are modeled with initial trees with two substitution sites (see Figure 6(a)) for the two discourse units they are predicating over.

So the question of relating the syntactic modeling and the discourse modeling arises. In particular, we wish to avoid this relation to rely on some intermediary step. Indeed, the latter has several drawbacks. First, it complicates the modeling of connectives that are ambiguous in their syntactic and discourse use, and prevents us from using standard grammar inference and disambiguation techniques. Second, while most of the syntax-semantics interfaces, in particular in TAG, aim at satisfying a compositional assumption (Gardent and Kallmeyer, 2003; Pogodalla, 2004; Kallmeyer and Romero, 2008; Nesson and Shieber, 2006), the syntax-discourse interface seems to escape it. Third, a better integration of the sentential and of the discourse components also seems an interest-

---

[1] It is not always the case, though. Bernard and Danlos (2016) propose different elementary trees, depending on the syntactical, semantic, and discourse properties of the conjunction.

ing feature if we want to better describe the interaction between discourse connectives and propositional attitude predicates (Danlos, 2013; Bernard and Danlos, 2016).

Finally, when generation instead of parsing is at stake, this architecture also prevents the reversibility of the grammars and requires ad-hoc post-processing. G-TAG, a TAG-based formalism dedicated to generation that includes elements of a discourse grammar, had this requirement (Danlos, 1998; Meunier, 1997; Danlos, 2000).

In this article, we describe how to interface a sentential and a discourse TAG-based grammar. We show how to link such two grammars and their proposed modelings of discourse connectives, overcoming the above mentioned issue. We use an encoding of TAG into Abstract Categorial Grammar (ACG, de Groote (2001)), a grammatical framework based on the simply typed λ-calculus. As we aim at reusing previous works such as existing TAG sentential grammars as well as discourse analysis, our approach relies on two key features of ACG: the ACG account of the TAG operations and the ACG-based syntax-semantics interface for TAG (Pogodalla, 2004; Pogodalla, 2009) on the one hand; and the modular ACG composition, in order to smoothly integrate the syntactical and discourse behavior of adverbial connectives without using a two-step analysis on the other hand. Note, however, that the operations we use in the ACG composition are *not available* as TAG operations. While the encoding of TAG into ACG is standard (de Groote, 2002; Pogodalla, 2009), our contribution is to use the interpreting device of ACG to relate (the ACG encoding of) a TAG sentential grammar and (the ACG encoding of) a TAG discourse grammar. The example grammars we use may be run and tested[2] on the ACG development software.[3]

2 TAG Based Discourse Grammars

As TAG grammars, D-LTAG and D-STAG do not differ from any other TAG grammar: they define elementary trees that can be combined using the

operations of substitution and adjunction. However, if some elementary trees are anchored by lexical items (the discourse markers) as in sentential grammars, the others are anchored by clauses resulting from the syntactic analysis. Contrary to sentential grammars that contain a lot of different elementary tree families, discourse grammars have a small set of such families. In this section, we focus on these elementary trees, anchored by discourse markers. We show how the structure of these trees influences the interaction between the sentential and the discourse grammars, and why this interaction calls for an intermediary processing step. For an in-depth presentation of these formalisms, we refer the reader to (Webber and Joshi, 1998; Forbes et al., 2003; Webber, 2004; Forbes-Riley et al., 2006) for D-LTAG and to (Danlos, 2009; Danlos, 2011) for D-STAG.

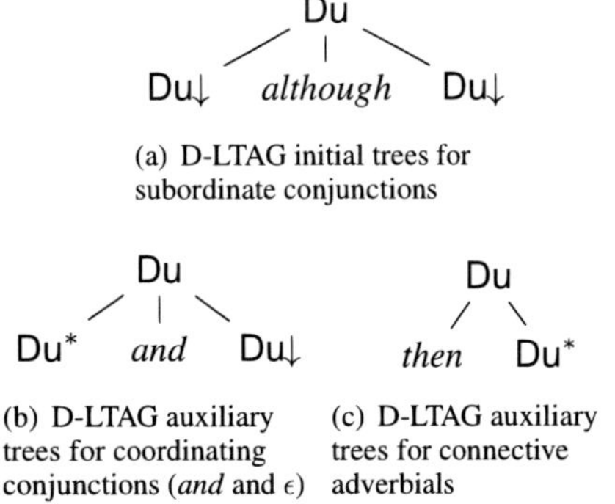

(a) D-LTAG initial trees for subordinate conjunctions

(b) D-LTAG auxiliary trees for coordinating conjunctions (*and* and ϵ)

(c) D-LTAG auxiliary trees for connective adverbials

Figure 6: D-LTAG elementary tree schemes

D-LTAG D-LTAG proposes three main families of elementary trees that capture different insights on discourse structures. Trees for subordinate conjunctions are modeled using *initial* trees with two substitution nodes for each of the arguments as Figure 6(a) shows. This reflects the predicate-argument structure of these connectives at the discourse level. But this contrasts with the syntactic account of these connectives: because they are outside the domain of locality of the verbs to which they can adjoin (at S or VP nodes), they typically are modeled using *auxiliary* trees (see Figure 7).

The second family of connectives is used to extend or to elaborate on clauses with auxiliary trees anchored by coordinate conjunctions (or by the empty connective). The first argument of the connective corresponds to the discourse unit the tree is

---

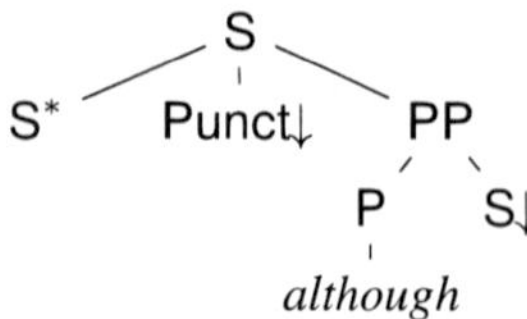

Figure 7: Syntactic modeling of subordinate conjunctions

adjoined to, and the second, the extending clause, corresponds to the clause that is substituted at the substitution node, as Figure 6(b) shows.

The third family also consists of auxiliary trees. But the latter are associated with a *single* clause as Figure 6(c) shows. The second argument comes from the *anaphoric* interpretation of the connectives anchoring such trees.

The two-stage process for parsing discourse proceeds as follows: first, each sentence gets a TAG analysis (derived and derivation trees) by a standard TAG. Then, each derivation tree is processed in order to identify the possible discourse connectives and their arguments from a syntactic point of view. The latter (one or two, depending on the connective) are added as initial trees with root Du to the discourse grammar, as well as the (discourse) elementary tree anchored by the connective. For instance, from the clausal derivation tree of Figure 8, the two arguments $\alpha^d_{s_1}$ and $\alpha^d_{s_2}$, and the connective $\beta^d_{s_3}$ are extracted. A similar extraction step takes care of the extraction of clause-medial adverbial connectives.

D-STAG Contrary to D-LTAG, D-STAG models all discourse connectives with auxiliary trees that are adjoined to the discourse unit they extend. The clause content that serves as second argument of the connective is substituted within this tree. Figure 9 shows some of the schemes for the elementary (auxiliary) trees of a D-STAG. The three internal Du nodes are available for adjunctions, achieving different effects on the semantic trees (following the principles of synchronous TAG, each discourse elementary tree is paired with a semantic tree). Together with a higher-order type for the semantic trees, this allows D-STAG to structurally generate DAG discourse structures.[4] But as the focus of this article is on the articulation between the sentential and the discourse grammar, we do

---

[4]Such structures are not easily available with D-LTAG, and this was a motivation to introduce D-STAG.

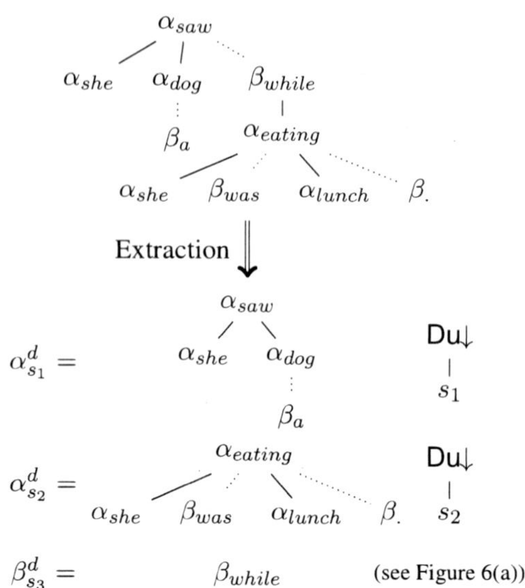

Figure 8: Discourse elementary tree extraction

not enter the details of the discourse-semantics interface here (see Danlos et al. (2015)).

D-STAG shares with D-LTAG the requirement of a transformation from the sequence of sentence analysis with a sentential grammar into a sequence of clauses and discourse connectives in a "discourse normal form". The reasons are basically the same as for D-LTAG: discourse connectives need to be identified in order to anchor their associated discourse elementary trees, as they differ from their syntactic elementary trees, and clause-medial extractions need to be managed at this level as well.

Medial Adverbial Extraction Looking at the elementary trees of Figure 9(a) (the problem is similar for D-LTAG elementary trees), we observe that the host clause of the adverbial are *substituted* into the elementary tree, at the Du↓ node. But at the sentential level, it is auxiliary trees anchored by the adverbials that adjoin into the host clause. When the adjunction occurs at the top S node, we get the same surface form in both cases. However, whenever the adjunction occurs at the VP node in the sentential grammar, this is not the case anymore: the adverbial is not fronted, and the discourse grammar cannot account for this position. An intermediary form, such as the discourse normal form in D-STAG, or the tree extraction in D-LTAG is then required. In order to get rid of this intermediary step, we should be

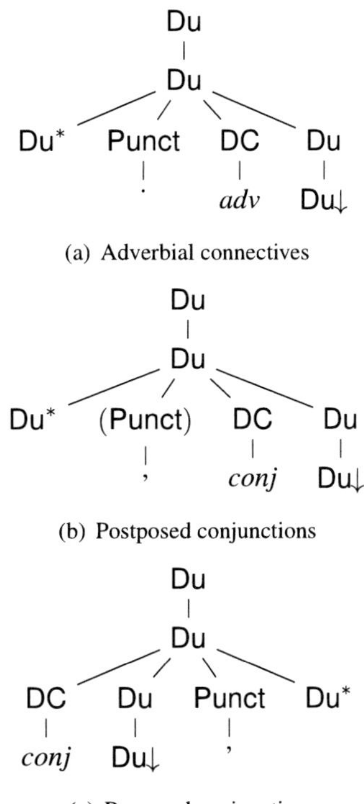

(a) Adverbial connectives

(b) Postposed conjunctions

(c) Preposed conjunction

Figure 9: D-STAG elementary trees

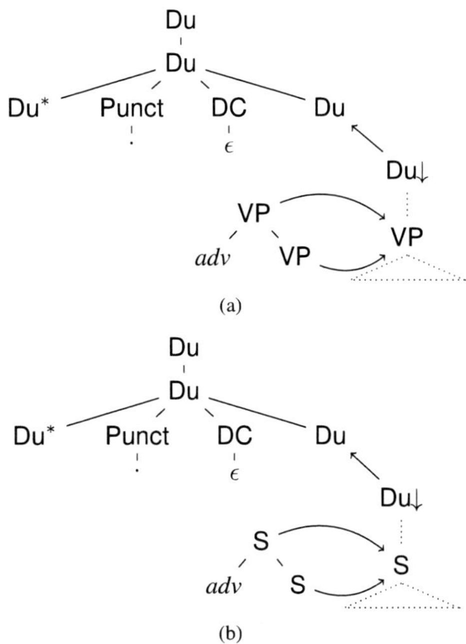

(a)

(b)

Figure 10: Auxiliary trees for discourse connectives

able to describe an operation that simultaneously substitutes a clause within the elementary tree of the discourse connective, and adjoins the auxiliary tree on the **VP** node. Figure 10(a) describes such an operation. The dotted lines would represent a dominance constraint that the tree to be substituted at **Du** $\downarrow$ should satisfy. It is also natural then to use the same approach for fronted discourse adverbials, as in Figure 10(b).

Because the adverb has to adjoin within the tree that is being substituted, describing such an operation seems not to be possible in TAG nor in multicomponent TAG (at least in a single step). It would be possible with D-Tree Substitution Grammars (Rambow et al., 2001), but then the derivation trees would be different, the synchronous syntax-semantics interface would have to be redefined, and the reversibility properties (for generation) would have to be stated. We instead use an encoding with ACG, where these properties naturally follow the standard encoding of TAG into ACG.

3   Abstract Categorial Grammars

ACG derives from type-theoretic grammars. Rather than a grammatical formalism on its own, it provides a framework in which several grammatical formalisms may be encoded (de Groote and Pogodalla, 2004), in particular TAG (de Groote, 2002). The definition of an ACG is based on type-theory, λ-calculus, and linear logic. In particular, ACG generates languages of linear λ-terms, which generalize both string and tree languages.

As key feature, ACG provides the user with a direct control over the parse structures of the grammar, the *abstract language*. Such structures are later on interpreted by a morphism, the *lexicon*, to get the concrete *object language*. We use the standard notations of the typed λ-calculus.

Definition (Types). Let A be a set of atomic types. The set $\mathcal{T}(A)$ of *implicative types* built upon A is defined with the following grammar:[5]

$$\mathcal{T}(A) ::= A \,|\, \mathcal{T}(A) \multimap \mathcal{T}(A)$$

Definition (Higher-Order Signatures). A *higher-order signature* Σ is a triple $\Sigma = \langle A, C, \tau \rangle$ where:

---

[5]We use the linear arrow $\multimap$ of linear logic (Girard, 1987) for the implication.

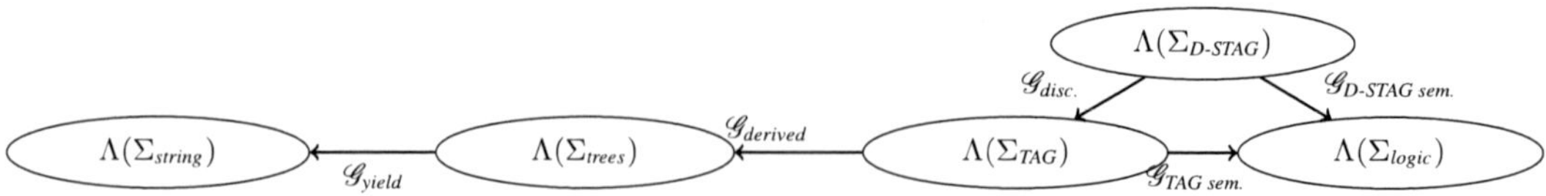

Figure 11: ACG architecture for a discourse and clause grammar interface

- A is a finite set of atomic types;

- C is a finite set of constants;

- $\tau : C \to \mathscr{T}(A)$ is a function assigning types to constants.

We note $\Lambda(\Sigma)$ the set of typed terms build on Σ. For $t \in \Lambda(\Sigma)$ and $\alpha \in \mathscr{T}(A)$, we denote that t has type α by $t :_\Sigma \alpha$ (possibly omitting the subscript).

Definition (Lexicon). Let $\Sigma_1 = \langle A_1, C_1, \tau_1 \rangle$ and $\Sigma_2 = \langle A_2, C_2, \tau_2 \rangle$ be two higher-order signatures. A lexicon $\mathscr{L} = \langle F, G \rangle$ from Σ_1 to Σ_2 is such that:

- $F : A_1 \to \mathscr{T}(A_2)$. We also note $F : \mathscr{T}(A_1) \to \mathscr{T}(A_2)$ its homomorphic extension;[6]

- $G : C_1 \to \Lambda(\Sigma_2)$. We also note $G : \Lambda(\Sigma_1) \to \Lambda(\Sigma_2)$ its homomorphic extension;[7]

- F and G are such that for all $c \in C_1$, $G(c)$ is of type $F(\tau_1(c))$ (i.e., $G(c) :_{\Sigma_2} F(\tau_1(c))$).

We also use $\mathscr{L}$ instead of F or G.

Definition (Abstract Categorial Grammar and vocabulary). An *abstract categorial grammar* is a quadruple $\mathscr{G} = \langle \Sigma_1, \Sigma_2, \mathscr{L}, \mathsf{S} \rangle$ where:

- $\Sigma_1 = \langle A_1, C_1, \tau_1 \rangle$ and $\Sigma_2 = \langle A_2, C_2, \tau_2 \rangle$ are two higher-order signatures. Σ_1 (resp. Σ_2) is called the *abstract vocabulary* (resp. the *object vocabulary*) and $\Lambda(\Sigma_1)$ (resp. $\Lambda(\Sigma_2)$) is the set of *abstract terms* (resp. the set of *object terms*).

- $\mathscr{L} : \Sigma_1 \to \Sigma_2$ is a lexicon.

- $\mathsf{S} \in \mathscr{T}(A_1)$ is the *distinguished type* of the grammar.

Given an ACG $\mathscr{G}_{name} = \langle \Sigma_1, \Sigma_2, \mathscr{L}_{name}, \mathsf{S} \rangle$, we use the following notational variants for the interpretation β (resp. u) of the type α (resp. of

the term t): $\mathscr{G}_{name}(\alpha) = \beta$ and $\alpha :=_{name} \beta$ (resp. $\mathscr{G}_{name}(t) = u$ and $t :=_{name} u$). The subscript may be omitted if clear from the context.

Definition (Abstract and Object Languages). Given an ACG $\mathscr{G}$, the *abstract language* is defined by

$$\mathcal{A}(\mathscr{G}) = \{ t \in \Lambda(\Sigma_1) \,|\, t :_{\Sigma_1} \mathsf{S} \}$$

The *object language* is defined by

$$\mathcal{O}(\mathscr{G}) = \{ u \in \Lambda(\Sigma_2) \,|\, \exists t \in \mathcal{A}(\mathscr{G}) \text{ s.t. } u = \mathscr{G}(t) \}$$

The process of recovering an abstract structure from an object term o is called *ACG parsing* and consists in finding the inverse image of $\{o\}$ under the lexicon (lexicon inversion). In this perspective, derivation trees of TAG are represented as terms of an abstract language, while derived trees (and yields) are represented by terms of some object languages. It is an object language of trees in the derived tree case and an object language of strings in the yield case. The class of *second-order ACG* is polynomially parsable with the usual complexity bounds ($O(n^3)$ for ACG encoding CFG, $O(n^6)$ for ACG encoding TAG, Kanazawa (2008)).

The lexicon, i.e., the way structures are interpreted, plays a crucial role in our proposal in two different ways. First, two interpretations may share the same abstract vocabulary, hence mapping a single structure into two different ones, typically a surface form and a semantic form. This composition, illustrated for instance by $\mathscr{G}_{derived}$ and $\mathscr{G}_{TAG\ sem.}$ sharing the Σ_{TAG} vocabulary in Figure 11, allows for the *semantic interpretation of derivation trees*. Second, the result of a first interpretation can itself be interpreted by a second lexicon when the object vocabulary of the first interpretation is the abstract vocabulary of the second one. This composition, illustrated for instance by the $\mathscr{G}_{yield} \circ \mathscr{G}_{derived}$ composition in Figure 11, allows for modularity and *partial specification of derivations*. This is how we relate the discourse derivation trees to the clausal derivation trees in $\mathscr{G}_{disc.}$.

---

[6] Such that $F(\alpha \multimap \beta) = F(\alpha) \multimap F(\beta)$.

[7] Such that $G(\lambda x.t) = \lambda x.G(t)$ and $G(t\ u) = G(t)\ G(u)$.

4 Examples

4.1 TAG as ACG

We present the TAG and D-STAG encoding using examples. This encoding follows (de Groote, 2001; de Groote, 2002; Pogodalla, 2009).

In order to encode a TAG into an ACG, we use a higher-order signature Σ_{TAG} whose atomic types include S, VP, NP, S_A, VP_A... where the X types stand for the categories X of the nodes where a substitution can occur while the X_A types stand for the categories X of the nodes where an adjunction can occur. For each elementary tree $\gamma_{lex.\ entry}$, there is a constant $C_{lex.\ entry}$ whose type is based on the adjunction and substitution sites as Table 1 shows. It additionally contains constants $I_X : X_A$ that are meant to provide a fake auxiliary tree on adjunction sites where no adjunction actually takes place in a TAG derivation. Terms built on this signature are interpreted by $\mathcal{G}_{derived}$ in the higher-order signature whose unique atomic type is τ the type of trees. In this signature, for any X of arity n belonging to the ranked alphabet describing the elementary trees of the TAG, we have

$$\text{a constant } X_n : \overbrace{\tau \multimap \cdots \multimap \tau}^{n \text{ times}} \multimap \tau.$$ Then $\mathcal{G}_{yield}$
interprets τ into σ, the type for strings, and X_n as $\lambda x_1 \cdots x_n . x_1 + \cdots + x_n$. For instance, the lexicon of Table 1 allows one to interpret two terms of $\Lambda(\Sigma_{TAG})$ representing a derivation with an adjunction at the S node (resp. at the VP node) of the given sentences as the equation (2a) (resp. (2b)) shows.

(2a) $\quad \mathcal{G}_{yield} \circ \mathcal{G}_{derived}(C_{went\ to}\ C^{\mathsf{S}}_{then}\ I_{\mathsf{VP}}\ C_{Fred}\ C_{Paris}) =$
$$then + Fred + went + to + Paris$$

(2b) $\quad \mathcal{G}_{yield} \circ \mathcal{G}_{derived}(C_{went\ to}\ I_{\mathsf{S}}\ C^{\mathsf{VP}}_{then}\ C_{Fred}\ C_{Paris}) =$
$$Fred + then + went + to + Paris$$

4.2 D-STAG as ACG

The ACG encoding of D-STAG follows the above mentioned principles to encode the derived and the derivation trees resulting from the D-STAG elementary trees of Figure 9. As a consequence, we get the same derivation trees. The main differences with (Danlos, 2009; Danlos, 2011) lie in the interpretations:

- $\mathcal{G}_{disc.}$ implements the interface between the discourse grammar and the sentential grammar, avoiding the intermediate step of building a discourse normal form (or the extraction step in D-LTAG). It is central to our proposal.

- $\mathcal{G}_{TAG\ sem.}$[8] implements the interpretation of the discourse structures. It slightly differs from (Danlos, 2011) in order to allow for a more unified view on the semantic types and to deal with the relative scope of quantifiers and discourse relations.

Sentence-Discourse Interface The higher-order vocabulary $\Sigma_{D\text{-}STAG}$ includes the usual atomic types to describe the sentence level (NP, VP, VP_A etc.) and new atomic types to describe the discourse level: Du, which is the type for discourse units, and the corresponding Du_A type representing adjunction sites. A typical constant introducing a discourse marker such as d^{S}_{then} has type
$$\mathsf{DC} \triangleq \mathsf{Du}_A \multimap \mathsf{Du}_A \multimap \mathsf{Du}_A \multimap \mathsf{Du} \multimap \mathsf{Du}_A$$
that reflects the auxiliary trees of D-STAG (Figure 9). For comparison, see the encoding of the C^{VP}_{then} encoding an auxiliary tree adjoining at a VP node). We also use a type T for full texts.

The key point to smoothly interface the sentential and the discourse grammar is to have the constant that describes a discourse marker d_{dm} of type DC at the discourse level interpreted using *the corresponding auxiliary tree C_{dm} at the right place*, i.e., as adjoining into the host clause. So, crucially, the interpretation specifies an adjunction of the auxiliary tree *into* the tree that is being substituted (i.e., the argument of Du type that is parameter of d_{dm} or, in D-STAG terms, the one plugged into the Du↓ node of the auxiliary trees of Figure 9). This operation mimics the insertion of the auxiliary tree in Figure 10.

In order to enable this adjunction, we interpret discourse units (with Du type) as *missing* a subordinate conjunction, a fronted adverbial, or a clause-medial adverbial. This corresponds to interpreting the atomic type Du as a second-order type such as $S_A \multimap VP_A \multimap S$.[9] We actually rather interpret Du as $S_A \multimap (VP_A \multimap VP_A) \multimap S$ in order to account for clause-medial adverbials occurring between to other adverbs such as in *John suddenly then passionately kissed her*.[10] Accord-

---

[8]Not discussed here but implemented in the example files.

[9]Another solution would be to have DC requires a ($S_A \multimap VP_A \multimap$ Du) type as fourth parameter. But the ACG would not be second-order anymore.

[10]It should be clear that from a technical point of view, both fronted and clause-medial missing adverbials could be dealt with the same way (i.e. with a $S_A \multimap VP_A \multimap$ S or a

Constants of Σ_{TAG}		Their interpretations by $\mathcal{G}_{derived}$
C_{Fred}	$: \mathsf{NP}$	$\gamma_{Fred} \;\; : \tau$
		$\gamma_{Fred} \;\; = \mathsf{NP}_1 \; Fred$
$C_{went\ to}$	$: \begin{array}{l} \mathsf{S}_A \multimap \mathsf{VP}_A \multimap \\ \mathsf{NP} \multimap \mathsf{NP} \multimap \mathsf{S} \end{array}$	$\gamma_{went\ to} \;\; : (\tau \multimap \tau) \multimap (\tau \multimap \tau) \multimap \tau \multimap \tau \multimap \tau$
		$\gamma_{went\ to} \;\; = \lambda S A sc.S(\mathsf{S}_2\; s\; (A\; (\mathsf{VP}_2\; (\mathsf{V}_1\; went)\; (\mathsf{PP}_2\; (\mathsf{Prep}\; to)\; c))))$
C^{S}_{then}	$: \mathsf{S}_A$	$\gamma^{\mathsf{S}}_{then} \;\; : \tau \multimap \tau$
		$\gamma^{\mathsf{S}}_{then} \;\; = \lambda x.(\mathsf{S}_2\; (\mathsf{Adv}_1\; then)\; x)$
C^{VP}_{then}	$: \mathsf{VP}_A \multimap \mathsf{VP}_A$	$\gamma^{\mathsf{VP}}_{then} \;\; : (\tau \multimap \tau) \multimap \tau \multimap \tau$
		$\gamma^{\mathsf{VP}}_{then} \;\; = \lambda A\; x.A\; (\mathsf{VP}_2\; (\mathsf{Adv}_1\; then)\; x)$

Table 1: Sample ACG lexicon encoding the TAG grammar of Figure 1

ingly, at the discourse level, the type of an intransitive verb will be $\mathsf{S}_A \multimap \mathsf{VP}_A \multimap \mathsf{VP}_A \multimap \mathsf{NP} \multimap \mathsf{S}$ instead of $\mathsf{S}_A \multimap \mathsf{VP}_A \multimap \mathsf{NP} \multimap \mathsf{S}$, allowing to specify the two VP_A auxiliary trees that can adjoin *before* and *after* the possible discourse marker. This leads us to the interpretation of Table 2. Note that even though the same name can occur on both sides of the $:=$ symbol, the atomic types and the constants on the left hand side belong to $\Sigma_{D\text{-}STAG}$ while the (possibly complex) types and the terms on the right hand side belong to $\Lambda(\Sigma_{TAG})$.

$$
\begin{array}{llll}
\mathsf{NP}_A & := \mathsf{NP}_A & \mathsf{N}_A & := \mathsf{N}_A \\
\mathsf{VP} & := \mathsf{VP} & \mathsf{Du}_A & := \mathsf{S}_A \\
\mathsf{VP}_A & := \mathsf{VP}_A \multimap \mathsf{VP}_A & \mathsf{T} & := \mathsf{S} \\
\mathsf{Du} & := \mathsf{S}_A \multimap (\mathsf{VP}_A \multimap \mathsf{VP}_A) \multimap \mathsf{S} & \mathsf{NP} & := \mathsf{NP} \\
\mathsf{S} & := \mathsf{S}_A \multimap (\mathsf{VP}_A \multimap \mathsf{VP}_A) \multimap \mathsf{S} & \mathsf{N} & := \mathsf{N} \\
\mathsf{S}_A & := \mathsf{S}_A \multimap \mathsf{S}_A & &
\end{array}
$$

$$
\begin{aligned}
&I_X & &: X_A \;\; := \lambda P.P \\
&d_{Fred} & &: \mathsf{NP} := \;\; C_{Fred} \\
&d_{went\ to} & &: \mathsf{S}_A \multimap \mathsf{VP}_A \multimap \mathsf{VP}_A \multimap \mathsf{S} \multimap \mathsf{S} \\
& & &:= \lambda S\; a_1\; a_2\; s\; o\; c\; m. \\
& & &\qquad C_{went\ to}\; (S\; c)(a_2(m(a_1 I_{\mathsf{VP}})))\; s\; o \\
&d_{in.\ anc.} & &: \mathsf{S} \multimap \mathsf{Du}_A \multimap \mathsf{Du} \\
& & &:= \lambda s\; m\; d_s\; d_v.\mathsf{mod}\; (s\; d_s\; d_v)\; m \\
&d_{anchor} & &: \mathsf{S} \multimap \mathsf{Du}_A \multimap \mathsf{Du} \\
& & &:= \lambda s\; m\; d_s\; d_v.\mathsf{mod}\; (s\; d_s\; d_v)\; m \\
&d^{\mathsf{S}}_{then} & &: \mathsf{Du}_A \multimap \mathsf{Du}_A \multimap \mathsf{Du}_A \multimap \mathsf{Du} \multimap \mathsf{Du}_A \\
& & &:= \lambda d_1\; d_2\; d_3\; s.\mathsf{cons}\; d_1\; d_2\; d_3\; (s\; C^{\mathsf{S}}_{then}\; (\lambda x.x)) \\
&d^{\mathsf{VP}}_{then} & &: \mathsf{Du}_A \multimap \mathsf{Du}_A \multimap \mathsf{Du}_A \multimap \mathsf{Du} \multimap \mathsf{Du}_A \\
& & &:= \lambda d_1\; d_2\; d_3\; s.\mathsf{cons}\; d_1\; d_2\; d_3\; (s\; I_{\mathsf{S}}\; C^{\mathsf{VP}}_{then})
\end{aligned}
$$

Table 2: $\mathcal{G}_{disc.}$ interpretation for the sentence-discourse interface[12]

We exemplify our approach on the examples (3). In D-STAG, the associated discourse rep-

---

$(\mathsf{S}_A \multimap \mathsf{S}_A) \multimap (\mathsf{VP}_A \multimap \mathsf{VP}_A) \multimap \mathsf{S}$ type). We leave it for further work to check the adequacy of the same phenomena occurring for fronted adverbials and how it compares with discourse connective modification or multiple connectives.

[12] mod and cons are two operators that have no other meaning that juxtaposing TAG derivation trees of elementary discourse units. They are interpreted as: $\mathsf{mod} := \lambda s\; m.m\; s$ (it performs the actual adjunction on the derived tree) and $\mathsf{cons} := \lambda s_1\; s_2\; s_3\; s\; x.s_1(s_2(\mathsf{S}_3\; x\; .\; (s_3\; s)))$ (it builds a derived tree, inserting a period between the derived trees corresponding to the elementary discourse units).

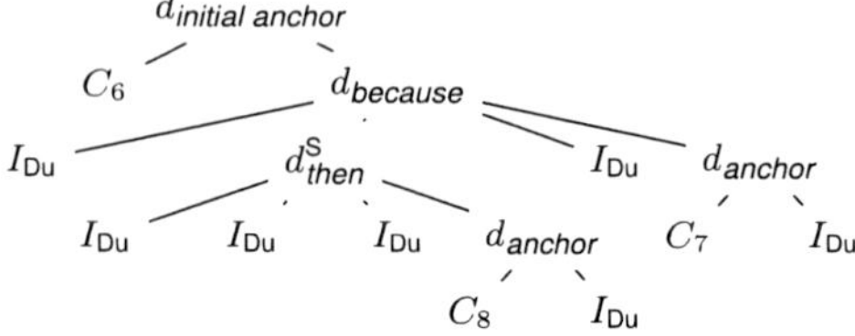

Figure 12: Discourse derivation trees

resentation is as in Figure 13, and the discourse derivation trees is the one of Figure 12 where the C_is correspond to the derivation trees of the bracketed discourse units of the examples. In D-STAG, the discourse derivation tree of course results from the discourse normal form F_6 because F_7 then F_8 that are the same for (3a) and (3b).

(3) a. [Fred went to the supermarket]$_6$ because [his fridge is empty]$_7$. Then, [he went to the movies]$_8$.

    b. [Fred went to the supermarket]$_6$ because [his fridge is empty]$_7$. [He]$_8$ then [went to the movies]$_8$.

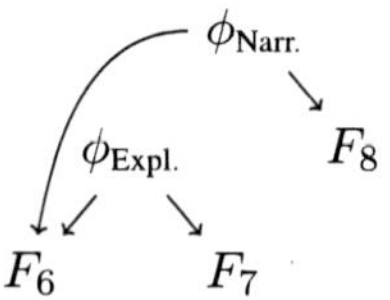

Figure 13: Discourse structure for (3a)

If we define the terms d_8 and d'_8 as in (4) and (5), we can compute their interpretations (6)-(11) using the lexicons of Tables 1 and 2. They show that both positions for the adverbs are now available directly from the abstract terms representing discourse derivations. Consequently, the two terms defined in (12) and (13) account for both sentences of (3). Note that they differ only in the constant they use for the adverb.

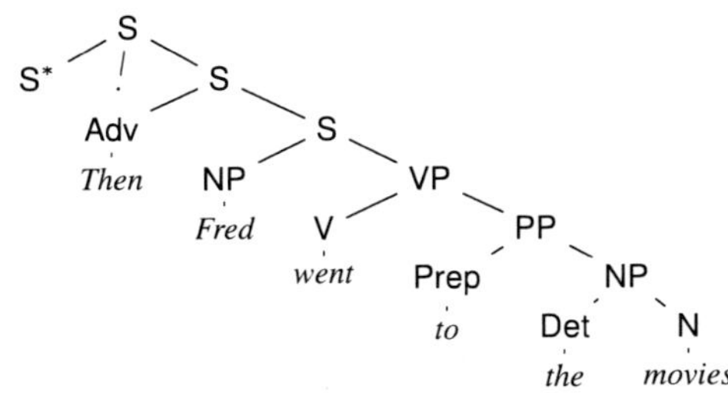

(a) Derived tree for d_8

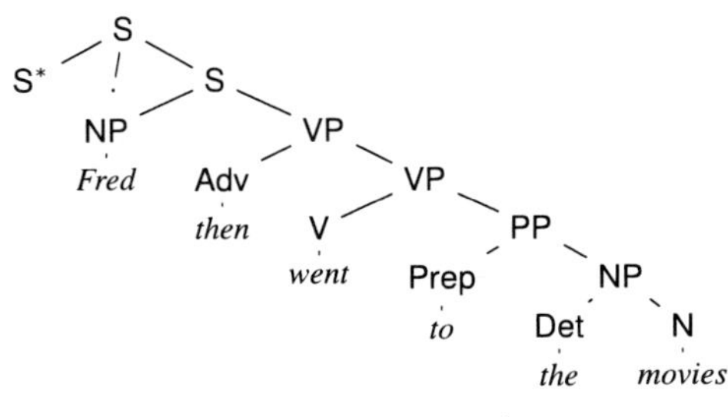

(b) Derived tree for d'_8

Figure 14: Interpretations as derived trees

(4) $\quad d_8 = d^{\mathsf{S}}_{then}\ I_{\mathsf{Du}}\ I_{\mathsf{Du}}\ I_{\mathsf{Du}}\ (d_{anchor}\ C_8\ I_{\mathsf{Du}}) : \mathsf{Du}_A$

(5) $\quad d'_8 = d^{\mathsf{VP}}_{then}\ I_{\mathsf{Du}}\ I_{\mathsf{Du}}\ I_{\mathsf{Du}}\ (d_{anchor}\ C_8\ I_{\mathsf{Du}}) : \mathsf{Du}_A$

5 Related Works

This problem of avoiding an intermediate step between a sentential and a discourse analysis has also been addressed within the framework of Combinatory Categorial Grammar (CCG, Steedman (2001); Steedman and Baldridge (2011)) by Nakatsu and White (2010). They propose a single grammar to treat both sentential and discourse phenomena using Discourse Combinatory Categorial Grammar (DCCG). This approach introduced "cue threading" where "connectives can be thought of as percolating from where they take scope semantically down to the clause in which they appear" (Nakatsu and White, 2010, p. 19). Here, the connective at the discourse level takes scope over its argument, but it is interpreted at the sentential level as an auxiliary tree adjoining within the clause.

6 Conclusion

This article shows how to interface TAG-based sentential and discourse grammars without resorting to a two step process. It relies on the interpretation of abstract terms encoding discourse derivation trees into terms encoding sentential derivation trees using ACG. The approach also allows us to build DAG discourse structures. ACG grammars have been implemented to compute (and parse) the surface forms and associate them with the relevant semantic forms. In this article, we only applied the approach to D-STAG, but it should be clear that it applies to D-LTAG as well. The approach is also suitable to model connective modifications (... *probably because it rains*). Our future work will concern multiple connectives (... *because then he discovered he was broke*), some of them we already account for. It will also concern the integration of discourse structure constraints such as the right frontier principle and the interaction with pronominal anaphora resolution.

Finally, discourse grammars are highly ambiguous. Hence the ACG we derive from such grammars also are ambiguous. We want to take advantage of our integrated approach to apply the disambiguation methods used in syntactic parsing. Moreover, as the analysis can now be dealt with at the level of the text, even with polynomial algorithms, the size of the input will be an issue. This calls for further analysis of discourse structuring, both in parsing and generation.

(6) $\quad \mathcal{G}_{disc.}(d_8) = \mathsf{cons}\ I_{\mathsf{S}}\ I_{\mathsf{S}}\ I_{\mathsf{S}}\ (\mathsf{mod}\ (C_{went\ to}\ C^{\mathsf{S}}_{then}\ I_{\mathsf{VP}}\ C_{Fred}(C_{the}\ (C_{movies}\ I_{\mathsf{N}})))\ I_{\mathsf{S}}) : \mathsf{S}_A$

(7) $\quad \mathcal{G}_{derived} \circ \mathcal{G}_{disc.}(d_8) = $ [see the tree representation in Figure 14(a)]

(8) $\quad \mathcal{G}_{yield} \circ \mathcal{G}_{derived} \circ \mathcal{G}_{disc.}(d_8) = \lambda x.x + . + Then + Fred + went + to + the + movies) : \sigma \multimap \sigma$

(9) $\quad \mathcal{G}_{disc.}(d'_8) = \mathsf{cons}\ I_{\mathsf{S}}\ I_{\mathsf{S}}\ I_{\mathsf{S}}\ (\mathsf{mod}\ (C_{went\ to}\ I_{\mathsf{S}}\ (C^{\mathsf{VP}}_{then}\ I_{\mathsf{VP}})\ C_{Fred}(C_{the}\ (C_{movies}\ I_{\mathsf{N}})))\ I_{\mathsf{S}}) : \mathsf{S}_A$

(10) $\quad \mathcal{G}_{derived} \circ \mathcal{G}_{disc.}(d'_8) = $ [see the tree representation in Figure 14(b)]

(11) $\quad \mathcal{G}_{yield} \circ \mathcal{G}_{derived} \circ \mathcal{G}_{disc.}(d'_8) = \lambda x.x + . + Fred + then + went + to + the + movies) : \sigma \multimap \sigma$

(12) $\quad d_3 = d_{in.\ anc.}\ C_6\ (d_{because}\ I_{\mathsf{Du}}\ (d^{\mathsf{S}}_{then}\ I_{\mathsf{Du}}\ I_{\mathsf{Du}}\ I_{\mathsf{Du}}\ (d_{anc.}\ C_8\ I_{\mathsf{Du}}))\ I_{\mathsf{Du}}\ (d_{anc.}\ C_7\ I_{\mathsf{Du}}))$

(13) $\quad d'_3 = d_{in.\ anc.}\ C_6\ (d_{because}\ I_{\mathsf{Du}}\ (d^{\mathsf{VP}}_{then}\ I_{\mathsf{Du}}\ I_{\mathsf{Du}}\ I_{\mathsf{Du}}\ (d_{anc.}\ C_8\ I_{\mathsf{Du}}))\ I_{\mathsf{Du}}\ (d_{anc.}\ C_7\ I_{\mathsf{Du}}))$

35

References

Anne Abeillé. 2002. *Une grammaire électronique du français*. Sciences du langage. CNRS Éditions.

Timothée Bernard and Laurence Danlos. 2016. Modelling discourse in stag: Subordinate conjunctions and attributing phrases. In David Chiang and Alexander Koller, editors, *Proceedings of the Twelfth International Workshop on Tree Adjoining Grammars and Related Framework (TAG+12)*. HAL open archive: hal-01329539.

Laurence Danlos, Aleksandre Maskharashvili, and Sylvain Pogodalla. 2015. Grammaires phrastiques et discursives fondées sur les TAG : une approche de D-STAG avec les ACG. In *TALN 2015 - 22e conférence sur le Traitement Automatique des Langues Naturelles*, Actes de TALN 2015, pages 158–169, Caen, France. Association pour le Traitement Automatique des Langues. HAL open archive: hal-01145994.

Laurence Danlos. 1998. G-TAG : Un formalisme lexicalisé pour la génération de textes inspiré de TAG. *Traitement Automatique des Langues*, 39(2). HAL open archive: inria-00098489.

Laurence Danlos. 2000. G-TAG: A lexicalized formalism for text generation inspired by Tree Adjoining Grammar. In Anne Abeillé and Owen Rambow, editors, *Tree Adjoining Grammars: Formalisms, Linguistic Analysis, and Processing*, volume 107 of *CSLI Lecture Notes*, pages 343–370. CSLI Publications. http://www.linguist.jussieu.fr/~danlos/Dossier%20publis/G-TAG-eng'01.pdf.

Laurence Danlos. 2009. D-STAG : un formalisme d'analyse automatique de discours basé sur les TAG synchrones. *T.A.L.*, 50(1):111–143. HAL open archive: inria-00524743.

Laurence Danlos. 2011. D-STAG: a formalism for discourse analysis based on SDRT and using Synchronous TAG. In Philippe de Groote, Markus Egg, and Laura Kallmeyer, editors, *14th conference on Formal Grammar - FG 2009*, volume 5591 of *LNCS/LNAI*, pages 64–84. Springer. DOI: 10.1007/978-3-642-20169-1_5.

Laurence Danlos. 2013. Connecteurs de discours adverbiaux : Problèmes à l'interface syntaxe-sémantique. *LinguisticæInvestigationes*, 36(2):261–275. HAL open archive: hal-00932184. DOI: 10.1075/li.36.2.05dan.

Philippe de Groote and Sylvain Pogodalla. 2004. On the expressive power of Abstract Categorial Grammars: Representing context-free formalisms. *Journal of Logic, Language and Information*, 13(4):421–438. HAL open archive: inria-00112956. DOI: 10.1007/s10849-004-2114-x.

Philippe de Groote. 2001. Towards Abstract Categorial Grammars. In *Association for Computational Linguistics, 39th Annual Meeting and 10th Conference of the European Chapter, Proceedings of the Conference*, pages 148–155. ACL anthology: P01-1033.

Philippe de Groote. 2002. Tree-Adjoining Grammars as Abstract Categorial Grammars. In *Proceedings of the Sixth International Workshop on Tree Adjoining Grammars and Related Frameworks (TAG+6)*, pages 145–150. Università di Venezia. URL: http://www.loria.fr/equipes/calligramme/acg/publications/2002-tag+6.pdf.

Katherine Forbes, Eleni Miltsakaki, Rashmi Prasad, Anoop Sarkar, Aravind K. Joshi, and Bonnie Lynn Webber. 2003. D-LTAG system: Discourse parsing with a Lexicalized Tree-Adjoining Grammar. *Journal of Logic, Language and Information*, 12(3):261–279. Special Issue: Discourse and Information Structure. DOI: 10.1023/A:1024137719751.

Katherine Forbes-Riley, Bonnie Lynn Webber, and Aravind K. Joshi. 2006. Computing discourse semantics: The predicate-argument semantics of discourse connectives in D-LTAG. *Journal of Semantics*, 23(1):55–106. DOI: 10.1093/jos/ffh032.

Claire Gardent and Laura Kallmeyer. 2003. Semantic construction in feature-based TAG. In *Proceedings of the 10th Meeting of the European Chapter of the Association for Computational Linguistics (EACL)*, pages 123–130. ACL anthology: E03-1030.

Claire Gardent. 1997. Discourse tree adjoining grammar. CLAUS Report 89, Universit, Saarbr, April.

Jean-Yves Girard. 1987. Linear logic. *Theoretical Computer Science*, 50(1):1–102. DOI: 10.1016/0304-3975(87)90045-4.

Aravind K. Joshi and Yves Schabes. 1997. Tree-adjoining grammars. In Grzegorz Rozenberg and Arto K. Salomaa, editors, *Handbook of formal languages*, volume 3, chapter 2. Springer.

Aravind K. Joshi, Leon S. Levy, and Masako Takahashi. 1975. Tree adjunct grammars. *Journal of Computer and System Sciences*, 10(1):136–163. DOI: 10.1016/S0022-0000(75)80019-5.

Laura Kallmeyer and Maribel Romero. 2008. Scope and situation binding for LTAG. *Research on Language and Computation*, 6(1):3–52. DOI: 10.1007/s11168-008-9046-6.

Makoto Kanazawa. 2008. A prefix-correct earley recognizer for multiple context-free grammars. In *Proceedings of the Ninth International Workshop on Tree Adjoining Grammars and Related Formalisms (TAG+9)*, pages 49–56, Tuebingen, Germany, June 7–8. http://tagplus9.cs.sfu.ca/papers/Kanazawa.pdf.

Daniel Marcu. 2000. *The Theory and Practice of Discourse Parsing and Summarization*. The MIT Press.

Frédéric Meunier. 1997. *Implantation du formalisme de génération G-TAG*. Ph.D. thesis, Université Paris 7 — Denis Diderot.

Crystal Nakatsu and Michael White. 2010. Generating with discourse combinatory categorial grammar. *Linguistic Issues in Language Technology*, 4. http://journals.linguisticsociety.org/elanguage/lilt/article/view/1277.html.

Rebecca Nancy Nesson and Stuart M. Shieber. 2006. Simpler TAG semantics through synchronization. In *Proceedings of the 11th Conference on Formal Grammar*, Malaga, Spain, 7. CSLI Publications. http://cslipublications.stanford.edu/FG/2006/nesson.pdf.

Sylvain Pogodalla. 2004. Computing Semantic Representation: Towards ACG Abstract Terms as Derivation Trees. In *Seventh International Workshop on Tree Adjoining Grammar and Related Formalisms - TAG+7*, pages 64–71, Vancouver, BC, Canada. HAL open archive: inria-00107768.

Sylvain Pogodalla. 2009. Advances in Abstract Categorial Grammars: Language Theory and Linguistic Modeling. ESSLLI 2009 Lecture Notes, Part II. HAL open archive: hal-00749297.

Livia Polanyi and Martin H. van den Berg. 1996. Discourse structure and discourse interpretation. In Paul J. E. Dekker and Martin Stokhof, editors, *Proceedings of the Tenth Amsterdam Colloquium*. ILLC/Department of Philosophy, University of Amsterdam. http://citeseerx.ist.psu.edu/viewdoc/summary?doi=10.1.1.56.221.

Owen Rambow, K. Vijay-Shanker, and David Weir. 2001. D-Tree Substitution Grammars. *Computational Linguistics*, 27(1):87–121. ACL anthology: J01-1004. DOI: 10.1162/089120101300346813.

Frank Schilder. 1997. Tree discourse grammar or how to get attached to a discourse? In *In Proceedings of the Tilburg Conference on Formal Semantics (IWCS-1997)*, pages 261–273. ftp://ftp.informatik.uni-hamburg.de/pub/unihh/informatik/WSV/schild97a.ps.gz.

Stuart M. Shieber and Yves Schabes. 1990. Synchronous tree-adjoining grammars. In *Proceedings of the 13th International Conference on Computational Linguistics*, volume 3, pages 253–258, Helsinki, Finland. http://www.eecs.harvard.edu/~shieber/Biblio/Papers/synch-tags.pdf. DOI: 10.3115/991146.991191.

Stuart M. Shieber. 2006. Unifying synchronous tree-adjoining grammars and tree transducers via bimorphisms. In *Proceedings of the 11th Conference of the European Chapter of the Association for Computational Linguistics (EACL-06)*, pages 377–384, Trento, Italy, 3–7 April. ACL anthology: E06-1048.

Radu Soricut and Daniel Marcu. 2003. Sentence level discourse parsing using syntactic and lexical information. In Marti Hearst and Mari Ostendorf, editors, *Proceedings of the 2003 Human Language Technology Conference of the North American Chapter of the Association for Computational Linguistics (HLT-NAACL 2003)*, pages 149–156. ACL anthology: N03-1030.

Mark Steedman and Jason Baldridge. 2011. Combinatory categorial grammar. In Robert Borsley and Kersti Börjars, editors, *Non-Transformational Syntax: Formal and Explicit Models of Grammar*, chapter 5. Wiley-Blackwell.

Mark Steedman. 2001. *The Syntactic Process*. MIT Press.

Bonnie Lynn Webber and Aravind K. Joshi. 1998. Anchoring a lexicalized tree-adjoining grammar for discourse. In Manfred Stede, Leo Wanner, and Eduard Hovy, editors, *Proccedings of the ACL/COLING workshop on Discourse Relations and Discourse Markers*. ACL anthology: W98-0315.

Bonnie Lynn Webber. 2004. D-LTAG: extending lexicalized TAG to discourse. *Cognitive Science*, 28(5):751–779. DOI: 10.1207/s15516709cog2805_6.

XTAG Research Group. 2001. A Lexicalized Tree Adjoining Grammar for English. Technical Report IRCS-01-03, IRCS, University of Pennsylvania. ftp://ftp.cis.upenn.edu/pub/xtag/release-2.24.2001/tech-report.pdf.

Modelling Discourse in STAG:
Subordinate Conjunctions and Attributing Phrases

Timothée Bernard
Université Paris Diderot
ALPAGE
timothee.bernard@inria.fr

Laurence Danlos
Université Paris Diderot
ALPAGE, IUF
laurence.danlos@inria.fr

Abstract

We propose a new model in STAG syntax and semantics for subordinate conjunctions (SubConjs) and attributing phrases – attitude/reporting verbs (AVs; *believe, say*) and attributing prepositional phrase (APPs; *according to*). This model is discourse-oriented, and is based on the observation that SubConjs and AVs are not homogeneous categories. Indeed, previous work has shown that SubConjs can be divided into two classes according to their syntactic and semantic properties. Similarly, AVs have two different uses in discourse: *evidential* and *intentional*. While evidential AVs and APPs have strong semantic similarities, they do not appear in the same contexts when SubConjs are at play. Our proposition aims at representing these distinctions and capturing these various discourse-related interactions.

1   Introduction

A text as a whole must exhibit some coherence that makes it more than just a bag of sentences. This coherence hinges on the *discourse relations* (DRs), that express the articulations between the different pieces of information of the text. There is still debate about the number and the nature of DRs, yet typical DRs include *Contrast, Consequence* or *Explanation* (Asher and Lascarides, 2003). In this paper we consider that DRs are two-place predicates that structure the text at the discourse level (1a) but also at the sentence level (1b). In these two examples, the *Consequence* relation is *explicit*, i.e. lexically signalled, but a DR can also be *implicit*, i.e. semantically inferred. This is for instance the case when *therefore* is removed

from (1b) to produce (1c).[1]

(1) a. *Fred was ill*. <u>Therefore</u>, **he stayed home**.

  b. *Fred was ill*, **he** <u>therefore</u> **stayed home**.

  c. *Fred was ill*, **he stayed home**.

Therefore is a *discourse connective* (DC), a group of lexical elements whose function is to signal that a DR holds between two spans of text.[2] DCs can be of different syntactic categories; we are specifically concerned here with subordinate conjunctions (SubConjs). SubConjs are generally considered a homogeneous category although previous work such as (Haegeman, 2004) has shown they can be divided into two classes with distinctive syntactic and semantic properties. Such properties are the possibility or impossibility of cleft sentences illustrated in (2) or the difference of scope observed in (3).

(2) a. It is <u>when</u> **he was twenty** that *Fred went to Brazil*.

  b. #It is even though he really wanted to come that Fred stayed home.

(3) a. He did not come because he was hungry: he came because he was thirsty.

  b. #He did not come even though he still had work to do: he came even though he was tired.

In addition to SubConjs, we are interested in *attitude verbs* and *reporting verbs* (AVs) – verbs

---

[1]Following the conventions of the PDTB (Prasad et al., 2007), we refer to the two arguments of DRs as Arg_1 and Arg_2 and use italics and bold face respectively to indicate the spans of text for each argument.

[2]There exist more complex markers constituting an open class, referred to as "AltLex" – "alternative lexicalization" (Prasad et al., 2010).

Proceedings of the 12th International Workshop on Tree Adjoining Grammars and Related Formalisms (TAG+12), pages 38–47,
Düsseldorf, Germany, June 29 - July 1, 2016.

like *say* or *believe*, which describe an action or a state but also report the stance of an agent towards a given semantic proposition – and attributing prepositional phrases (APPs; e.g. *according to*). These have particular interactions with DCs in general and SubConjs in particular. Some of these phenomena could probably be correctly analysed with a purely semantic treatment of *at-issueness* inspired from (Potts, 2005) and (Scheffler, 2013). However, we think a proper treatment of the syntactic aspects as well requires a different formalism. The goal of this work is to model these various lexical elements in a Synchronous Tree Adjoining Grammar (STAG, (Shieber and Schabes, 1990)). Current models so far (see (Nesson and Shieber, 2006), or (Danlos, 2009) which focuses specifically on discourse analysis) do not incorporate most of the properties mentioned in this paper.

The paper is organised as follows. Section 2 presents relevant work related to DCs, AVs and some of their interactions. Section 3 exposes and summarises the properties we are aiming for with our model. Then, Section 4 describes our STAG proposition. Section 5 discusses this model and introduce a possible evolution.

2 Relevant Work

2.1 Non-Alignment of Syntactic and Discourse Arguments

According to a number of authors (see (Dinesh et al., 2005) for English and (Danlos, 2013) for French), in a sentence like (4a) the speaker intends to contrast her belief with the belief of Sabine; hence the inclusion of *Sabine thinks* in Arg_2. On the contrary, in (4b) the speaker does not intend to oppose her belief with the one of Sabine, but rather Fred's stay in Peru with his (alleged) absence of stay in Lima; hence the exclusion of *Sabine thinks* from the argument of the DR. In this last case, we observe that the (semantic/discourse) argument of the DR is included in but not equal to the propositional content of the (syntactic) argument of the DC.[3]

Such non-alignments of the syntactic and discourse arguments ("mismatches" in the following) often arise with *attitude verbs* and *reporting verbs* (AV): when an AV together with the clause it introduces is an argument of a DC, the AV may (4a)

---

[3]Another argument for this distinction is that *Sabine thinks* can be felicitously removed from (4b) while it cannot from (4a).

or may not (4b) be included in the discourse argument of the corresponding DR. Following (Asher et al., 2006), we say the AV is *intentional* in the first case and *evidential* in the second. One can notice that an evidential AV is equivalent to the expression *according to Sabine*.

(4) a. *Fred went to Peru* <u>although</u> **Sabine thinks he never left Europe**.

   b. *Fred went to Peru* <u>although</u> Sabine thinks **he has never been to Lima**.

It is interesting to note, as highlighted in (Hunter and Danlos, 2014), that contrarily to *although* not all DCs can be found with such mismatches. It is the case, for instance, of *because*, as illustrated in (5). (Hunter and Danlos, 2014), using the DR hierarchy of the PDTB, observes that a DC lexicalising a COMPARISON or an EXPANSION relation can often be found with a mismatch, whereas it seems impossible for a DC lexicalising a TEMPORAL or a CONTINGENCY relation.

(5) a. *Fred could not come* <u>because</u> **he was not in town**.

   b. #Fred could not come because Sabine thinks he was not in town.

2.2 Two Types of Adverbial Clauses

An adverbial clause is a subordinate clause that functions as an adverb. It is the case of *after he ate* (temporal meaning) and *although he was starving* (concessive meaning) in (6).

(6) a. *Fred left* <u>after</u> **he ate**.

   b. *Fred left* <u>although</u> **he was starving**.

Traditionally, adverbial clauses are considered a rather homogeneous syntactical category. But a particular distinction between two types of adverbial clauses is proposed by (Haegeman, 2004):

- on the one hand, the *central adverbial clauses* (CAC), which add an information (time, place, etc.) about the eventuality described in the matrix clause;

- on the other hand, the *peripheral adverbial clauses* (PAC), whose function is to structure the discourse (expressing a concession, providing background information, etc.).

In (7), *while he was a student* specifies the date, and *if it is sunny* expresses a necessary condition, of the event in their respective matrix clause; they both are CACs. In (8), *while Sabine has never left Europe* expresses a fact contrasting with, and *if it is sunny* justifies the interrogation in, their respective matrix clause; they both are PACs.

(7) a. *Fred went to Brazil* <u>while</u> **he was a student**.

    b. <u>If</u> **it is sunny**, *I'll go outside*.

(8) a. *Fred has been to Brazil* <u>whereas</u> **Sabine has never left Europe**.

    b. <u>If</u> **it is sunny**, *why aren't you playing outside?*

Several phenomena are studied in (Haegeman, 2004) – coordination, ellipsis, ambiguity, or phenomena related to scope, prosody, typography, etc. –, tending to show a greater integration of CACs into their matrix clause than PACs. Two of these phenomena are of particular interest for this work:

- "Main clause negation may scope over central adverbial clauses, but peripheral adverbial clauses cannot fall within the scope of a negative operator in an associated clause";

- "in addition to tense, other adverbial operators may also have scope over central adverbial clauses but they do not scope over peripheral adverbial clauses".

These two phenomena are illustrated in (9) – for negation – and (10) – for adverbs. These examples each present a pair of sentences with parallel construction: the first contains a CAC and the second a PAC. In line with (Haegeman, 2004)'s observation, the negation scopes over the whole sentence in (9a) while it only scopes over the matrix clause in (9b). Similarly, the adverb scopes over the whole sentence in (10a) while it only scopes over the matrix clause in (10b).

(9) a. *Fred did*n't *go to Brazil* <u>because</u> **he wanted to learn Portuguese** (but for another reason).

    b. *Fred has not been to Brazil* <u>whereas</u> **Sabine travels there often**.

(10) a. *Fred* often *wake up in the middle of the night* <u>because</u> **he is scared**.

    b. *Fred often takes the bus* <u>while</u> **Sabine prefers walking**.

It should also be noted that a CAC cannot contain an epistemic modal if it is *speaker-oriented* (as in (11a) but not in (11c) where *may* is mainly "John-oriented"), while a PAC can (see 11b). Expressed with the terms of (Hunter and Danlos, 2014): the syntactic and discourse arguments of a conjunction must be aligned in the case of a CAC, while there can be a mismatch with PACs.

(11) a. #Mary accepted the invitation without hesitation after John may have accepted it. [from (Haegeman, 2004)]

    b. *The ferry will be fairly cheap*, <u>while/whereas</u> **the plane** may/will probably **be too expensive**. [from (Haegeman, 2004)]

    c. *John is worried* <u>because</u> **he may be ill**.

In this paper, a SubConj introducing a CAC is called a *CConj* and a SubConj introducing a PAC is called a *PConj*. It is important to keep in mind that, as illustrated in (7b) and (8b), a same SubConj, depending on its meaning, can alternatively introduce a CAC or a PAC.

3   Desired Properties of the Model

Before exposing our STAG model, we list in this section the properties that we want to include. First, we want our model to be able to account for the possibilities (with PConjs) and impossibilities (with CConjs) of syntax-discourse mismatch presented in section 2.1. Then, as explained in section 2.2, the model should allow V-modifiers of a matrix clause – such as a negation or an adverb – to scope over a CAC but not over a PAC. Finally, two other interesting properties are presented in the following section, related to the scope of AVs and the meaning of attributing prepositional phrases (*according to NP, in NP's opinion*).

3.1   Scope of AVs

The scope ambiguity for V-modifiers described in (Haegeman, 2004) seems to also apply to some S-modifiers such as AVs. A sentence of the form *Sabine thinks A because B* can either mean that it is because of B that Sabine thinks A (narrow scope) or that Sabine thinks that A, that B and the A-because-of-B relation (wide scope).[4] This generalises well to other CConjs, however things seem different for PConjs.

There has been a lot of discussion since Frege (Frege, 1948) about the semantics of a PConj such as *although*. Like a *presupposition*, the concessive meaning of *although* can project through *presupposition holes* (negation, epistemic modals, etc.), but it also projects through *presupposition plugs* such as AVs. Indeed, *although* is often cited as a *conventional implicature* trigger since (Grice, 1975), which are characterised in (Potts, 2005) with 4 properties: *non-cancellability, not at-issueness, scopelessness* and *speaker-orientedness*. From these properties one can explain many of the observation in (Haegeman, 2004).[5]

It is also interesting to remark that there is a strong interpretation bias associated with PConjs like *although*: for instance, out of context, (12a) seems intuitively to imply that Fred was actually sick. Yet, saying that the Arg_2 of a *Concession* is never at-issue (i.e. that it cannot be targeted by any operator, like the concessive part of the meaning) would be taking shortcuts. Indeed, (12a) can be felicitously followed by (12b) even though it negates Arg_2. So in such a case, *he was sick* is under the semantic scope of *Sabine thinks*. That is why we believe such an utterance is ambiguous: the Arg_2 may (wide scope) or may not (narrow scope) be under the semantic scope of the AV; the latter being a default reading. Note that we do not relate this difference to a matter of centrality vs. peripherality; in both cases the lexicalised relation is the same speaker-oriented *Concession* and is not at-issue.

(12) a. Sabine thinks *Fred came to work* although **he was sick**.

    b. But she is wrong, he had recovered several days ago.

c. Although **he was sick**, Sabine thinks *Fred came to work*.

Although we lack space to support this claim, we believe that those properties about at-issueness, speaker-orientedness and scope ambiguity are shared among PConjs. Even if PConjs are strongly biased towards the narrow scope reading, we still want our model to be able to handle both interpretations. Furthermore, the difference between them is not only a semantic one; only when the AV has narrow scope can the adverbial clause be anteposed (with no shift in meaning) as in (12c) – this applies to PConjs and CConjs equally.

3.2 Attributing Prepositional Phrases

In the context of this paper, we can consider that an evidential AV such as *Sabine thinks* is semantically equivalent to an attributing prepositional phrases (APP) such as *according to Sabine* (13a). It might then come as a surprise that APPs can felicitously be found with CConjs (13b), which otherwise do not accept evidential AVs. In fact, the situation is not symmetrical; with a CConj, the APP does not scope only over Arg_2 but also over the DR lexicalised by the CConj. (13b) is indeed semantically equivalent to (13c). We want our model to predict the correct semantics for sentences including an APP. Note that APPs are adverbials, and thus can also appear in clause-medial position (13d).[6]

(13) a. *Fred could not come* <u>even though</u>, according to Sabine, **he was really looking forward to it**.

b. *Fred could not come* <u>because</u>, according to Sabine, **he was not in town**.

c. Fred could not come and, according to Sabine, it is because he was not in town.

d. *Fred could not come* <u>even though</u> **he was**, according to Sabine, **really looking forward to it**.

4 Our Proposition in STAG

We now turn to STAG and propose new structures for AVs and SubConjs, in addition to a slight vari-

---

[4]We are here implicitly dealing with the causal *because*, which introduces a CAC, whereas there also exists a pragmatic *because* as in *It has rained because the ground is wet*. Such pragmatic DCs are particular in many ways and even though we believe they introduce PACs, we won't consider them in detail here.

[5]One reviewer points out that *although* can be embedded under negation as in *Fred didn't leave ALTHOUGH Lucy arrived, but because of it*. We think that in such a case, the subordinate clause behaves as a central one and that *although* can be satisfactorily modelled with an ambiguity between PConj and CConj.

[6]We are aware that not all APPs are equivalent in terms of acceptability. In particular, some of our examples are more natural if *in X's opinion* is substituted for *according to X*. For the sake of simplicity, however, we have chosen to only use this latter expression.

ation of traditional phrase structures. These modifications reflect the properties described in the previous sections.

4.1 AVs and APPs

AVs – as other bridge verbs – are usually modelled in TAG as anchors of auxiliary trees that adjoin on the S-node of the clause they introduce (Joshi, 1987). Auxiliary trees for these verbs are motivated by long distance extractions as in *He is the man Paul believes [...] Ringo said Yoko loves*, where *NP believes/said* is similar to *according to NP* (see Fig. 1 for a model of APPs). However this equivalence seems unwarranted for intentional AVs: such a verb describes the state or action (of believing, of saying, etc.) that is the argument of the DR, the introduced clause being a central element of this eventuality but not the eventuality in itself. Intentional AVs, contrarily to evidential ones, do not appear as semantic modifier of the clause they introduce.

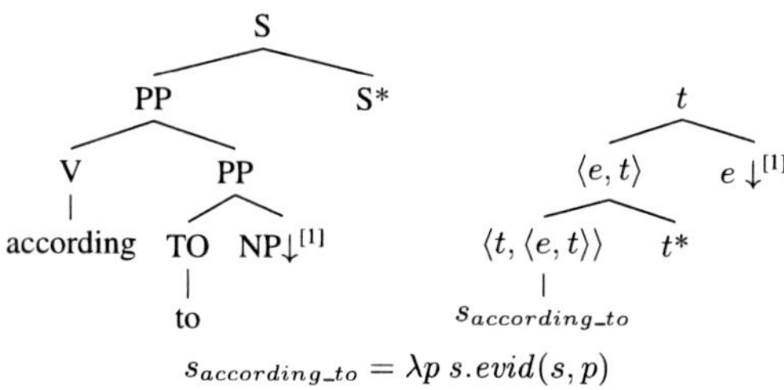

$$s_{according\_to} = \lambda p\, s.evid(s, p)$$

Figure 1: APP: $\beta_{\text{according to}}$ (the commas are omitted for readability)

Therefore, to take into account the two evidential and intentional uses of AVs, we propose an initial TAG pair (Fig. 2) in addition to the auxiliary one traditionally used (Fig. 3). In our model their semantics is also slightly different: evidential AVs use predicates – marked here without apostrophe unlike intentional predicates – that are "erased" when in a peripheral DR. This is achieved by introducing rewriting rules of the form:

$$Contrast(p, think(a, q)) \rightarrow Contrast(p, q)$$

Conversely, unnatural mismatches can be avoided by discarding any analysis displaying an evidential AV predicate as argument of a central DR:

$$Explanation(p, think(a, q)) \rightarrow \bot$$

Thanks to these rules, our model will be able to get the correct semantics and to account for the possibilities and impossibilities of mismatch.

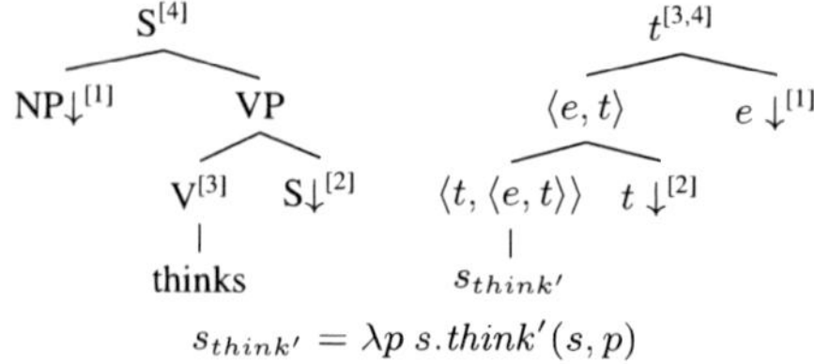

$$s_{think'} = \lambda p\, s.think'(s, p)$$

Figure 2: Intentional AV: α_{think}

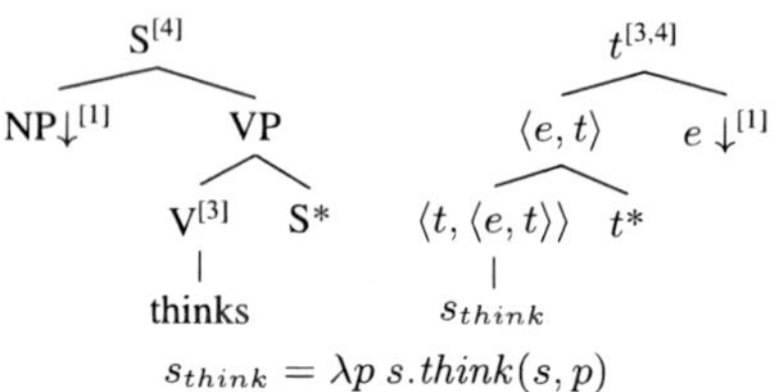

$$s_{think} = \lambda p\, s.think(s, p)$$

Figure 3: Evidential AV: β_{think}

4.2 Subordinate Conjunctions

In the same vein, the difference in syntax and semantics between CACs and PACs can be explained with different structures for CConjs and PConjs as in Fig. 4 and Fig. 5.[7] The syntax of all SubConjs is usually modelled homogeneously, be it with an auxiliary tree as in TAG (XTAG Research Group, 2001) or with an initial one as in D-LTAG (Webber, 2004), but this is not the case in our proposition. Because we model PConjs with a substitution node even for the left argument instead of the adjunction node of CConjs, we can assure that any modifier of the left argument (such as a negation) is only local and cannot scope over the whole $Arg_1 \wedge Arg_2 \wedge R(Arg_1, Arg_2)$ proposition, while this is possible with CConjs.

Also note that the link [3] for CConjs allows APPs such as *according to Sabine* in (13b) to scope over both the Arg_2 and the DR. With PConjs, the APP must adjoin on the right argument, which *a priori* would also be possible with CConjs but is in fact excluded by the semantic rule for evidentials within a central DR (an APP is considered as evidential). Not all S-modifiers should be allowed to adjoin on [3], in particular no AVs; a feature should then be used to restrict link [3] to natural adjunctions only.

<hr>

[7]The presence of the SBAR-node for CConjs is necessary because of the possibility of cleft sentences (*It is because A that B*), which shows that there exists such a constituent. No cleft sentences are observed with PConjs.

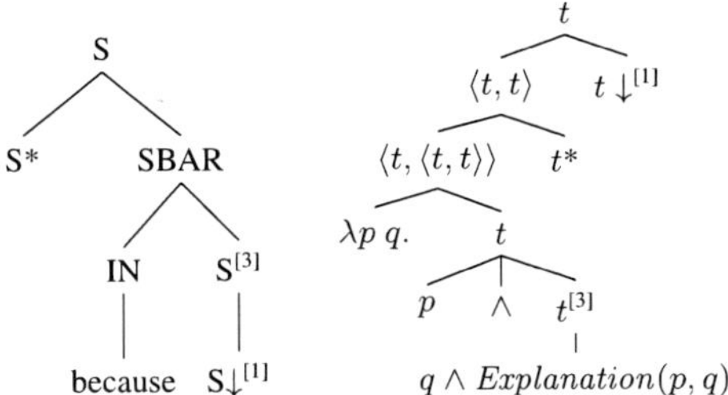

Figure 4: CConj: β_{because}

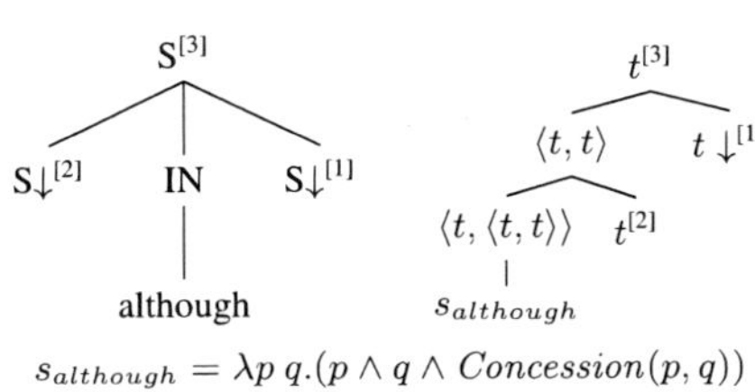

$$s_{although} = \lambda p\, q.(p \wedge q \wedge Concession(p, q))$$

Figure 5: PConj: α_{although}

4.3 Sentence Structures

Following (Nesson and Shieber, 2006), we consider that sentence structures have two different adjunction sites in their semantic tree for V-modifiers (such as negation and adverbs) and S-modifiers (such as AVs). Because multiple adjunctions on the same node are allowed and are used to represent various scope ambiguities, doing so avoids (unnatural) interpretations of a V-modifier scoping over a S-modifier. However, CConjs are sentence modifiers like AVs but, as seen in the previous sections, they do present scope ambiguity when confronted with verbal modifiers such as negation. This is why, as illustrated in Fig. 6, we consider adding to sentence structures another adjunction site on the S-node (link [3]) whose semantic counterpart is at the same node as verbal modifiers' one. We can use features to restrict the other S-site (link [2]) to AVs and APPs, and conversely to force them to adjoin there.

Fig. 7 shows the derivations trees obtained from the adjunction of a negation (or any verbal modifier) on the matrix clause of a SubConj. Our model correctly predicts that the negation can have local *or* global scope in the case of a CConj, but only local scope in the case of a PConj.

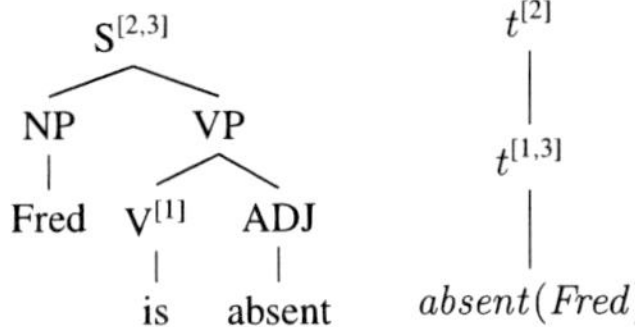

Figure 6: A sentence structure; link [2] is restricted to AVs and APPs, other S-modifiers adjoin at [3].

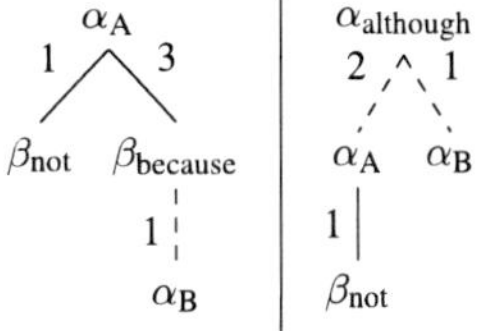

Figure 7: The derivation trees for $\neg A\ CONJ\ B$ with a CConj (left) or a PConj (right). Because in α_A links [1] and [3] are at the same semantic node, the left tree is a scope neutral representation yielding one syntactic tree but two semantic ones depending on the order of the adjunctions.

5 Discussion

5.1 Standard STAG

Tab. 1 shows the derivation trees for sentences of the form *A CONJ Sabine thinks B* as in (4). We lack space to display all the derived trees corresponding to this configuration, however Fig. 8 shows the trees obtained with a PConj and an evidential AV (top-right possibility in Tab. 1). The syntactic trees do not depend on the use (intentional or evidential) of the AV, whereas the semantic trees do, but only in the substitution of the evidential s_{think} term for the intentional $s_{think'}$ one. This slight difference, in addition to the semantic rules stated earlier, accounts for the correct semantic of these various interpretations and the exclusion of analyses where an evidential AV is an argument of a CConj. Remains for PConjs, however, an ambiguity that only the semantics of the various elements involved can solve.

Tab. 2 shows the derivation trees for sentences of the form *Sabine thinks A CONJ B*, that is with the AV in sentence-initial position as in (12a). In this configuration, *A CONJ B* may be an S-constituent introduced by the AV; the latter is not then part of the arguments of the relation lexicalised by CONJ and is called here "external". Note that in this case and without context, the in-

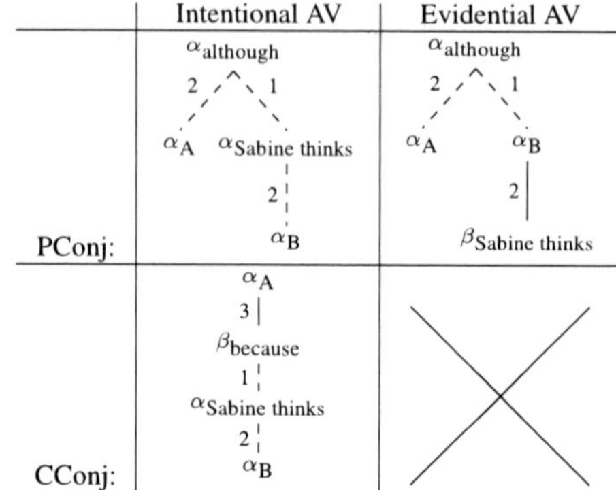

Table 1: Derivation trees for sentences of the form *A CONJ Sabine thinks B*.

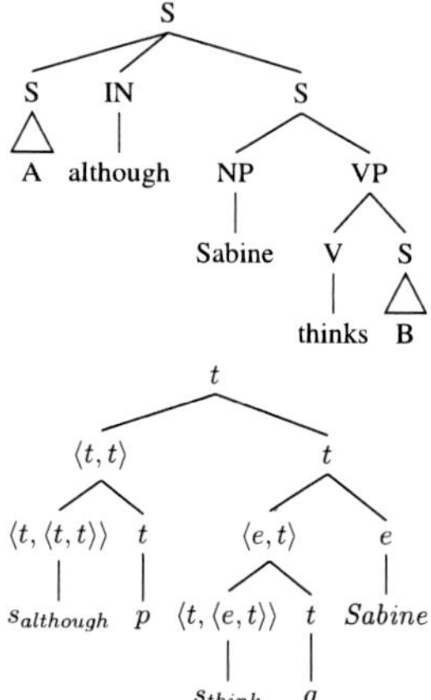

Generated formula:
$$p \wedge think(Sabine, q) \wedge Concession(p, q)$$

Figure 8: Result of the analyse of *A although Sabine thinks B* with an evidential AV.

tentional or evidential status of the AV is undetermined; we have chosen to use the traditional β_{thinks} pair. As before, this configuration presents ambiguities that can only be resolved with the help of the semantics of the particular DR.

Fig. 9 shows the two syntactic trees obtained in this configuration with the PConj *although*, depending on the role of the AV (on the top: intentional or evidential; at the bottom: external). Note that our model analyses the evidential case with a syntax-discourse mismatch on Arg_1. Indeed, in the top tree *Sabine thinks A* is the syntactic argument of *although*, whereas if the AV is evidential, only the propositional content of *A* constitutes the Arg_1 of *Concession*. This analysis is supported by the possibility of anteposition of the subordi-

nate clause in intentional and evidential cases illustrated in (12c): the anteposition of *although B* appears natural from the top tree and not from the bottom one.

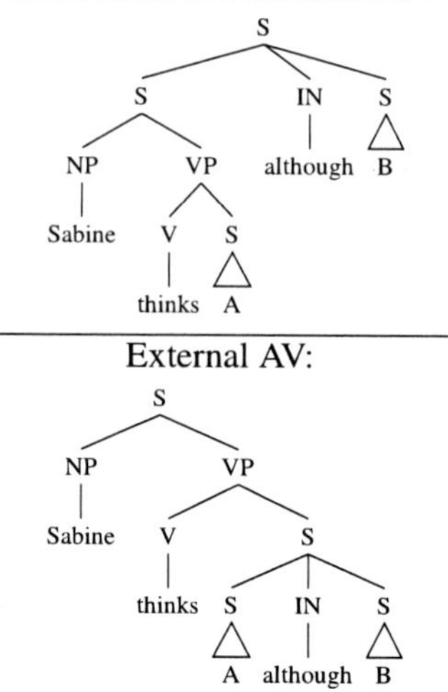

Figure 9: Syntactic derived trees for sentences of the form *Sabine thinks A although B*. Note that with *although* (a PConj), the tree at the bottom corresponds to a less likely reading that must be forced by the context.

Finally, Fig. 10 shows the analyses for *A CONJ, according to Sabine, B*. Note how the additional link [3] in CConjs lead to a correct interpretation of (13b) where the APP scopes over both the DR and its Arg_2 as stated in section 3.2.

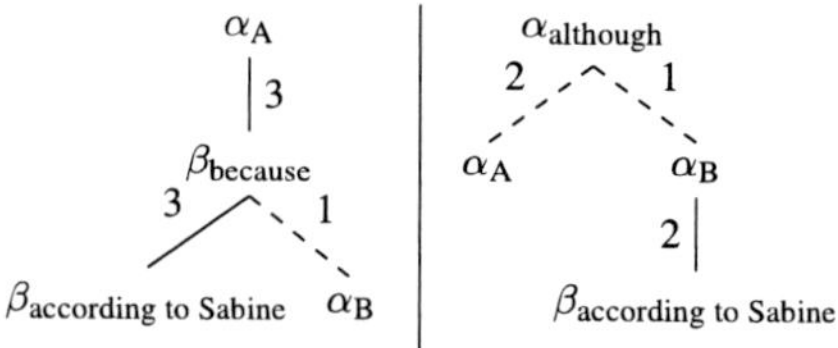

Figure 10: The derivation trees for *A CONJ, according to Sabine, B* with a CConj (left) or a PConj (right).

5.2 Towards Multi-Component TAG

We have proposed the link [3] in CConj (see Fig. 4) in order to handle modifiers such as APPs that are inserted between a CConj and the rest of the introduced clause while scoping over the DR and the Arg_2. However, we previously mentioned that such modifiers can also be found

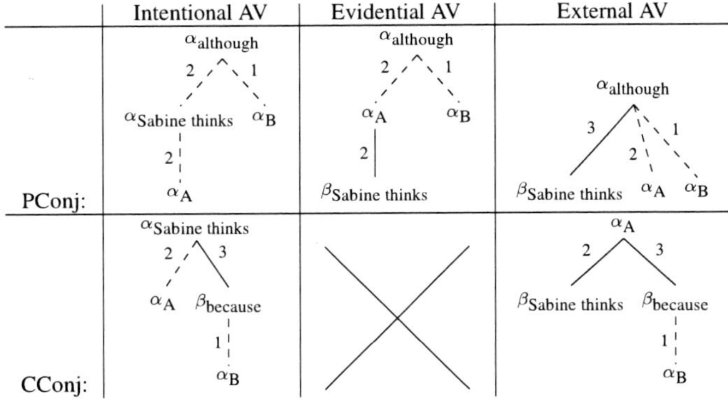

Table 2: Derivation trees for sentences of the form *Sabine thinks A CONJ B*.

in middle position with the same meaning as illustrated in (13d). This clearly poses a problem for our current approach, because an APP in middle position must adjoin on the right argument and thus cannot scope over the DR itself. It seems we can overcome this problem with the help of Multi-Component Tree Adjoining Grammars (MCTAG) in a fashion similar to what is done for noun phrases in (Nesson and Shieber, 2007). We won't give here a fully detailed MCTAG proposition, but rather sketch the main aspects of it.

Our idea is that when an S-constituent is the syntactic argument (be it left or right) of a Sub-Conj, its modifiers can have a local scope (i.e. within this constituent), or, in the case of a CConj, also a wider scope (which depends on whether the S-constituent is on the left or right of the CConj). These scope phenomena could be dealt with homogeneously by considering a two-component structure for the S-constituents as shown in Fig. 11. One component provides the content of the sentence while the other one – a vestigial (S*, t*) one – would serve the purpose of "pluging in" the correct node of the SubConj's semantic tree for subsequent adjunctions. Links [1,2] in Fig. 11 are for local scope and links [3,4] for (possibly) wider scope. Because of this multi-component structure, we probably don't need an adjunction site for the left argument of CConjs anymore, as they can be modelled with two substitution sites as shown in Fig. 12.

With such a model, sentences with a CAC containing a clause-initial APP like (13b) could be analysed as in Fig. 13. The derivation tree for sentences with clause-medial APP would be almost identical: the APP would adjoin on the link [3] of α_B instead of the link [4].

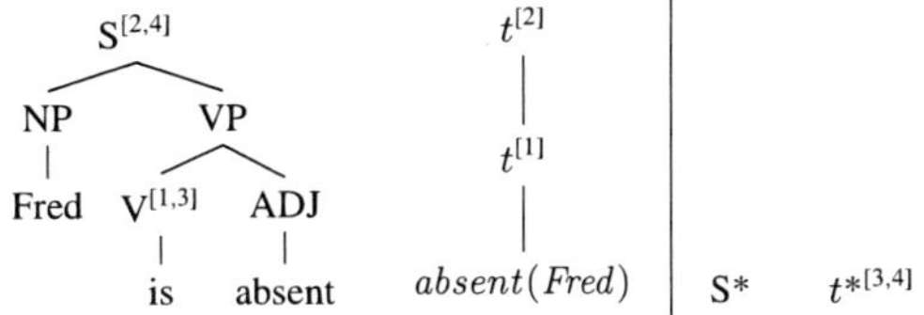

Figure 11: A sketch of MCTAG structure for S-constituents.

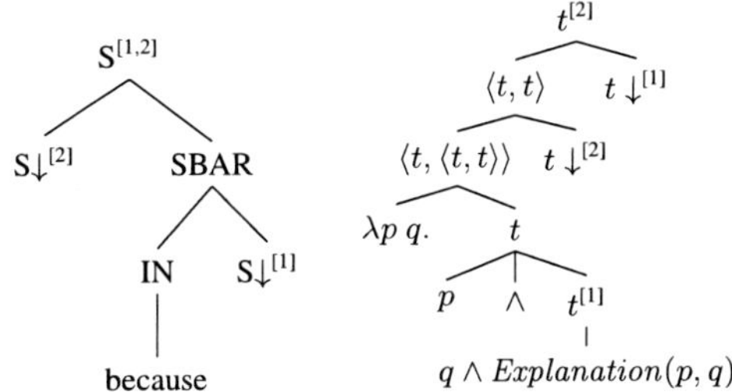

Figure 12: A sketch of MCTAG structure for CConjs.

6 Conclusion

We have first recalled the notion of syntax-discourse mismatch and related it to the two intentional and evidential uses of AVs. Then, we have presented the distinction made in (Haegeman, 2004) between central and peripheral adverbial clauses. Additional syntactic and semantic phenomena were mentioned, which have motivated our STAG model. This model is enriched with new structures for AVs and SubConjs that reflect the distinctions and properties previously highlighted.

Yet, it is still too constrained regarding the relatively free position of attributing prepositional phrases. This lead us to consider the Multi-

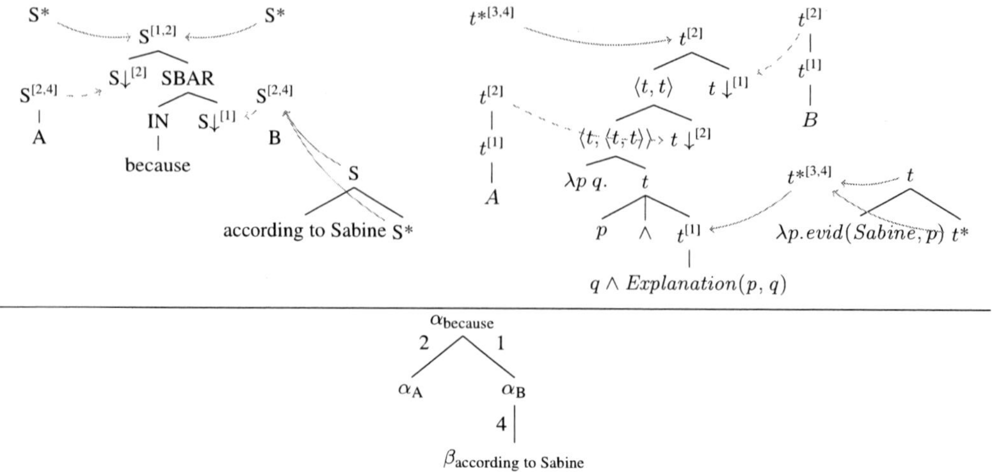

Figure 13: MCTAG analysis of sentences with a CAC containing a clause-initial APP like (13a).

Component TAG formalism, which we believe is more suitable for modelling fine-grained phenomena in discourse. Only a sketch of an MCTAG model is given here; we plan on developing these ideas in the future. Furthermore, projection properties not mentioned here will probably require us to refine our proposal, before extending our approach to the other categories of discourse connectives. Among them, adverbials are the most problematic; their ability to be integrated inside one of their argument has lead previous TAG-based accounts – namely D-LTAG (Webber, 2004) and D-STAG (Danlos, 2009) – to resort to a complex parsing process with an intermediate step. While more recent work has been successful in getting rid of this additional step in an elegant way (Danlos et al., 2016), it requires a substantial change in formalism (the use of *Abstract Categorial Grammars* (de Groote, 2001)). Further investigation with MCTAG may confirm whether such a change is necessary.

References

N. Asher and A. Lascarides. 2003. *Logics of Conversation*. Cambridge University Press.

N. Asher, J. Hunter, P. Denis, and B. Reese. 2006. Evidentiality and intensionality: Two uses of reportative constructions in discourse. In *Workshop on Constraints in Discourse Structure*, Maynooth, Ireland.

L. Danlos, A. Maskharashvili, and S. Pogodalla. 2016. Interfacing Sentential and Discourse TAG-based Grammars. To appear in the proceedings of the 12th International Workshop on Tree Adjoining Grammars and Related FormalismsTAG+12 (TAG+12), Düsseldorf, Germany., June.

L. Danlos. 2009. D-STAG: a Formalism for Discourse Analysis based on SDRT and using Synchronous TAG. In P. de Groote, editor, *Proceedings of FG'09*. INRIA.

L. Danlos. 2013. Connecteurs de discours adverbiaux: Problèmes à l'interface syntaxe-sémantique. *Linguisticae Investigationes*, 36(2):261–275, December.

P. de Groote. 2001. Towards Abstract Categorial Grammars. In *Proceedings of the 39th Annual Meeting on Association for Computational Linguistics*, ACL '01, pages 252–259, Stroudsburg, PA, USA. ACL.

N. Dinesh, A. Lee, E. Miltsakaki, R. Prasad, A. Joshi, and B. Webber. 2005. Attribution and the (Non-)Alignment of Syntactic and Discourse Arguments of Connectives. In *Proceedings of the Workshop on Frontiers in Corpus Annotations II: Pie in the Sky*, pages 29–36, Ann Arbor, Michigan, June. ACL.

G. Frege. 1948. Sense and Reference. *The Philosophical Review*, 57(3):209–230.

H. Grice. 1975. Logic and conversation. In P. Cole and L. Jerry, editors, *Syntax and semantics 3: Speech acts*, pages 41–58. Academic Press, San Diego, CA.

L. Haegeman. 2004. The syntax of adverbial clauses and its consequences for topicalisation. In M. Coene, G. De Cuyper, and Y. D'Hulst, editors, *Current Studies in Comparative Romance Linguistics*, number 107 in APiL, pages 61–90. Antwerp University.

J. Hunter and L. Danlos. 2014. Because We Say So. In *Proceedings of the EACL 2014 Workshop on Computational Approaches to Causality in Language*, CAtoCL, pages 1–9, Gothenburg, Sweden, April. ACL.

A. Joshi. 1987. An introduction to Tree Adjoining Grammars. *Mathematics of Language*, 1:87–115.

R. Nesson and S. Shieber. 2006. Simpler TAG semantics through synchronization. In *Proceedings of FG 2006*, pages 129–142, Malaga, Spain.

R. Nesson and S. Shieber. 2007. Extraction Phenomena in Synchronous TAG Syntax and Semantics. In *Proceedings of the NAACL-HLT 2007/AMTA Workshop on Syntax and Structure in Statistical Translation*, SSST '07, pages 9–16, Stroudsburg, PA, USA. ACL.

C. Potts. 2005. *The logic of conventional implicatures*. Oxford University Press Oxford.

R. Prasad, E. Miltsakaki, N. Dinesh, A. Lee, A. Joshi, L. Robaldo, and B. Webber. 2007. The Penn Discourse Treebank 2.0 Annotation Manual. *IRCS Technical Reports Series*, December.

R. Prasad, A. Joshi, and B. Webber. 2010. Realization of Discourse Relations by Other Means: Alternative Lexicalizations. In *Proceedings of the 23rd International Conference on Computational Linguistics*, pages 1023–1031, Beijing, China, August.

T. Scheffler. 2013. *Two-dimensional Semantics. Clausal Adjuncts and Complements.* De Gruyter Mouton, Berlin/Boston.

S. Shieber and Y. Schabes. 1990. Synchronous Tree-adjoining Grammars. In *Proceedings of the 13th Conference on Computational Linguistics - Volume 3*, COLING '90, pages 253–258, Stroudsburg, PA, USA. ACL.

B. Webber. 2004. D-LTAG: extending lexicalized TAG to discourse. *Cognitive Science*, 28(5):751–779, September.

XTAG Research Group. 2001. A Lexicalized Tree Adjoining Grammar for English. Technical Report IRCS-01-03, IRCS, University of Pennsylvania.

Argument linking in LTAG:
A constraint-based implementation with XMG

Laura Kallmeyer and **Timm Lichte** and **Rainer Osswald** and **Simon Petitjean**
University of Düsseldorf, Germany
{kallmeyer,lichte,osswald,petitjean}@phil.hhu.de

Abstract

This paper develops a first systematic approach to argument linking in LTAG, building on typologically oriented work in Van Valin (2005). While Van Valin's argument linking mechanism is procedurally defined, we propose a constraint-based implementation. The advantage is that we can separate between the linguistic generalizations to be captured and algorithmic considerations. The implementation is couched into the metagrammar framework eXtensible MetaGrammar (XMG).

1 Introduction

The syntax-semantics interface of Lexicalized Tree Adjoining Grammar (LTAG) builds on the assumptions that (i) the elementary tree of a predicate contains slots for the arguments of the predicate, (ii) this elementary tree is paired with a semantic representation with semantic arguments, (iii) there is a linking between syntactic argument slots and semantic arguments that makes sure that the filling of an argument node in the syntax triggers the insertion of a corresponding semantic representation into the linked semantic argument position. This holds for the unification-based approach from Kallmeyer and Joshi (2003), Gardent and Kallmeyer (2003) and Kallmeyer and Romero (2008) using predicate logic, for the approach based on synchronous TAG (Shieber, 1994; Nesson and Shieber, 2006; Nesson and Shieber, 2008) and also for the frame-based approach of Kallmeyer and Osswald (2013). However, none of these approaches has implemented a theory which explains why only certain patterns of argument linking are allowed. In Fig. 1, for instance, the elementary tree for *ate* is paired with the upper frame while the lower frame is not grammatical

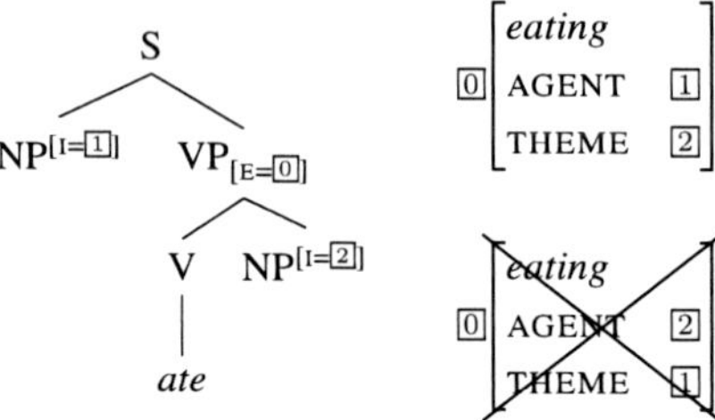

Figure 1: Simple linking example

in combination with this tree because of the incorrect linking. The AGENT has to be contributed by the subject while the THEME slot is filled via the object substitution node.

The principles and constraints underlying linking have been extensively investigated (Levin and Rappaport Hovav, 2005; Wechsler, 2015). Dowty (1991), for instance, introduces proto-AGENT and proto-PATIENT as intermediate roles linking syntax to semantics. Van Valin (2005) presents an elaborated linking algorithm based on the *macroroles* ACTOR and UNDERGOER and on the *actor-undergoer-hierarchy*. This algorithm is not fully formalized, however, and it is formulated in a procedural way that mixes constraints which express linguistic generalizations with algorithmic aspects. The latter point is problematic insofar as Van Valin's linking system is intended to be used both for language understanding and language generation. It is thus desirable for a formalization and implementation of the system to keep the principles and constraints separate from aspects of processing order.

Based on Van Valin's proposal, this paper provides a constraint-based implementation of linking principles that captures the systematic relation between syntactic arguments and semantic roles. These constraints restrict the set of possible ele-

Proceedings of the 12th International Workshop on Tree Adjoining Grammars and Related Formalisms (TAG+12), pages 48–57,
Düsseldorf, Germany, June 29 - July 1, 2016.

mentary pairs of tree and semantic representation. In other words, they act on the level of elementary structures in the grammar and are therefore part of the metagrammar, together with syntactic tree fragments and fragments of semantic representations. This is the part of the grammar that provides a systematic constraint-based definition of the set of elementary trees along with the semantic representations they can be paired with (Crabbé and Duchier, 2004; Duchier et al., 2004). We will use the metagrammar compiler XMG (Crabbé et al., 2013; Lichte and Petitjean, 2015) with frames as semantic representations (Kallmeyer and Osswald, 2013). Since argument linking is independent from the choice of the semantic representation, our analysis could also be applied to an LTAG syntax-semantics interface using one of the other frameworks mentioned above.

2   The syntax-semantics interface

We assume familiarity with the basic notions of LTAG (Joshi and Schabes, 1997; Abeillé and Rambow, 2000), enriched with syntactic feature structures in the usual way (Vijay-Shanker and Joshi, 1988).

Following Kallmeyer and Osswald (2013), we pair syntactic trees with frame-semantic representations, which instantiate a slightly extended variant of typed feature structure. An example is given in Fig. 2. We use *interface features* on the syntactic nodes that are responsible for triggering semantic composition (i.e., frame unification) via the syntactic feature unifications during substitution and adjunction. These features here are I (for "individual") and E (for "event"), whose values are variables that also occur in the frames. Upon substituting the elementary tree of *John* into the subject NP slot of the elementary tree of *ate*, the variables ① and ③ get equated, hence triggering the unification of the frame of *John* with the AGENT component of the frame of *ate*.

In the rest of the paper, we will be focusing on the properties of single elementary entries of verbs such as *ate*.

3   Constraints on elementary entries

Given that in LTAG, the set of composition operations is rather small, the actual domain of linguistic theorizing lies mainly in the way elementary entries like that of *ate* in Fig. 2 are designed, or rather constrained. Hence, constraints pertain-

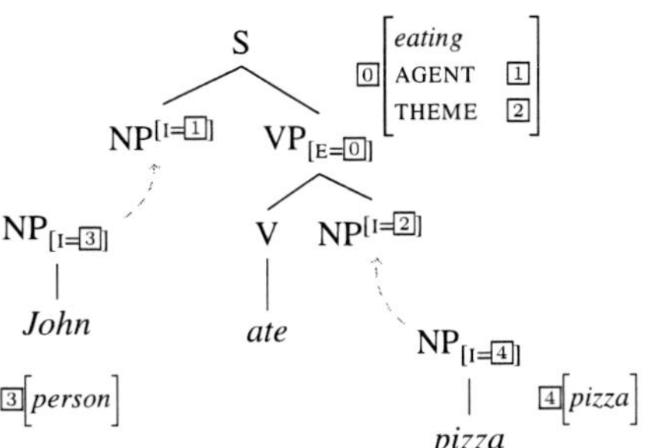

Figure 2: Sample derivation

ing to the tree structure, the frame-semantic representation, and the linking among the two make up an important part of theories expressed within this framework. These constraints on elementary structures constitute what is commonly called a metagrammar, the general outline of which is shown in Fig.3.

3.1   Constraints on tree structure

The most explicit and systematic proposal to constrain the shape and structure of elementary trees was made in works of Robert Frank (1992; 2002).[1] Based on the Fundamental TAG Hypothesis ("Every syntactic dependency is expressed locally within an elementary tree."), the inner structure (Condition on Elementary Tree Minimality) and the number of non-terminal leaf nodes (θ-Criterion for TAG) are covered, the latter aspect, of course, being the more relevant here. The θ-Criterion for TAG states that there is a bijective mapping between "θ-roles", i.e. semantic arguments, and non-terminal leaf nodes. This is met, for example, in the tree of *ate* based on the shown *eating* frame. Yet there is no particular constraining on what this mapping might look like. In other words, it is unclear how to prevent the deficient linking pattern in Fig. 1 from coming into existence. This is exactly the gap that our contribution is supposed to fill.

One important remaining issue is the status of the θ-Criterion for TAG when dealing with semantic frames. In its original formulation, the θ-Criterion requires the numbers of syntactic and semantic arguments to be equal, whereas modifiers are neglected. However, in a frame, there is no principled distinction between arguments and modifiers anymore – both get represented as ordinary functional attributes. Hence, combining

---

[1]But see also Abeillé and Rambow (2000).

the θ-Criterion, as is, with frame semantics would have the unwanted effect that modifiers are represented as nonterminal leaves just like arguments. This is unwanted because it would increase the number and size of elementary trees massively, though not ad infinitum due to the functional nature of frame attributes (therefore being reminiscent of the treatment of optional arguments). Possible remedies could be to apply the θ-Criterion to descriptions of lexical frames where modifiers have not yet entered, or to insert a mediating valency layer that helps to abstract away from the full set of semantic roles (cf. Lichte, 2015). However, this discussion touches the issue of argument-modifier distinction more generally, and therefore should be treated elsewhere.

3.2 Constraints on frame structure

Following Kallmeyer and Osswald (2013), we formalize semantic frames as typed feature structures with base labels and relations. The frame constraints used in this paper are basically Horn clauses built from atomic attribute-value descriptions of the form $\text{P}:a$ and $\text{P} \doteq \text{Q}$, where P and Q are (possibly empty) feature paths and a is a type (including $\top$ and $\bot$). For example, the constraint that *eating* involves an ACTOR and a THEME but no PATH can be formalized in this logic as follows:

$$eating \Rightarrow \text{ACTOR}:\top \wedge \text{THEME}:\top$$
$$eating \wedge \text{PATH}:\top \Rightarrow \bot$$

3.3 Constraints on argument linking

The linking constraints in the metagrammar basically combine tree constraints with frame constraints. For instance, regarding the elementary entry of *ate* in Fig. 2, one such constraint could be paraphrased as "in an active sentence, the AGENT is realized as the subject, and the THEME is realized as the object". We will learn about a systematic and typologically oriented linking theory in Section 5, which will be the starting point for our implementation in Section 6. The overall structure of the metagrammar, together with the metagrammar compiler, is shown in Fig. 3.

4 eXtensible MetaGrammar

The framework of eXtensible MetaGrammar (XMG, Crabbé et al., 2013) provides description languages and dedicated compilers for generating a wide range of linguistic resources.[2] Descriptions

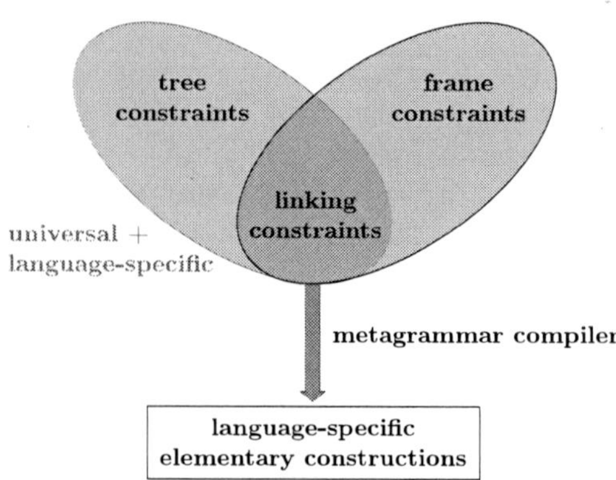

Figure 3: Metagrammar components

are organized into *classes*, alluding to the class concept in object-oriented programming. Similarly, classes have encapsulated name spaces and inheritance relations may hold between them. The crucial elements of a class are *dimensions*. They can be equipped with specific description languages and are compiled independently, thereby enabling the grammar writer to treat the levels of linguistic information separately.

As our focus is on argument linking, the following three class dimensions, which contain the three different sorts of constraints mentioned in Fig. 3, are most relevant to us: **<syn>** holds tree constraints that express dominance and precedence relations among nodes. Moreover, the nodes may carry (untyped) feature structures. **<frame>** holds frame descriptions, i.e. descriptions of typed feature structures. Feature structure *constraints*, on the other hand, are specified globally outside classes. Finally, **<iface>** is an interface dimension where (non-typed) feature structures are used to share information between other dimensions and classes. This dimension will obviously serve as a place for expressing linking constraints. The general structure of a class then looks as follows:

```
class classname
import someOtherClass[]
export ?someVariable
declare ?someVariable
{
    <syn>{ ... };
    <frame>{ ... };
    <iface> { ... }
}
```

Note that **import**, **export**, and **declare** behave similarly to the corresponding constructs in object-oriented programming. The operator ; ex-

---

[2] https://sourcesup.cru.fr/xmg/

presses the conjunction of contents. One can also express disjunction with the operator `|`.

The description language used inside **`<frame>`** is a simple recursive bracket notation with the following ingredients:

```
?variable1 [
   type1, type2 , ... ,
   feature2:?variable2,
   feature3:?variable3[ ... ]
]
```

Variables here correspond to the boxed variables in Fig. 1 and 2 and are optional as well. Also note that there can be more than one atomic type specified (making up conjunctive types). Features and their values are separated with the colon (`:`), and values can be either variables, or feature structures. See Lichte and Petitjean (2015) for a detailed definition. The descriptions inside the **`<iface>`** dimension look very similar, the main difference being that the feature-value separator is the equal sign (`=`) for historical reasons. As far as the description language in **`<syn>`** is concerned, we will ignore it for now and use graphical representations in the further presentation.

As mentioned before, feature structure constraints (and type constraints), which hold globally for all frame structures inside the classes, are specified externally (see, again, Lichte and Petitjean, 2015). They are constructed in the following way, building on the description language from (Kallmeyer and Osswald, 2013) as sketched in Section 3.2:

Constraint ::= *Description* **->** *Description*
Description ::= `type ... type` |
  `feature ... feature:type` |
  `feature ... feature = feature ... feature`

-> is the implication operator, `feature ...`
`feature` stands for a path in the feature structure, and `feature ... feature =`
`feature ... feature` for a path equation. The atomic types which can be used in the constraints are defined by the user. To this set are added the predefined types $+$ and $-$, standing for $\top$ (the most generic type) and $\bot$ (the "false" type).

Note that constraints are treated differently in the compiler: type constraints (with only types on the left-hand side) are precompiled into a type hierarchy, that is, the constraints on types are used to compute the set of valid conjunctive types. The result is a maximal model of the type constraints, meaning that all combinations of atomic types which are not explicitly prohibited are authorized.

The remaining set of constraints is checked at runtime.

Based on a set of constraints, XMG compiles full models (i.e., trees and frames such as in Fig. 2), which then enter into parsing. Hence, under this perspective, the metagrammar constraints act as lexical constraints proper. Note, however, that metagrammar constraints could also be used in parsing more directly (de la Clergerie, 2013).

5 Argument linking in Van Valin (2005)

In this section, we describe the core generalizations on argument linking proposed in Van Valin (2005), which will serve as a basis for our constraint-based implementation of argument linking in elementary trees. The basic idea is to assign the macroroles ACTOR (AC) and UNDERGOER (UG) to certain semantic arguments, which are then syntactically realized in a specific way that depends on the language and the voice type expressed in the elementary tree, among others. For the purposes of this paper, we put aside the linking of a possible third, non-macrorole argument, which is typically realized with oblique case or by a prepositional phrase.

The relation between semantic roles and macroroles is captured in the *actor-undergoer hierarchy* shown in Fig. 4. Since our approach employs frame-semantic representations, we do not make use of the positional encoding in logical structures sketched in the top line of the figure but build directly on the associated semantic roles. Depending on its semantic role, an event participant obtains a higher or a lower rank with respect to the hierarchy. For example, Fig. 4 implies that a STIMULUS argument gets assigned a lower rank than an EXPERIENCER argument. (Note that rank 1 is considered the highest rank while rank 4 is the lowest rank.)

The relation between the actor-undergoer hierarchy and the macrorole assignment is then as follows: If a rank 1 argument is present, it is the actor. If a rank 4 argument is present, it is the undergoer. A rank 2 argument is the actor if there is no rank 1 argument. A rank 2 argument is the undergoer if there is a rank 1 argument and no rank 3 or rank 4 undergoer. A rank 3 argument is the undergoer if it is not the actor and if there is no rank 4 argument. A rank 3 argument cannot be an actor unless it is at the same time a rank 1 argument. In this latter case, it counts as rank 1 in our constraints.

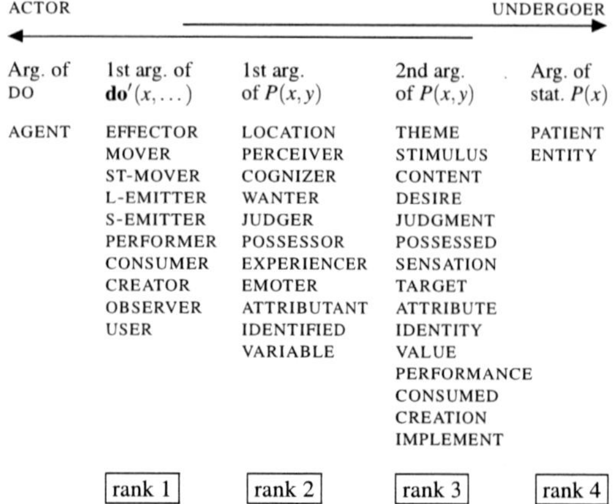

Figure 4: Actor-undergoer hierarchy with semantic roles; adapted from Van Valin (2005, p. 58)

Macrorole assignment is only one of the steps of the linking algorithm laid out in Van Valin (2005); the subsequent step is concerned with the morphosyntactic realization of arguments based on the assigned marcroroles. This step is dependent on the language type and it is also sensitive to voice-modulation, among others. In the case of English, for instance, if a transitive verb is anchored to an active-voice elementary tree, which can be seen as the default anchoring, then the highest ranking argument, i.e. the actor, is realized as the *privileged syntactic argument*, i.e. in subject position, while the undergoer is realized as the direct object. In passive voice, on the other hand, the undergoer becomes the privileged syntactic argument while the actor may be optionally realized by a *by*-clause. The general observation is that in languages with an accusative syntactic system such as German and English, the highest ranking argument is by default realized as the privileged syntactic argument. In particular, the macrorole assignment does not matter for intransitive verbs (since there is only one argument); the single argument becomes the privileged syntactic argument, which receives nominative case in German (1-b).

(1) a. Der   Junge   zerbrach
       the.NOM boy[AC].NOM broke
       den   Teller.
       the.ACC plate[UG].ACC
    b. Der   Teller   zerbrach.
       the.NOM plate[UG].NOM broke

In ergative languages, by contrast, the *lowest* argument with respect to the hierarchy is by default selected as the privileged syntactic argument, which appears in the absolutive case. If the language is syntactically accusative but morphologically ergative then the highest ranking argument becomes the privileged syntactic argument while the lowest ranking argument receives absolutive case. This is illustrated in the following Warlpiri examples (Van Valin, 2005, p. 109; taken from Hale 1973): the actor in (2-a) and the undergoer in (2-b) both receive absolutive case.

(2) a. Ngaju-∅   ka-rna   purla-mi.
       1SG[AC]-ABS PRES-1SG shout-NPAST
       'I am shouting.'
    b. Ngaju-rlu   ka-rna-∅
       1SG[AC]-ERG PRES-1SG-3SG
       wawiri-∅   pura-mi.
       kangaroo[UG]-ABS cook-NPAST
       'I am cooking the kangaroo.'

As mentioned at the beginning of this section, the linking rules just sketched capture only the very core of Van Valin's system, namely the case of intransitive and simple transitive verbs where all arguments are macrorole arguments. In addition, the lexicon may contain verbs with two arguments of which only one is a macrorole argument, which means that the other argument is realized by an oblique case or a prepositional phrase according to certain rules. Similarly, there are rules, which are partly language-specific, for assigning dative, instrumental or another oblique case to the non-macrorole argument of verbs with three arguments. Moreover, these verbs often permit variable undergoer choice, which is then reflected in alternations such as the dative and the locative alternation. Finally, languages differ with respect to whether the privileged syntactic argument of a construction is restricted to macrorole arguments (as in German or Italian), or whether also non-macrorole arguments can serve as the privileged syntactic argument (as, e.g., in Icelandic). While the implementation presented in the following is restricted to the basic linking of macroroles described above, the long-term goal is to successively extend the implementation towards a full coverage of Van Valin's linking system.

6 Constraint-based implementation of Van Valin (2005)

6.1 Universal constraints on semantic frames

As a first element of our linking system, we define universal constraints on semantic roles and on macroroles. Macroroles are taken to be attributes in our semantic frames, just like semantic roles.

A selection of these constraints is given in Fig. 5. The constraints are notated with the XMG syntax. They correspond to formulas in the frame logic introduced in Kallmeyer and Osswald (2013), the last constraint in Fig. 5 for instance corresponds to *change-of-state* $\Rightarrow$ PATIENT $\doteq$ RESULT PATIENT in this logic. The first two constraints express the fact that rank 1 arguments (= EFFECTOR) are actors while rank 4 arguments are undergoers. The next two constraints are two of many constraints on hierarchical relations between roles. The roles listed in Fig. 4 under a specific rank, for instance rank 2, are hierarchically ordered. The last three constraints in this list are constraints for lifting semantic roles from the recursive structure of an event to a higher level. Take for instance the frame at the top of Fig. 6 for a *smashing* event, which is analyzed as a causation involving an activity as the causing event. The 5th constraint in Fig. 5 tells us that in a *causation* event, the EFFECTOR of the embedded CAUSE is also the EFFECTOR of the entire *causation*.

To support these constraints, XMG's frame dimension has been extended, compared to Lichte and Petitjean (2015), such that it allows not only single attributes but also sequences of attributes on the left-hand sides of the $\phi_1 -> \phi_2$ implications.

The example in Fig. 6 shows how these constraints enrich the frame structure by adding new attributes to it. At the top, we have the frame representing lexical semantics of *smash*. A smashing event is a causation where an effector performs some activity and, as a result of this, a patient changes its state into the state of being smashed. The second frame in Fig. 6 shows the enriched frame we obtain when applying the constraints from Fig. 5 to this first frame.

6.2 Semantic argument classes

The universal constraints introduced so far take care of the fact that rank 1 arguments are actors and rank 4 arguments are undergoers. But for rank 2 and rank 3 arguments, macrorole assignment is more complicated. In the following, we introduce

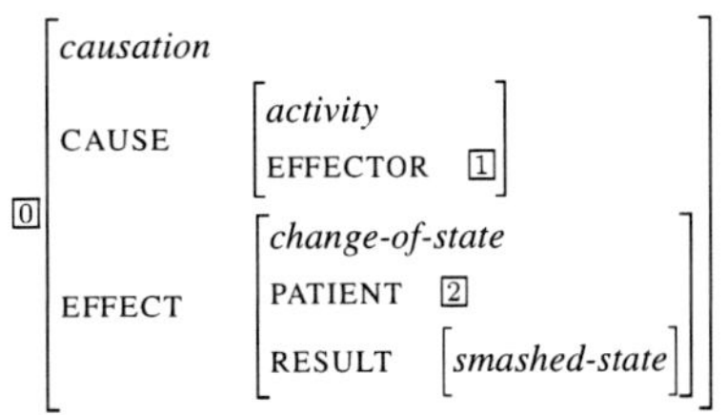

Applying the constraints from Fig. 5 yields

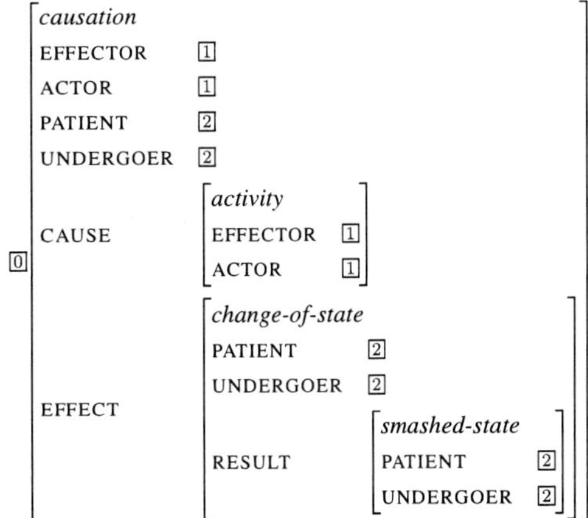

Figure 6: Frame for *smashing*

XMG classes for these arguments and for the different ways of linking them to the macroroles. In contrast to the universal constraints, these classes describe possible frame fragments, i.e., they are used as being existentially quantified whenever they are integrated into some class that gets compiled in the MG. Fig. 7 gives the classes for the arguments with a disjunction of the possible semantic roles. In all the XMG classes given in this section, `?e` and `?x` are XMG variables that are always exported.

Concerning macrorole assignment, we have to make sure that for combinations of these arguments, macroroles are assigned in accordance with the constraints stated above. To this end, we use interface features. Interface features are a special dimension in our XMG classes, the `<iface>` dimension. They form an untyped non-recursive feature structure. When combining two classes, the interface features have to unify. In other words, their values (where specified) have to be equal. For our purposes, we need the following linking interface features: A feature `highest-rank` that gives the highest rank in the combination of arguments, and boolean features `und-lower2` and `und-lower3` that indicate whether there is an undergoer of rank lower than 2 (resp. 3).

constraint	explanation
`effector:+ -> effector=actor`	if an effector exists, then it is the actor
`patient:+ -> patient=undergoer`	a patient is always an undergoer
`mover:+ -> mover=effector`	a mover is always an effector
`emoter:+ -> emoter=experiencer`	an emoter is always an experiencer
`cause effector:+ ->` `    cause effector=effector`	if the cause of a causation has an effector, then this is also the effector of the entire causation
`effect patient:+ ->` `    effect patient=patient`	if the effect of a causation has a patient, this is also the patient of the causation event
`change-of-state ->` `    patient=result patient`	the patient of a change-of-state is the patient of the embedded result state

Figure 5: Universal constraints for semantic roles and macroroles

```
class argRank1
<frame>{?e[event, effector:?x] |
  ?e[event, mover:?x] |
  ?e[event, st-mover:?x] | ...}

class argRank2
  <frame>{?e[event, location:?x] |
  ?e[event, perceiver:?x] | ...}

class argRank3
  <frame>{?e[event, theme:?x] |
  ?e[event, stimulus:?x] | ...}

class argRank4
  <frame>{?e[event, patient:?x] |
  ?e[event, entity:?x] }
```

Figure 7: XMG classes for rank i arguments

```
class Rank2_actor
import argRank2[]
<frame>{?e[event, actor:?x]};
<iface>{[highest-rank=r2,highest-arg=?x,
  rank2=?x]}

class Rank2_undergoer
import argRank2[]
<frame>{?e[event,undergoer:?x]};
<iface>{[highest-rank=r1,rank2=?x,
  und-lower2=false,lowest-arg=?x]}

class Rank2_no_macrorole
import argRank2[]
<iface>{[highest-rank=r1,
  und-lower2=true,rank2=?x]}

class Rank2_no_arg
<frame>{?e[event]}
```

Figure 8: Rank-specific XMG classes for the different macrorole assignments: classes for rank 2

These features are needed for macrorole assignment. In addition, we also need the following interface features for linking the resulting semantic frame with a syntactic tree: features `ranki` that give the frame node of the argument with rank i, if it is present, and features `highest-arg` and `lowest-arg` where `highest-arg` gives the frame node of the argument with the highest rank while `lowest-arg` gives the one with the lowest rank provided there exists a higher ranked argument.

As a further step of factorizing possible argument realizations in the metagrammar, for each rank, we then introduce new classes for arguments of this rank a) being an actor, b) being an undergoer, c) without macrorole and d) not realized (if applicable). Fig. 8 gives these classes for rank 2, where all four cases are possible. For each possibility, the interface features are set accordingly. For instance, if a rank 2 argument is an undergoer (see the second class in Fig. 8), there has to be a higher argument

(highest-rank=r1) and there cannot be any other lower undergoer (und-lower2=false, und-lower3=false).

The classes for rank 3 arguments are given in Fig. 9. Such an argument can either be the undergoer (no rank 4 argument is present) or without macrorole (there is a rank 4 argument) or not realized. In the latter case, captured in the class `class Rank3_no_arg`, the interface features state that either there is no undergoer lower than rank 2, which allows for combinations with the first two rank 2 classes in Fig. 8. Or there is a rank 4 undergoer. In this case, a rank 2 undergoer is excluded via the assignment und-lower2=true.

Finally, for each rank i, we have a class `Ranki` that is just a disjunction of the different possibilities captured in the `Ranki_...` classes, and, furthermore, there is a general class `event` that com-

```
class Rank3_undergoer
import argRank3[]
{<frame>{?e0[event, undergoer:?x]};
 <iface>{[und-lower3=false,
     und-lower2=true, rank3=?x,
     lowest-rank=r3, lowest-arg=?x]}}

class Rank3_no_macrorole
import argRank3[]
{<iface>{[und-lower3=true, rank3=?x]}}

class Rank3_no_arg
<frame>{?e[event]};
{<iface>{[und-lower2=false]} |
   <iface>{[und-lower2=true,
     und-lower3=true]}}
```

Figure 9: Classes for different macrorole assignments for arguments of rank 3

bines these Rank*i* classes (see Fig. 10).

```
class Rank2
  {?arg=Rank2_actor[] |
   ?arg=Rank2_no_arg[] |
   ?arg=Rank2_undergoer[] |
   ?arg=Rank2_no_macrorole[]};
  ?e=?arg.?e

class event
import Rank1[] Rank2[] Rank3[] Rank4[]
```

Figure 10: XMG classes Rank2 and event

XMG compiles the class event into all possible semantic role combinations while computing the correct macrorole assignments, creating thereby all possible event frames.

6.3 Linking syntax and semantics

The part of the MG described in the previous two sections is language-independent. Depending on the language, the arguments with the highest and the lowest rank are realized differently in the syntax (see section 5). In the following, we will only introduce the XMG classes for syntax-semantics linking for English.

Recall that the interface feature highest-arg gives the argument with the highest rank and that lowest-arg gives the one with the lowest, provided there is a higher one. Besides these two, we also use the interface features rank*i* for linking.

A simplified version of the syntactic XMG classes implemented for English is given in Fig. 11. The two classes for subject and object combine into the class n0Vn1 for transitive verbs. Note that in our actual implementation, Subject if further decomposed and, furthermore, a range of

```
class Subject
<syn>{             S
               ___/ \___
          NP[I=?arg1]   VP[I=?e]
                          |
                        V[VOICE=?Voice]  };
{{?Voice=active;
   <iface>{[highest-arg=?arg1]}} |
{?Voice=passive;
   <iface>{[lowest-arg=?arg1]}}}

class Object
<syn>{        VP[I=?e]
            __/ \__
          V   NP[I=?arg2]   };
{<iface>{[rank2=?arg2]} |
   <iface>{[rank3=?arg2]} |
   <iface>{[rank4=?arg2]}}

class n0Vn1
import Subject[] Object[] event[]
```

Figure 11: Language-specific XMG classes for English (simplified)

additional boolean interface features is used in order to constrain the combinations of arguments of different ranks in the two syntactic argument slots. The Subject class expresses that in active sentences, the highest-arg fills the subject slot while in passive sentences, this slot is filled by the lowest-arg. Further boolean interface features check that in these cases, highest-arg and lowest-arg are actually given.

When limiting the semantic argument classes argRank*i* to just one single semantic role, the XMG compiler yields 16 different frames when compiling the class event (each argument rank can be present or absent and the rank combination determines the macrorole assignments) and a total of 25 tree frame pairs when compiling n0Vn1, which corresponds to the correct 25 linking patterns that we expect here: In active sentences, either a) the subject is of rank 1, then there are 3 possible object ranks and the other two ranks can be each present or absent in the frame or b) the subject is of rank 2, then the object has rank 3 or 4 and the rank among $\{3, 4\}$ that is not object can be present or not in the frame or c) the subject has rank 3 and the object rank 4. In passive sentences, either a) the subject is of rank 4, then the object can be 3 or 2 and the remaining two ranks can be present or absent in the frame, or b) the subject is of rank 3, the object of rank 2 and rank 1 is present or absent in the frame. Furthermore, a rank 2 argument requires a rank 3 argument that could, however, be promoted to the rank 1. The implementation yields a total of 23 linking patterns. Note that this simplified implementation of nOVn1 leaves out a lot of possibilities for argument realizations. It considers only the case of canonical subject and object positions and does not take the possibility into account that the highest argument in passive constructions can be realized as a *by*-PP. All these other cases would of course lead to more tree frame pairs.

Our analysis allows for tree frame pairs where only some of the arguments listed in the frame have corresponding syntactic slots. In other words, we implement a relaxation of the θ-criterion for LTAG mentioned in section 3 that requires that each syntactic argument slot in the elementary tree of a predicate corresponds to a semantic argument slot in the frame but not necessarily vice versa. To what extend the stronger version of the θ-criterion, requiring a bijection between syntactic and semantic arguments, should be applied, is an open question (see section 7).

6.4 Lexical insertion

When combining a lexical item, for instance *smashed* paired with the frame from Fig. 6, with an unanchored class such as nOVn1, the two event frames unify. Due to our relaxed implementation of the θ-criterion, this unification can enrich the lexical frame with further semantic roles and there might even be roles coming from the lexical element that do not have a corresponding syntactic argument slot. Sometimes this might be desired. The semantics of *walk* for instance does not necessarily contain a GOAL component. Such a component can however be added by a directed-motion construction as in (3).

(3) John walked into the house.

One way to prevent additional roles from being added is to constrain the frame via the interface features. We have implemented this for the example of *smash* to the effect that when anchoring our nOVn1 class with the lemma *smash*, we obtain only the elementary tree frame pair where we have active voice, the EFFECTOR linked to the subject and the PATIENT linked to the object.

7 Conclusion

We proposed a constraint-based formulation of the principles underlying the linking algorithm from Van Valin (2005), instead of a procedural specification. The advantage is not only that we can separate between the linguistic generalizations to be captured and algorithmic considerations. There is also a straightforward way to implement this with XMG and, within this metagrammar framework, to connect it with existing implementations of LTAG, allowing for a neat separation between language-specific and language-independent linking constraints. From a less technical perspective, the presented work can be seen as the first attempt to fill an important gap in the theory of the shape of elementary entries that Frank's θ-Criterion left open.

Acknowledgments

We thank the three anonymous reviewers for helpful comments. The work presented in this paper was financed by the Deutsche Forschungsgemeinschaft (DFG) within the CRC 991.

References

Anne Abeillé and Owen Rambow. 2000. Tree Adjoining Grammar: An Overview. In Anne Abeillé and Owen Rambow, editors, *Tree Adjoining Grammars: Formalisms, Linguistic Analysis and Processing*, pages 1–68. CSLI.

Benoit Crabbé and Denys Duchier. 2004. Metagrammar Redux. In *International Workshop on Constraint Solving and Language Processing*, Copenhagen.

Benoit Crabbé, Denys Duchier, Claire Gardent, Joseph Le Roux, and Yannick Parmentier. 2013. XMG: eXtensible MetaGrammar. *Computational Linguistics*, 39(3):1–66.

Éric Villemonte de la Clergerie. 2013. Exploring beam-based shift-reduce dependency parsing with DyALog: Results from the SPMRL 2013 shared task. In *4th Workshop on Statistical Parsing of Morphologically Rich Languages (SPMRL'2013)*, Seattle.

David Dowty. 1991. Thematic proto-roles and argument selection. *Language*, 67(3):547–619.

D. Duchier, J. Le Roux, and Y. Parmentier. 2004. The Metagrammar Compiler: an NLP application with a Multi-Paradigm Architecture. In *Proceedings of the 2nd international Mozart-Oz Conference MOZ 2004, Lecture Notes in Computer Science, Vol. 3389, Springer*, Charleroi, Belgium.

Robert Frank. 1992. *Syntactic Locality and Tree Adjoining Grammar: Grammatical, Acquisition and Processing Perspectives*. Ph.D. thesis, University of Pennsylvania.

Robert Frank. 2002. *Phrase Structure Composition and Syntactic Dependencies*. MIT Press, Cambridge, Mass.

Claire Gardent and Laura Kallmeyer. 2003. Semantic Construction in FTAG. In *Proceedings of EACL 2003*, pages 123–130, Budapest.

Aravind K. Joshi and Yves Schabes. 1997. Tree-Adjoning Grammars. In G. Rozenberg and A. Salomaa, editors, *Handbook of Formal Languages*, pages 69–123. Springer, Berlin.

Laura Kallmeyer and Aravind K. Joshi. 2003. Factoring Predicate Argument and Scope Semantics: Underspecified Semantics with LTAG. *Research on Language and Computation*, 1(1–2):3–58.

Laura Kallmeyer and Rainer Osswald. 2013. Syntax-driven semantic frame composition in Lexicalized Tree Adjoining Grammar. *Journal of Language Modelling*, 1:267–330.

Laura Kallmeyer and Maribel Romero. 2008. Scope and situation binding in LTAG using semantic unification. *Research on Language and Computation*, 6(1):3–52.

Beth Levin and Malka Rappaport Hovav. 2005. *Argument Realization*. Cambridge University Press, Cambridge.

Timm Lichte and Simon Petitjean. 2015. Implementing semantic frames as typed feature structures with XMG. *Journal of Language Modelling*, 3(1):185–228.

Timm Lichte. 2015. *Syntax und Valenz. Zur Modellierung kohärenter und elliptischer Strukturen mit Baumadjunktionsgrammatiken*. Number 1 in Empirically Oriented Theoretical Morphology and Syntax. Language Science Press, Berlin.

Rebecca Nesson and Stuart M. Shieber. 2006. Simpler TAG semantics through synchronization. In *Proceedings of the 11th Conference on Formal Grammar*, Malaga, Spain, 29–30 July.

Rebecca Nesson and Stuart M. Shieber. 2008. Synchronous vector tag for syntax and semantics: Control verbs, relative clauses, and inverse linking. In *Proceedings of the Ninth International Workshop on Tree Adjoining Grammars and Related Formalisms (TAG+ 9)*, Tübingen, Germany.

Stuart M. Shieber. 1994. Restricting the weak-generative capacity of synchronous Tree-Adjoining Grammars. *Computational Intelligence*, 10(4):271–385.

Robert D. Van Valin, Jr. 2005. *Exploring the Syntax-Semantics Interface*. Cambridge University Press.

K. Vijay-Shanker and Aravind K. Joshi. 1988. Feature structures based tree adjoining grammar. In *Proceedings of COLING*, pages 714–719, Budapest.

Stephen Wechsler. 2015. *Word Meaning and Syntax*. Oxford Surveys in Syntax and Morphology. Oxford University Press, Oxford.

Verbal fields in Hungarian simple sentences and
infinitival clausal complements

Kata Balogh
DFG Collaborative Research Centre 991
Heinrich-Heine-Universität Düsseldorf
Katalin.Balogh@hhu.de

The paper presents an analysis of Hungarian sentence articulation driven by discourse-semantic functions such as *topic* and *focus*, hence the information structure of the utterance. In this paper extensions of the standard LTAG framework are proposed to represent the information structure driven positions in simple sentences. The elementary trees are generated by the meta-grammar, using the XMG tool for grammar writing. The verbal fields will also be investigated in complex sentences with infinitival clausal complements. I will discuss challenging phenomena, such as scrambling of the different verbal fields, and verbal modifier climbing.

1 Introduction

The core topic of this paper is the analysis of the verbal fields in Hungarian simple sentences and infinitival clausal complements. Hungarian is challenging for computational linguistic applications, given its flexible word order and discourse configurational type, where syntactic positions are not driven by grammatical functions, but rather by discourse-semantic functions such as *topic* and *focus*. In this paper I propose an analysis in Lexicalized Tree-Adjoining Grammar [LTAG; (Joshi and Schabes, 1997)] with an extension to the representation of information structure, the driving device for sentence articulation in Hungarian. The elementary trees are generated by the meta-grammar, using the eXtensible MetaGrammar tool [XMG; (Crabbé et al., 2013)].

Next to simple sentences, the paper also presents the proposal of an analysis of complex sentences with infinitival clausal components. The analysis of Hungarian infinitival clauses faces a list of interesting issues, regardless of the given framework. In the analysis we need to capture the fact that the embedded infinitival clause has

its own verbal fields and that the arguments of the matrix verb and the embedded infinitival can be mixed. The analysis of infinitival clausal complements is challenging for standard LTAG, since it cannot handle discontinuity and scrambling phenomena (Becker and Rambow, 1990; Becker et al., 1991), caused by the mixing of the arguments in different verbal fields. This paper proposes some modifications in order to capture these phenomena: (i) using multi-component TAG [MCTAG] (Weir, 1988; Nesson et al., 2010), and (ii) extending the feature sets to represent stress-positions.

1.1 LTAG in a nutshell

Tree-Adjoining Grammar (TAG) is a tree-rewriting formalism, where the elementary structures are trees. A TAG is a set of *elementary trees* with two combinatorial operations: *substitution* and *adjunction*. The set of elementary trees is the union of a finite set of *initial trees* and *auxiliary trees*. A derivation in TAG starts with an initial tree (α) and proceeds by using either of the two operations. By *substitution* a non-terminal leaf node is replaced by an initial tree (β), while by *adjunction* an internal node is replaced by an auxiliary tree (γ).

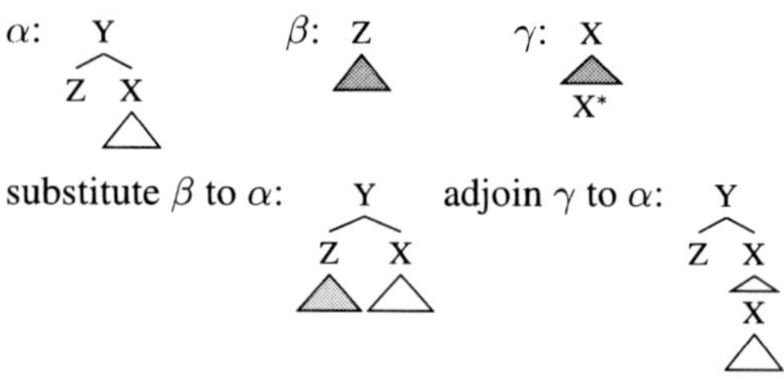

Figure 1: Substitution and adjunction

In a Lexicalized TAG [LTAG] each elementary tree contains at least one lexical element, its *lexical anchor* ($\diamond$). To increase the expressive power

Proceedings of the 12th International Workshop on Tree Adjoining Grammars and Related Formalisms (TAG+12), pages 58–66,
Düsseldorf, Germany, June 29 - July 1, 2016.

of the formalism, adjunction constraints are additionally introduced to restrict whether adjunction is mandatory and/or which trees can be adjoined at a given node. In particular for natural language analyses another extension of TAG is proposed, using feature structures as non-terminal nodes. Among the reasons for a Feature-based TAG [F-TAG] two important ones are generalizing agreement and case marking via underspecification. A great advantage of F-TAG with respect to grammar writing is the result of smaller grammars that are easier to maintain, as well as the possibility of modeling adjunction constraints. The shape of the elementary trees is driven by linguistic principles (Abeillé and Rambow, 2000; Frank, 2002), reflecting the syntactic/semantic properties of linguistic objects. Syntactic design principles determine, for example, that subcategorization is expressed locally within the elementary tree of the predicate. In the grammar architecture *tree families* are defined, sets of tree templates representing a subcategorization frame and collecting all syntactic configurations the subcategorization frame can be realized in.

2 Verbal fields in simple sentences

With respect to information structure, Hungarian sentence structure distinguishes two fields: the *postverbal* and the *preverbal* field (see e.g. É. Kiss, 2005). The *postverbal field* by default hosts the 'argument positions' the order of which is free: the word order variations do not signal grammatical roles and are associated with the same semantic content. The *preverbal field* hosts the so-called 'functional projections', the order of which is fixed. Sentence initially we find the topic(s), followed by quantifier(s) and the narrow focus, which is placed in the immediate preverbal position:[1]

Topic* < Quantifier* < Focus < Verb [...]

A designated syntactic position immediately preceding the verb is important in Hungarian for several reasons. This position hosts narrow focus, sentential negation, the verbal modifier (verbal particles, bare nouns, infinitives etc.), partially in complementary distribution. In 'neutral sentences' – utterances without narrow focus or sentential negation –, the immediate preverbal position is occupied by the verbal modifier (VM) as il-

lustrated in (1a). When the sentence contains sentential negation (1b) or narrow focus (1c) the VM stands postverbally.

(1)   a. Pim meg-hívta Marit.
          Pim VM-invited Mary.acc
          'Pim invited Mary.'

       b. Pim nem hívta   meg Marit.
          Pim neg invited VM Mary.acc
          'Pim did not invite Mary.'

       c. Pim MARIT   hívta   meg.
          Pim Mary.acc invited VM
          'It is Mary whom Pim invited.'

The verbal modifier is in complementary distribution with both the narrow focus and the sentential negation. However, narrow focus and negation can co-occur; see (2).

(2)   Pim MARIT   nem hívta   meg.
    Pim Mary.acc neg invited VM
    'It is Mary whom Pim did not invite.'

The position of the VM depends on whether narrow focus or sentential negation is present in the sentence. The narrow focus and sentential negation must stand in the immediate preverbal position, forcing the VM to appear postverbally.

2.1 Functional positions

In Hungarian, sentence articulation is driven by discourse semantics rather than by grammatical function. Instead of defining structural positions for grammatical functions (e.g. subject) we need to define structural positions for topic and focus. Accordingly, the elementary trees in a given tree family need to encode the possible topic/focus structures. In the following, I will illustrate the system via the transitive tree family with two NP arguments. Both arguments can be either in postverbal position, in topic position and in focus position. Hence, the tree family of transitive verbs must contain the elementary trees for all structures: VP-NP-NP, NP$_{top}$-VP-NP, NP$_{foc}$-VP-NP, NP$_{top}$-NP$_{top}$-VP, NP$_{top}$-NP$_{foc}$-VP. Instead of merely listing the structures, the XMG tool is used to generate the set of elementary trees, so that generalizations on positions can also be expressed (see section 3).

2.2 Representing information structure

The representation of information structure comes on a par with the elementary tree, following the proposals by (Kallmeyer and Romero, 2008) and

---

[1]Next to topic, focus and quantifiers, the preverbal field also hosts sentential negation, optative operators (*bárcsak* 'if only') and interrogative operators.

(Kallmeyer and Osswald, 2012). Each elementary tree is linked to a frame-based semantic representation. The syntactic operations (substitution and adjunction) trigger the unification of the semantic representations, thereby deriving the meaning representation of the sentence. Next to the meaning representation, the representation of the information structure is proposed, mediated by the meta-variables on the nodes.

The notion of *information structure* [InfS] covers a wide range of phenomena such as topic, comment, focus, background, given, new, contrast etc. The central aim in the current analysis is to represent InfS in a way that we can derive the basic focus structures: *sentence focus*, *predicate focus* and *narrow focus*. These structures are nicely reflected in the Hungarian sentence articulation by the structural distinction of the topic of the sentence and the comment, which we take as the *focus domain*. The focus domain is either as a whole the focus of the sentence (predicate focus) or it contains narrow focus.

(3)   a.   Q: What happened?

A: Meg-hívta   Pim Marit.
VM-invited Pim Mary.acc

'[Pim invited Mary.]^{F}' → sentence focus

b.   Q: What did Pim do?

A: Pim meg-hívta   Marit.
Pim VM-invited Mary.acc

'Pim [invited Mary.]^{F}' → predicate focus

c.   Q: Whom did Pim invite?

A: Pim MARIT   hívta   meg.
Pim Mary.acc invited VM

A′: MARIT   hívta   meg Pim.
Mary.acc invited VM Pim

'Pim invited [Mary]^{F}.' → narrow focus

In the elementary tree of the predicate, the feature INFS indicates the positions related to information structure. The values *topic* and *focus* indicate the positions for the sentence topic and the narrow focus respectively, while the value *pred* indicates the syntactic predicate.

Each elementary tree is linked to a representation of the information structure, uniformly given as an attribute-value matrix. The attributes TOP (topic) and FOC-DOM (focus domain) represent the *topic–comment* distinction. The focus domain can be further divided into FOC (indicating narrow focus) and NON-FOC (non-focus part of the fo-

cus domain).[2] The background part in the *focus–background* distinction can be derived as the unification of the NON-FOC and the TOP values.

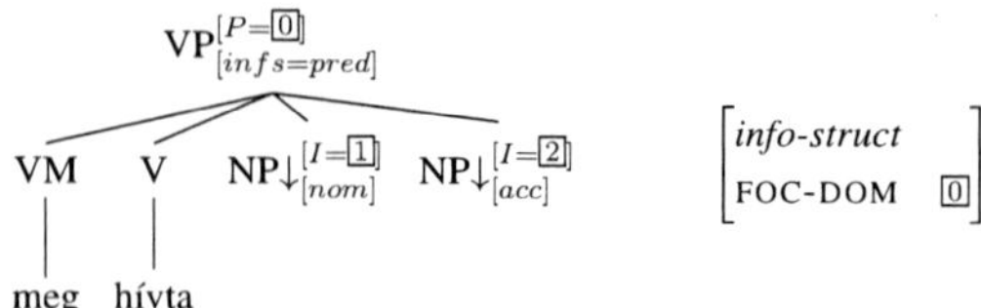

Figure 2: Elementary tree of *meg-hívta* for sentence focus

Figure 2 illustrates the elementary tree of the verb *meg-hívta* ('invited') for structures with sentence focus (3a). The resulting InfS representation signals the whole predication (P=⓪) being the focus-domain, and since it is not divided further, it represents sentence focus.

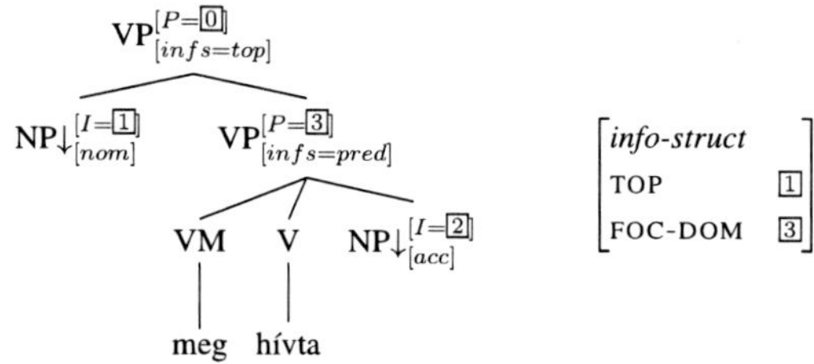

Figure 3: Elementary tree of *meg-hívta* for predicate focus

Figure 3 shows the elementary tree for predicate focus structure (3b). The InfS representation signals the syntactic predicate (P=③) as the focus-domain, while the element occupying the topic position (I=①) is represented as the sentence topic.

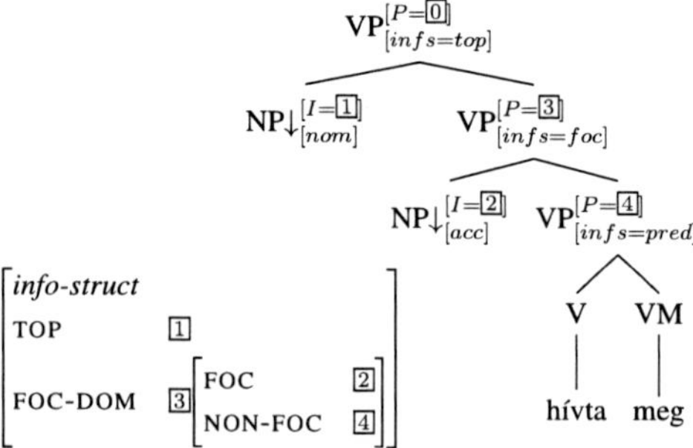

Figure 4: Elementary tree of *hívta meg* for narrow focus

Figure 4 illustrates the elementary tree of the verb for a construction containing both a topic and

<hr>

[2] The notions of *focus domain* and *non-focus* are inspired by (Van Valin Jr., 2005).

a narrow focus (3c-A). The focus domain is divided into the narrow focus (FOC) and the non-focus, that contributes to the background.

The different information structures can be further mapped to the information status of the given elements, in terms of *givenness*. The representations of different topic/focus structures and their relation to the discourse is under investigation and will be presented in a later stage of the analysis.

3 Topic and focus positions

As already noted above, the tree families of the verbs must contain all possible structures reflecting the information structure of the utterance. The arguments of the verbs can occupy three structural positions, resulting in various structures. For example, transitive verbs must have two argument slots, each with three possibilities. Instead of merely listing these structures, the XMG tool is used to generate the set of elementary trees, so that generalizations can also be expressed.

3.1 XMG in a nutshell

An LTAG grammar is a set of elementary trees which contain most linguistic information. However, this set contains identical tree fragments, leading to multiple structure sharing. The XMG tool provides the elementary trees for a given grammar, such that it factors out redundant parts of a given tree set by identifying identical tree fragments in the set of elementary trees. An additional abstraction level is introduced, the *metagrammar*, where generalizations can be expressed. The meta-grammar is a declarative system that combines re-usable tree fragments – *classes* – by conjunction and disjunction.

```
Class  ::= Name → Content
Content ::=
   Descr | Name |
   Content ∧ Content | Content ∨ Content
Descr ::=
```
$$n_i \to n_j \mid n_i \to^+ n_j \mid n_i \to^* n_j \mid n_i \prec n_j \mid$$
$$n_i \prec^+ n_j \mid n_i \prec^* n_j \mid n_i[f_1 : v_1, ..., f_n : v_n] \mid$$
$$n_i(c_1 : cv_1, ..., cf_n : cv_n) \mid \text{Descr} \wedge \text{Descr}$$

The content of a class can be either a simple tree fragment or a conjunction / disjunction of two tree fragments. In the description of a tree fragment the dominance $\to$ and precedence $\prec$ relations of the nodes are given, where $\to^+$ and $\prec^+$ stand for their transitive closure and $\to^*$ and $\prec^*$ for their transitive, reflexive closure. At each node we refer to the features associated with it

by $n_i[f_1 : v_1, ..., f_n : v_n]$ and each node can be marked for substitution, footnode, anchor, etc. by $n_i(c_1 : cv_1, ..., cf_n : cv_n)$.

```
class CanSubj
declare ?S ?VP ?NP
{<syn>{
node ?S (color=black) [cat=s] ;
node ?NP (color=black,mark=subst) [cat=np] ;
node ?VP (color=white) [cat=vp] ;
?S -> ?NP ; ?S -> ?VP ; ?NP » ?VP } }
```

Figure 5: Tree description of the class of canonical subject in English

Tree fragments can be combined by conjunction and disjunction resulting in tree templates, e.g.:

```
Subject → CanSubject ∨ WhNpSubject
Object → CanObject ∨ WhNpObject
```

In the combination of the tree fragments nodes get unified. Node equations are carried out by node polarization: annotating the nodes with colors (e.g. `color = black`), which declare implicitly how a given node can be unified with others. This method is based on a color matrix, according to which (i) a black node can unify with zero, one or more white nodes, producing a black node, (ii) a white node must be unified with a black node producing a black node, and (iii) a red node cannot be unified with any other node. The resulting tree fragment is a satisfying model only if it does not contain any white nodes.

3.2 Implementation using XMG

The class of transitive verbs must contain the verbal projection and two arguments, the subject (`Subj`) and the object (`Obj`).

```
Trans → VProj ∧ Subj ∧ Obj
```

Both arguments have three possible positions: postverbal (`ArgPos`), topic (`TopPos`) or focus (`FocPos`) position and get the appropriate case marking.

```
Subj → (ArgPos ∨ TopPos ∨ FocPos) ∧ Nom
Obj → (ArgPos ∨ TopPos ∨ FocPos) ∧ Acc
```

NP case marking is generalized via the classes Nom, Acc, ... as:

```
Nom → n[cat:np,top:[case:nom]]
Acc → n[cat:np,top:[case:acc]]
```

The core is the class of the verb projection, VProj, that must be either one of the three tree fragments:

```
VProj → VProj1 ∨ VProj2 ∨ VProj3
```

The above fragments are defined according to whether there is a verbal modifier present, and in which order it appears relative to the verb. Considering the VM-V order as default (non-inversion), the INV feature determines whether inversion is present (values *yes* / *no*). In case the sentence contains no VM, the INV feature is irrelevant / not applicable (value *na*).

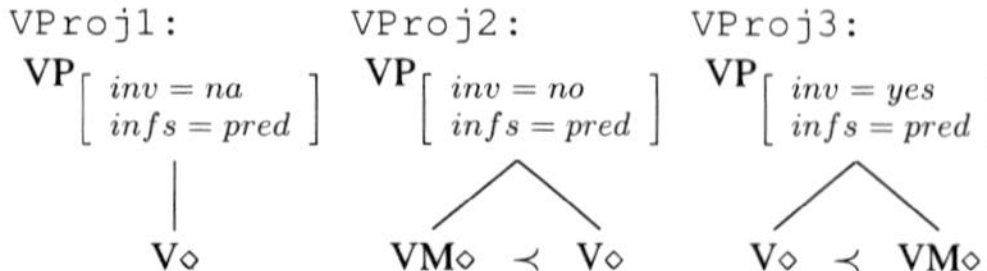

Figure 6: Tree fragments for verb projection

For the argument position the class `ArgPos` is defined. As illustrated in section 2, in the post-verbal field the order of the arguments is free. At the VP node the feature INFS represents the information structural function of the constituent, with value *pred* representing the syntactic predicate.

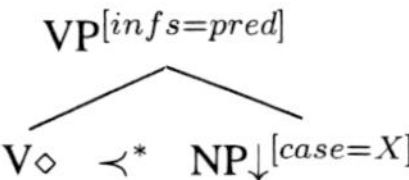

Figure 7: Tree fragment for argument position

The class of the verb projection combines with one or more argument positions, where the order of the arguments are free. This latter is made possible by the reflexive, transitive closure ($\prec^*$) of the precedence relation between the V node and the argument NP node. The case marking of the argument is underspecified.

By the above fragments we can generate the elementary trees for deriving all possible argument orders in the post-verbal field for a given predicate. For example, the tree family of a transitive verb will contain the structures (among others) for cases in which both arguments are postverbal:

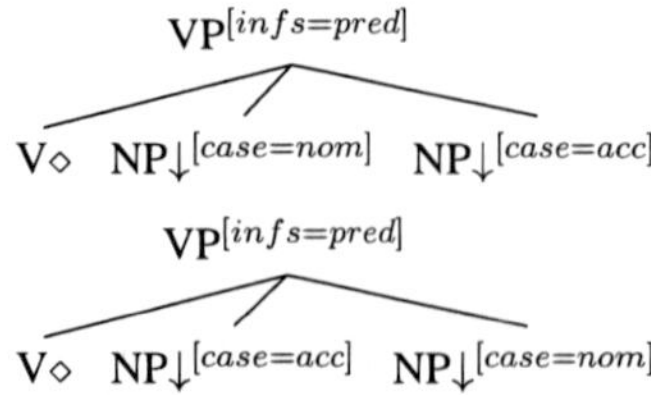

In the pre-verbal field we have fixed structural positions for the *topic* and *focus*.[3] The classes for these positions are defined respectively as:

---

[3] In Hungarian, (distributive) quantifiers have a designated position, too, between the topic(s) and the focus. Regarding

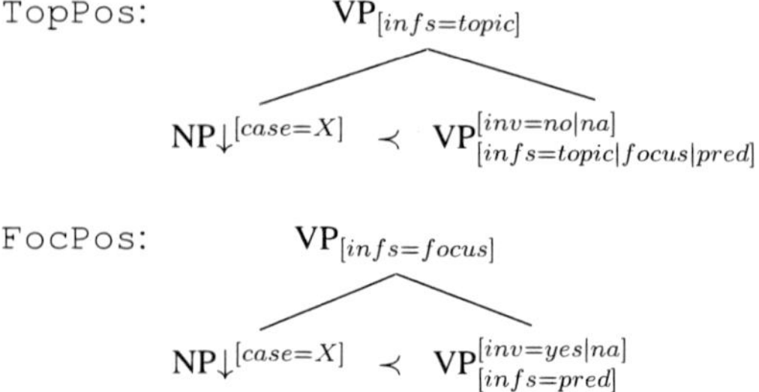

Figure 8: Tree fragments for topic and positions

According to the hierarchical order of the pre-verbal positions, a topic can be followed by another topic, the focus or the predicate, while focus can only be followed by the predicate. These ordering constraints are captured by the bottom features of the respective VP footnotes, while the top features of these nodes constrain the VM-V inversion. Focus induces inversion (*inv=yes|na*), while topics do not (*inv=no|na*). For both, a combination with a non-VM verb is of course possible.

The tree fragments above define the post-verbal position and the two functional positions (topic, focus) in a uniform way, capturing the generalizations behind them. Using the above tree fragments the meta-grammar generates the elementary trees, by which the grammar can derive all possible structures in simple sentences, possibly containing topic and focus positions. The non-grammatical structures – e.g. topic following focus, focus without VM-V inversion etc. – are ruled out correctly.

4 Infinitival embedded clauses

In this section I propose an analysis of infinitival complements and the structure and relation of the verbal fields of the matrix verb and the infinitival embedded verb. In Hungarian two types of control verbs can be distinguished: the ones that take main stress (e.g. *fél* 'is afraid') versus the ones that avoid main stress (e.g. *akar* 'want'), referred to as 'stress-bearing verbs' and 'stress-avoiding verbs' respectively. These two verb classes differ in syntactic behavior with respect to the placement of the verbal modifier of the embedded infinitive. In Hungarian the main stress falls on the *leftmost* element of the phonological phrase, hence, in neutral sentences the main stress falls on the VM.

---

the space limitations, the analysis of quantifiers is not discussed in this paper.

Example (4a) illustrates the stress-avoiding verb (*akar* 'want'), which induces the climbing of the VM of the infinitival verb.

(4)   a. Pim el akarja (el-*)olvasni a levelet.
          Pim VM wants (VM-)read.inf the book.acc
          'Pim wants to read the letter.'
      b. Pim (el*) fél el-olvasni a levelet.
          Pim (VM) afraid VM-read.inf the book.acc
          'Pim is afraid to read the letter.'

The VM *el-* is the modifier of the infinitival *olvasni*, but it must appear in the pre-verbal position of the matrix verb. In this way the VM *el-* receives the main stress instead of the matrix verb. In (4b) the VM of the infinitival stays in its own pre-verbal position, VM climbing is no grammatical. Koopman & Szabolcsi (2000) classifies different verb types as (i) the group of *auxiliaries*: that do not bear main accent and induce VM-climbing, (ii) *non-auxiliaries 1*: that bear main accent and do not induce VM-climbing and (iii) *non-auxiliaries 2* with mixed behavior.

In case of clausal complements we have multiple verbal fields, belonging to both the finite and the infinite verbs.

(5) $[preV_1]\ V_1\ [\ postV_1\ ]\ [\ preV_2\ ]\ V_2\ [\ postV_2\ ]$

(6)   András meg-tanította a diákokat   a
      Andrew VM-taught   the students.acc the
      mondatot   csak LFG-ben elemezni.
      sentence.acc only LFG.in analyze.inf
      'Andrew taught the students to analyze the sentence only in LFG.'

      (from (Szécsényi, 2009))

Syntactically interesting cases are the sentences in which arguments of the embedded verb are topicalized or focused. Szécseényi's (2009) example above provides evidence of the existence of the separate pre-verbal field of the embedded infinitive, hosting the focus expression *csak LFG-ben* 'only in LFG'. However, broader data suggest that the preferred position of a focused or topicalized argument of the infinitive is in the pre-verbal field of the matrix verb (see examples (7) and (8)).

In the following examples the embedded infinitive is *el-olvasni* 'VM-read.inf', containing a verbal modifier, while the matrix verb does not have a VM. Topics preferably stand in the preverbal field of the matrix verb (7b, 8b), however, it is also grammatical in the preverbal field of the embedded verb (7a, 8a). Focused constituents stand in the preverbal field of the matrix verb (7c, 8c). Next

to these preferred positions, the sentence articulation is also sensitive to the type of the matrix verb (auxiliary vs. non-auxiliary), providing different structures.

(7)   a. $^?$Pim fél   [a levelet]^T el-olvasni.
          Pim afraid the letter.acc VM-read.inf
      b. Pim [a levelet]^T fél   el-olvasni.
          Pim the letter.acc afraid VM-read.inf
          'Pim is afraid to read the letter.'
      c. Pim [a LEVELET]^F fél   el-olvasni.
          Pim the letter.acc   afraid VM-read.inf
          'It is the letter, that Pim is afraid to read. '

(8)   a. $^?$Pim el akarja [a levelet]^T olvasni.
          Pim VM wants the letter.acc read.inf
      b. Pim [a levelet]^T el akarja olvasni.
          Pim the letter.acc VM wants read.inf
          'Pim wants to read the letter.'
      c. Pim [a LEVELET]^F akarja el-olvasni.
          Pim the letter.acc   wants VM-read.inf
          'It is the letter, that Pim wants to read. '

4.1   Proposal: from LTAG to TL-MCTAG

Closely related to scrambling, the position of the verbal modifier of the embedded verb in stress avoiding versus stress bearing control verbs poses interesting questions to the analysis.[4]

The structures reflecting the verbal fields of the control verbs and the infinitives can both be generated along the lines of the analysis of simple sentences. See, e.g., the elementary tree of *el-olvasni* 'to read' with a topicalized argument:

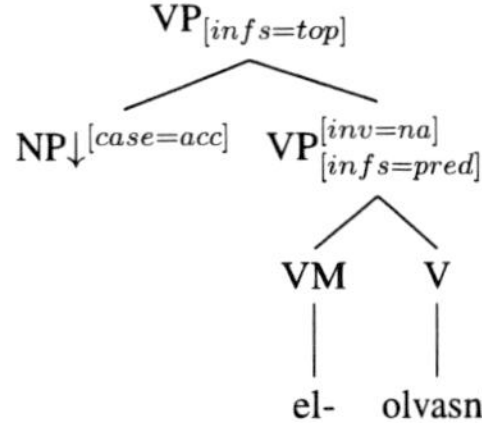

The core of the problem with an LTAG analysis here is caused by scrambling of the arguments and the verbal modifier in the different verbal fields of the matrix verb and the embedded verb. Using the standard LTAG formalisms it is not possible to capture VM-climbing (4a), since it proposes elementary trees for sentence embedding, such that sentential complements being represented as a footnode (S*), and the elementary

---

[4]Hungarian infinitival clauses pose several more interesting issue to deal with, for example the verb-object agreement between the matrix verb and the object of the infinitive. For more issues around infinitival clauses in Hungarian see (Koopman and Szabolcsi, 2000) and (Szécsényi, 2009).

tree of the matrix verb (*akar* 'wants') being ad-joined into the elementary tree of the embedded verb. The standard LTAG analysis derives straight-forwardly the structures, in which the matrix verbs and its arguments are not split. This involves sentences with a stress-bearing control verb with different possible topic/focus structures, e.g.

(9) a. Pim^T fél   el-olvasni   a levelet.
         Pim   like.mod VM-read.inf the letter.acc
         'Pim is afraid to read the letter.'

     b. A levelet^T Pim^F fél   el-olvasni.
         the letter.acc Pim   like.mod VM-read.inf
         'It is Pim, who is afraid to read the letter.'

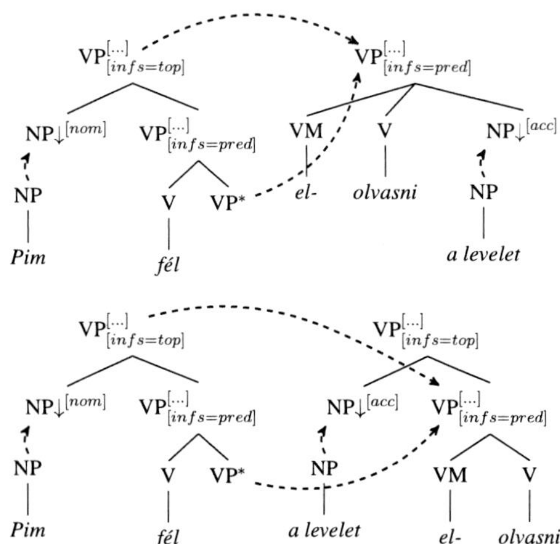

Figure 9: Standard LTAG analysis of (9a) and (9b)

The analysis in Figure 9 correctly derives the structures for stress-bearing verbs (4b), however this structure is not grammatical for stress-avoiding verbs as *akar* 'want'.

(10) *Pim akarja el-olvasni   a levelet.
       Pim   wants VM-read.inf the letter.acc

This structure should be ruled out for stress-avoiding verbs, but must be derived for stress-bearing verbs. Furthermore, Hungarian has a number of control verbs compatible with both VM-climbing and VM in situ structures. For such verbs it should be possible to derive both structures .

(11) a. Pim szeretne el-olvasni   egy levelet.
          Pim like.mod VM-read.inf a   letter.acc
          'Pim would like to read a book.'

      b. Pim el   szeretne olvasni egy levelet.
          Pim VM like.mod read.inf the letter.acc
          'Pim would like to read a book.'

In cases of VM-climbing (4a,11b), the tree of the matrix verb (*akar*) should split into more pieces when adjoined to the tree of the embedded verb (*el-olvasni*). This core problem for the standard LTAG analysis also arises when the arguments of the two verbs are mixed in the pre-verbal field of the matrix verb. As shown before, the preferred position of the topicalized or focused argument of the infinitive is in the pre-verbal field of the finite verb, hence arguments of different verbs can mix. See, for example, the sentence in which the object of the infinitive is focused and the subject of the finite verb is topicalized.

(12) Pim a LEVELET^F fél   el-olvasni.
      Pim the letter.acc   afraid VM-read.inf
      'It is the letter, what Pim is afraid to read.'

The problems of the analysis discussed above are due to the fact that standard LTAG cannot capture discontinuity (scrambling, extraposition etc.) in general (Becker and Rambow, 1990; Becker et al., 1991). In order to overcome the problems of our analysis, the use of Multicomponent TAG [MCTAG] is proposed. MCTAG is a modified TAG formalism, that allows elementary structures as set of trees. For natural language grammars the tree-local MCTAG [TL-MCTAG] (Weir, 1988; Nesson et al., 2010) is considered, which comes with the restriction that all trees in the set have to attach to the same elementary tree. TL-MCTAG is strongly equivalent to standard LTAG, thus by using this formalism we can overcome the problems of scrambling and VM-climbing without losing any of the attractive formal and computational properties of LTAG.

The first necessary modification of our original analysis is the position of the VM. In order to make VM-climbing possible, we need more structure below the given VP node, hence the previously proposed flat structure must be revised.

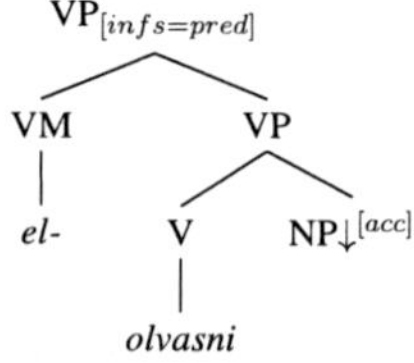

Figure 10: VM-V structure revised

Evidently, the structures with a topicalized/focused argument must be revised accordingly. Such a structure allows adjunction at the VP node right above the V, thereby allowing the VM-V verbal complex to split. This is one of the necessary conditions for capturing VM-climbing. However, this is merely the first step. The problem of the discontinuity of the finite verbs and its (topicalized) argument is still unresolved. Obviously, we need to deal with cases, where both the finite verbs and the embedded infinitive come with a split structure regarding the arguments and the verbal modifier. The solution is provided by TL-MCTAG, taking the elementary structures of the matrix verbs (*akar*, *fél*) as sets of trees.

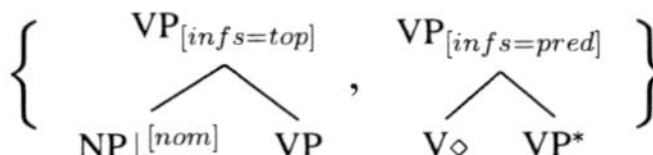

Figure 11: Elementary tree set for control verbs

Through this modification of the analysis we can derive the correct VM-climbing structure of stress avoiding verbs by allowing the first tree in the tree set to adjoin at the root VP node of the infinitival tree, and the second tree at the inner VP node right above the V. However, with these elementary tree sets we also derive the non-grammatical structures for both stress-bearing and stress avoiding verbs. The difference between these two verb classes relies on their relation with the prosodical structure of the sentence, that motivates the extension of the analysis by features representing stress positions. In Hungarian, the main stress falls on the left edge of the phonological phrase, hence in the default VM-V order the VM bears the main stress, while the V is unstressed. This is reflected in the elementary trees of verbs, e.g.:

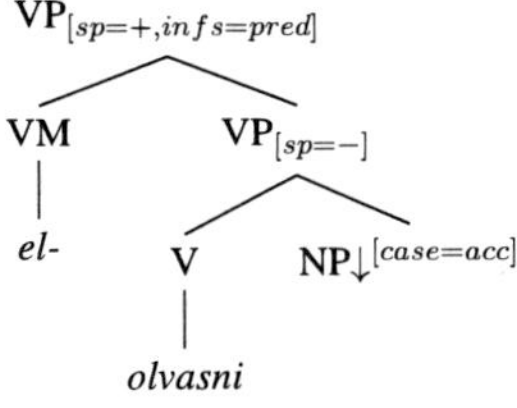

Figure 12: Features for stress positions

Stress-bearing verbs (*fél* 'is afraid') are marked for a stress position ([sp=+]) and thereby can only be adjoined at the root VP node of the tree of the infinitive. Adjoining at the inner VP node is ruled

out by a feature clash between the footnode of *fél* and the target node.

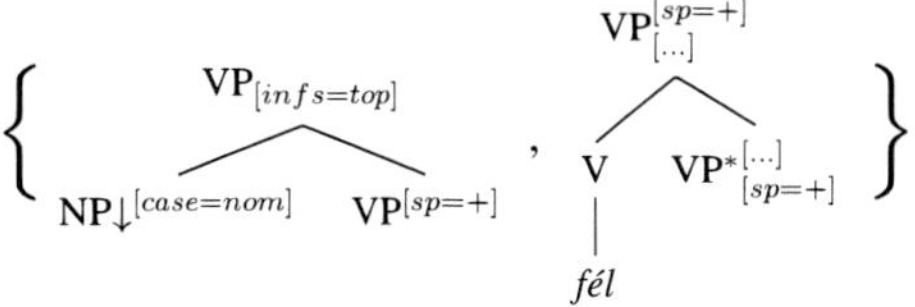

Stress-avoiding verbs (*akar* 'want') are marked for a non-stress position ([sp=−]) and hereby the second tree in the set can only be adjoined at the inner VP node of the tree of the infinitive.

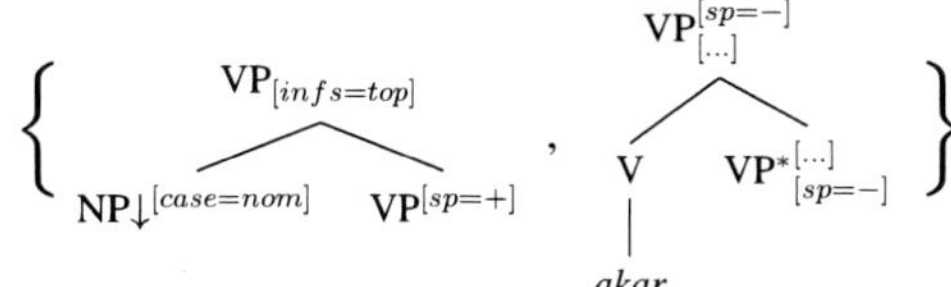

Verbs allowing for both structures come with a SP feature with an underspecified value, and thus can be equally derived in both structures.

5   Conclusion

This paper proposes an analysis of the verbal fields in Hungarian sentences articulation. I discussed several issues for an LTAG analysis of the information structure driven syntactic positions in simple sentences and in infinitival clausal complements. As information structure is the main device driving sentence articulation, an extension is proposed for representing different topic–focus structures. The elementary trees – reflecting the possible structures – are generated by the meta-grammar, using the eXtensible MetaGrammar tool. As shown in the paper, the flexible word order in Hungarian simple sentences is relatively easy to capture, generating all possible structures, while expressing the important generalizations on the functional positions.

Next to the analysis of the verbal fields in simple sentences, the paper proposed an analysis of complex sentences with infinitival clausal components. The analysis of Hungarian infinitival clauses faces a list of interesting issues. It is especially challenging for standard LTAG, since it cannot handle discontinuity and scrambling phenomena, caused here by the mixing of the arguments and the verbal modifier of different verbs. The proposed analysis shows that the challenges can be overcome by using TL-MCTAG extended with features to represent stress positions.

References

Anne Abeillé and Owen Rambow. 2000. Tree Adjoning Grammar: An overview. In Anne Abeillé and Owen Rambow, editors, *Tree Adjoning Grammars: Formalisms, Linguistic Analyses and Processing*, pages 1–68. CSLI Publications, Stanford.

Tilman Becker and Owen Rambow. 1990. Formal aspects of long distance scrambling. *Unpublished Paper*.

Tilman Becker, Aravind K. Joshi, and Owen Rambow. 1991. Long-distance scrambling and tree adjoining grammars. In *Proceedings of the 5th meeting of the European Chapter of the Association for Computational Linguistics (EACL)*, Berlin, Germany.

Benoit Crabbé, Denys Duchier, Claire Gardent, Joseph Le Roux, and Yannick Parmentier. 2013. XMG: eXtensible MetaGrammar. *Computational Linguistics*, 39(3).

Katalin É. Kiss. 2005. *The Syntax of Hungarian*. Cambridge University Press.

Robert Frank. 2002. *Phrase Structure Composition and Syntactic Dependencies*. MIT Press, Cambridge, MA.

Aravind K. Joshi and Yves Schabes. 1997. Tree-Adjoning Grammars. In G. Rozenberg and A. Salomaa, editors, *Handbook of Formal Languages*, pages 69–123. Springer, Berlin.

Laura Kallmeyer and Rainer Osswald. 2012. An analysis of directed motion expressions with lexicalized tree adjoining grammars and frame semantics. In L. Ong and R. de Queiroz, editors, *WoLLIC 2012, Lecture Notes in Computer Science LNCS 7456*, pages 34–55. Springer.

Laura Kallmeyer and Maribel Romero. 2008. Scope and situation binding in LTAG using semantic unification. *Research on Language and Computation*, 6(1):3–52.

Hilda Koopman and Anna Szabolcsi. 2000. *Verbal Complexes*. MIT Press.

Rebecca Nesson, Stuart M. Shieber, and Giorgio Satta. 2010. Complexity, parsing, and factorization of tree-local multicomponent tree-adjoining grammar. *Computational Linguistics*, 36(3):443–480.

Krisztina Szécsényi. 2009. *An LF-driven Theory of Scrambling in Hungarian Infinitival Constructions*. Ph.D. thesis, Szeged University, Hungary.

Robert Van Valin Jr. 2005. *Exploring the syntax-semantics interface*. Cambridge University Press.

David J. Weir. 1988. *Characterizing Mildly Context-Sensitive Grammar Formalisms*. Ph.D. thesis, University of Pennsylvania.

Modelling the *ziji* Blocking Effect and Constraining Bound Variable Derivations in MC-TAG with Delayed Locality

Dennis Ryan Storoshenko
University of Calgary
Craigie Hall C205, 2500 University Dr NW
Calgary, AB, Canada
`dstorosh@ucalgary.ca`

Abstract

MC-TAG derivations using delayed locality (i.e. non set-local composition) have been used to model long distance binding in natural language. In this paper, I explore the possibility within Synchronous TAG that tree sets composing via delayed locality may have many possible syntactic derivations for a single semantic form. Using the Mandarin (Chinese) anaphor *ziji* as a test case, I show that the blocking effect which is described in other generative frameworks as a constraint on covert movement can be modelled as arising from constraints across possible derivation families for a given tree set. Further observing the interaction of *ziji* with other bound variables in the language, I propose that anti-locality effects in variable binding arise when a more specialized bound variable is available. This has consequences for the definition of a typology of bound variables.

1 Variable Binding in STAG

Variable binding in Synchronous TAG (STAG) has been modelled as a phenomenon which exploits delayed locality. Building on the definition of delayed-local derivations presented in Chiang and Scheffler (2008), bound variables can be modelled as multi-component sets (MCSs) in both the syntax and semantics. As formulated in Storoshenko and Han (2015), Figure 2 shows that the bound variable obligatorily composes non-locally, with the α components substituting into the argument position of the predicate selecting the variable, while the β components compose directly with the antecedent. This is most crucial on the semantics side, where the variable's auxiliary tree com-

poses with the "scope part" of a STAG generalized quantifier, as in Figure 3. The bound variable carries a function from $\langle e,t \rangle$ to $\langle e,t \rangle$ which accomplishes the variable binding, in a form similar to Büring's (2005) Binder Index Evaluation Rule. On the syntax side, the β component acts as solely an agreement check. The English bound variable pronoun *her* is lexically specified for third person feminine φ-features; in this case there is no gender specification on *a student*, so the combination goes through. For nominals with inherent gender specification, for example *every boy*, the resulting feature clash would block the derivation. In this way, agreement is treated as a purely syntactic phenomenon, with no manifestation in the semantics. As written, these trees could compose into a sentence such as *A student loves her father*.

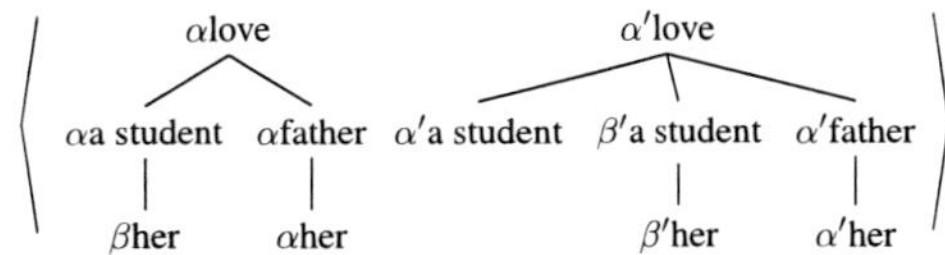

Figure 1: Derivation trees for *A student loves her father*

Following the derivation trees in Figure 1, delayed locality is observed in the composition of the members of the *her* MCS, while the only other MCS present has composed tree-locally[1]. Chiang and Scheffler define a delay as the set of derivation tree nodes including the members of the MCS, and all nodes on a path between members of the MCS, but excluding the common dominating node. Storoshenko and Han extend this notion into a measure for the size of a delay by taking the cardinality of that set. The derivations in Figure 1 will have a delay (d) value of four for the pronoun.

---

[1]Though the DP anchored by *father* could also be represented as a MCS.

Proceedings of the 12th International Workshop on Tree Adjoining Grammars and Related Formalisms (TAG+12), pages 67–76,
Düsseldorf, Germany, June 29 - July 1, 2016.

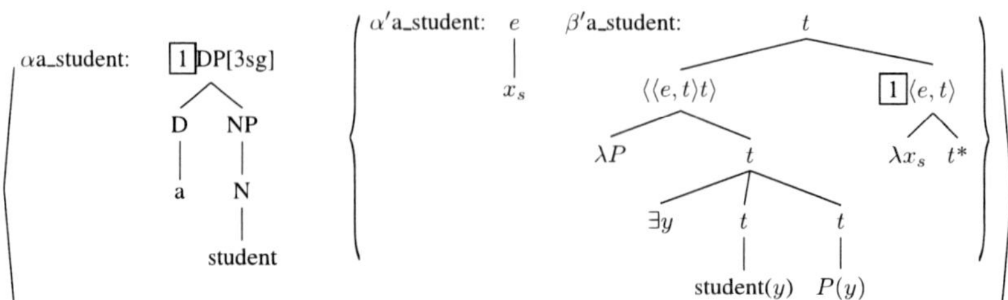

Figure 2: Tree sets for bound variable pronoun *her*

Figure 3: Sample Quantifier Tree Set

Beyond referring to the delay as a whole, they further define the length l of a delayed local MCS combination as $d - n$, where n is the number of MCS members. Thus, for the bound variable pronoun in the derivation trees of Figure 1, $l=2$. The reason for applying this characterization of a delay becomes clear when considering the quantifier tree sets. As defined, even a tree-local MCS combination will have a trivial delay consisting only of its own derivation tree nodes, yielding a d value of two, though the l value for this MCS combination will be zero. This is a more intuitive match with a singleton tree combination on the syntax side, as it is not immediately obvious at a glance that the two derivations are in fact isomorphic. With derivational isomorphism defined based on the equivalency of l values for any given lexical item's combinations on both sides of the STAG derivation, as well as respecting all linked nodes, the quantifier's combination can be said to be maximally isomorphic (borrowing the term from Storoshenko and Han (2015)), as $l=0$ in both cases. It is this notion of "maximal" isomorphism that I will assume to underlie all further claims of isomorphism.

2 *Ziji* and The Blocking Effect

The key data modelled in this paper all derive from the behaviour of the Mandarin (Chinese) anaphor *ziji*, described extensively in the literature since Cole et al. (1990). In brief, there are five different phenomena which need to be accounted for. The first is the fact that *ziji* can allow both local and long-distance antecedents, as shown in (1).

(1) Zhangsan$_i$ renwei [Lisi$_j$ zhidao [Wangwu$_k$
    Zhangsan think   Lisi know   Wangwu
    xihuan ziji$_{i/j/k}$.]]
    like   self
    'Zhangsan thinks that Lisi knows that Wangwu likes self.'

In this respect, *ziji* is not dissimilar to its Korean cognate *caki*, which is discussed in Storoshenko and Han (2015). Where the two diverge is in the manifestation of the so-called blocking effect illustrated in (2):

(2) Zhangsan$_i$ renwei [**wo**$_j$ zhidao [Wangwu$_k$
    Zhangsan think **I**   know   Wangwu
    xihuan ziji$_{*i/*j/k}$.]]
    like   self
    'Zhangsan thinks that I know that Wangwu likes self.'

In this sentence where the subject of the middle clause is a first person pronoun, *ziji* is restricted not only to a third person antecedent, but only to the most local one. Descriptively, the presence of an intervening antecedent with mismatched φ-features blocks the anaphor from binding by the highest subject, even though that subject is also third person. However, the situation is different in the local domain:

(3) Zhangsan$_i$ yiwei [**wo**$_j$ hui ba **ni**$_k$ dai
    Zhangsan thought I   will BA you take
    hui ziji$_{*i/j/k}$ de jia.]
    back self's   DE home
    'Zhangsan thought I will take you back to self's house.'

As seen in (3), *ziji* is not inherently restricted to third person antecedents (unlike *caki* and the English *her* from above). In the local domain, *ziji* may be bound by either the first or the second person antecedent. This is a more general property of *ziji*, which can be bound by an antecedent of any φ-feature value, within the constraints of the blocking effect. For example, a version of (1) where all clauses had first person subjects would equally be grammatical. Finally, there is the observation that even when the blocking condition is respected, *ziji* may not take a non-local non-subject antecedent:

(4) Zhangsan$_i$ gaosu Lisi$_j$ [Wangwu$_k$
     Zhangsan tell   Lisi   Wangwu
     piping-le   ziji$_{i/*j/k}$.]
     criticize-ASP self
     'Zhangsan told Lisi that Wangwu criticized self.'

Again unlike Korean, the anaphor may not take Lisi as a potential antecedent. However, even though *Lisi* is not considered a possible antecedent, a first person pronoun in that position induces a blocking effect, even though this was not observed in the local domain. Based on these data, the five different properties of *ziji* which need to be modelled are enumerated again below:

1. Local and long distance antecedents are possible
2. φ-feature mismatch in a c-command chain induces blocking across clauses
3. Any antecedent may be viable in the lowest clause
4. The anaphor can in principle take any φ-feature valued antecedent
5. Higher clause antecedents must be subjects

Sohng's (2004) analysis of *ziji* follows the tradition of the original Cole et al. analysis in making use of covert movement to capture all of the relevant facts, accounting for the various differences between Korean *caki* and Mandarin *ziji* as being the result of the difference in φ-features between the two. While the formal mechanisms here will of course be different, STAG not having any notion of covert movement to fall back on, the final analysis will draw on Sohng's key insight. The intricate pattern of data observed will be here be modelled as an interplay between the mechanisms used to capture agreement and a set of well-formedness constraints on STAG derivations.

3 Modelling Core Cases

Above, I showed the agreement checking mechanism that has been previously proposed for bound variables in STAG: a feature value on the degenerate DP node which combines in the syntax with the variable's antecedent. However, this is not the only agreement-checking mechanism which has been proposed in the TAG literature. Working in LTAG, Kallmeyer and Romero (2007) provide an account for reflexive pronouns where agreement is checked via a degenerate T' node, part of the MCS for the reflexive. The intuition here is that by having agreement check with the functional projection of the verb, a tree-local derivation for the reflexive is ensured. My proposal is simple: the unique φ-feature deficiency of *ziji* versus *caki* is derived by adding this additional degenerate node to the syntax side of the bound variable's MCS, as in Figure 4.

Based on these MCS definitions, it is clear where the notion of delay length will become relevant, as there are asymmetric sets on the syntax and semantic sides. Ultimately, the semantics will define the minimum l value for any given derivation, as the delay needed for semantic composition will be directly determined by the intended meaning of the sentence: α'ziji will substitute at the appropriate argument position while β'ziji will adjoin to the scope part of the desired antecedent[2] Between the two MCSs in Figure 4, I assume the following symmetric compositions: αziji and α'ziji will need to substitute at linked nodes, while βziji$_{DP*}$ and β'ziji will also be required to adjoin into the tree sets of the antecedent. With no matched component to force a fully isomorphic derivation via a linked node, βziji$_{T*}$ is essentially free to attach at any node with a matching label, constrained only by the φ-feature value. I will begin with the assumption that both adjoining sites must have no incompatible features, with the α variables valued via unification with features at the adjoining sites. However, to capture all the facts within a single account, it will emerge that the equivalence of the two feature unifications is relaxed under certain structural relationships between the two agreeing members of the *ziji* MCS. Moving forward, I will not be presenting any information on the semantic derivations, choosing to focus exclusively on the syntax. Full STAG

---

[2]Proper names are assumed to also have generalized quantifier scope parts to provide the necessary binding.

$$\left\langle \left\{ \begin{array}{l} \alpha ziji_{DP}\ \mathrm{DP} \\ \quad | \\ \quad \mathrm{D} \\ \quad | \\ \quad ziji \end{array} \quad \beta ziji_{DP*}\ \mathrm{DP}^*[\phi = \alpha] \quad \beta ziji_{T'*}\ \mathrm{T}'^*[\phi = \alpha] \right\} \left\{ \begin{array}{l} \alpha' ziji{:}\ e \\ \quad\ | \\ \quad\ x_a \end{array} \quad \beta' ziji{:}\ \begin{array}{c} \langle e,t \rangle \\ \overbrace{\qquad\qquad} \\ \langle\langle e,t \rangle\langle e,t \rangle\rangle \quad \langle e,t \rangle^* \\ | \\ \lambda P \lambda z.[\lambda x_a.P(z)](z) \end{array} \right\} \right\rangle$$

Figure 4: Tree Sets for *ziji*

derivations in the syntax and semantics for many of the predicates used here can be found in existing work, and no changes in the mechanics of deriving variable binding are being proposed in this paper.

For the sake of illustration, one syntactic predicate tree appears in Figure 5. Predicates such as *renwei* "think" and *zhidao* "know" will be simpler transitive verbs, still recursive on C′, with all of these able to either recursively join to each other, or a CP-rooted embedded clause such as *xihuan* "like" or *piping* "criticize" having a DP terminal node at the object position which will be the substitution site for $\alpha ziji$. The ditransitive *gaosu* "tell" is represented using a standard VP-shell structure. The only crucial detail to note is that in a ditransitive predicate, the T′ node is c-commanded by the subject, but not the indirect object.

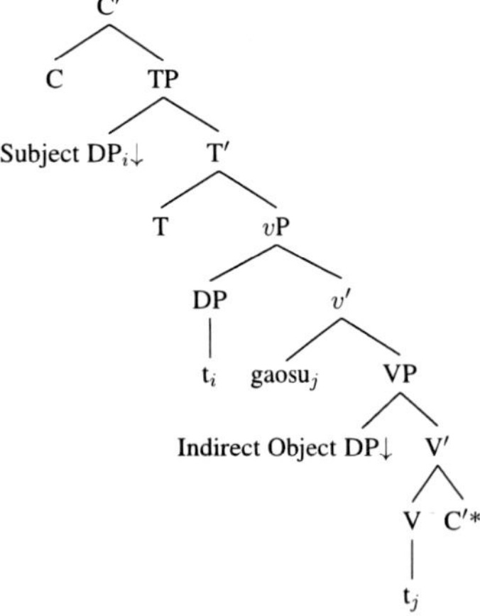

Figure 5: Sample Embedding Predicate *gaosu* "tell"

The three readings for (1) will emerge from the DPs into which $\beta ziji_{DP*}$ and its associated semantic tree adjoin. Multiplying this out by the three clauses each with their own T′ nodes yields nine possible derivation trees, three for each reading. These are given in full in Figure 6, though all further examples will be summarized as in Table 1. In these tables, the l value for the semantic combi-

nation of *ziji* will correspond to the cell matching the predicate of which *ziji* is an argument with the intended antecedent for that reading; the leftmost column in all cases.

Table 1: Tabular representation of Figure 6

T′* at:	xihuan	zhidao	renwei
DP* at: Wangwu	$\delta 1$: $l{=}1$	$\delta 2$: $l{=}2$	$\delta 3$: $l{=}3$
Lisi/Wo	$\delta 4$: $l{=}2$	$\delta 5$: $l{=}2$	$\delta 6$: $l{=}3$
Zhangsan	$\delta 7$: $l{=}3$	$\delta 8$: $l{=}3$	$\delta 9$: $l{=}3$

Based on this table, it is immediately clear that not all possible derivations are licit. For the situation where *Wangwu* is the antecedent, placing the $\beta ziji_{T'*}$ in any clause higher than the one containing $\alpha ziji$ will create a longer delay in the syntax than the semantics, making $\delta 2$ and $\delta 3$ not (maximally) isomorphic STAG derivations. Conversely, when *Zhangsan* is the antecedent, all placements of $\beta ziji_{T'}$ yield a formally isomorphic derivation, under the terms defined above. I label this set of isomorphic derivations as a derivational family: a set of isomorphic derivations (as defined by sharing equal l values for all MCS compositions) which yield identical semantic outputs. Removing spurious derivations yields the final set of possible derivations for (1) in Table 2. The lowest antecedent is derived via a singleton derivation, while the other two are represented with derivational families.

Table 2: Isomorphic Derivations for (1)

T′* at:	xihuan	zhidao	renwei
DP* at: Wangwu	$\delta 1$: $l{=}1$		
Lisi	$\delta 4$: $l{=}2$	$\delta 5$: $l{=}2$	
Zhangsan	$\delta 7$: $l{=}3$	$\delta 8$: $l{=}3$	$\delta 9$: $l{=}3$

Taking these same values for the blocking effect example in (2) yields the derivations in Table 3. However, two of the isomorphic derivations, $\delta 4$

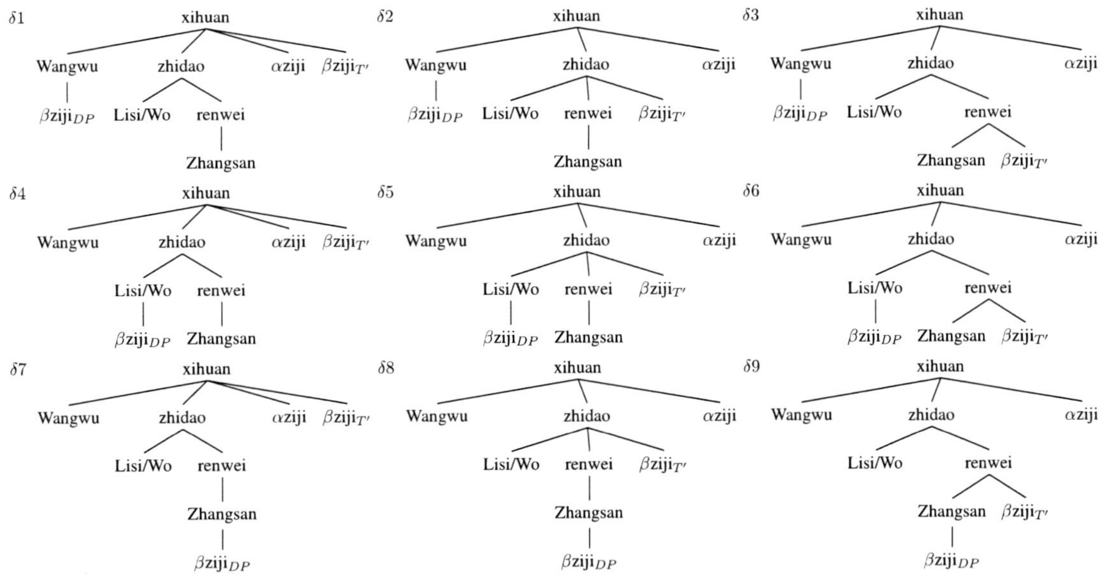

Figure 6: Derivation Trees for (1) and (2)

and $\delta 8$ (indicated in bold in the table), will result in a feature clash as the $\beta ziji$ components will adjoin at locations with different φ feature values.

Table 3: Isomorphic Derivations for (2)

T$'$* at:	xihuan	zhidao	renwei
DP*: at Wangwu	$\delta 1$: $l=1$		
Wo	$\delta\mathbf{4}$: $l=2$	$\delta 5$: $l=2$	
Zhangsan	$\delta 7$: $l=3$	$\delta\mathbf{8}$: $l=3$	$\delta 9$: $l=3$

This clash is what I propose to be at the root of the blocking effect. Following on the definition of a derivational family, I propose the Fully Functional Family (FFF) constraint:

(5)   FULLY FUNCTIONAL FAMILY (FFF): If one member of a derivational family violates a syntactic constraint, all members of the family are rendered infelicitous.

Applying this constraint to the set of derivations in Table 3, only the derivation belonging to the most local antecedent survives.

(3) presents a more complex situation. Here, the lowest clause is a ditransitive, while *ziji* is further embedded inside of a possessive DP structure. The partial derivation for this this example is presented in Figure 7. With three possible antecedents and

Figure 7: Partial Derivation Tree for (3)

two clauses, here there are six possible derivations, presented in Table 4. Non-isomorphic derivations have already been removed, and those creating a feature clash are again bolded.

Table 4: Isomorphic Derivations for (3)

T$'$* at:	dai hui	yiwei
DP* at: Ni	$\delta\mathbf{1}$: $l=2$	
Wo	$\delta 3$: $l=2$	
Zhangsan	$\delta\mathbf{5}$: $l=3$	$\delta 6$: $l=3$

Recall that the possible antecedents here were *ni* and *wo*. The correct prediction is made for *Zhangsan*, whose derivational family is eliminated by virtue of the FFF, and for *wo*, where the first person subject values T$'$ in the only isomorphic derivation. Note that a hypothetical $\delta 4$ would exist, where $\beta ziji_{T'*}$ attaches to the higher clause with a third person subject. However, that derivation is not isomorphic, and does not survive into the (singleton) family, avoiding the feature clash. A similar $\delta2$ would exist, but is also non-isomorphic. The unexpected result here is that $\delta1$ yields a feature clash, and yet the reading is grammatical.

Refining the definition of how a feature clash results resolves this issue. The distinction to make here is in the relationship of the elements in the final derived syntax tree; I assume the higher clause to be a transitive verb auxiliary tree recursive on C', while the embedded clause is a CP-rooted ditransitive-like structure. In $\delta5$, βziji$_{DP*}$ is adjoined to the subject in the higher clause, at a position c-commanding βziji$_{T'*}$ adjoined to the T' node of the lower clause. This c-command relationship, I claim, is required for the feature clash to be triggered. Looking at $\delta1$, an opposite relationship occurs, where βziji$_{T'*}$ dominates βziji$_{DP*}$. Here, the features do not enter into the necessary configuration to be checked, and $\delta1$ is not actually a clash. To fully implement this would require a revision to the original *ziji* trees such that it is not a formal part of the MCS that the two feature unifications must match: βziji$_{DP*}$ would receive a value for its α, while βziji$_{T'*}$ would have a distinct value β for its φ features, and the constraint described here would be that if βziji$_{DP*}$ c-commands βziji$_{T'*}$, then $\alpha = \beta$.

This c-command relationship comes into play when it comes to discussing (4) and the closely-related (6):

(6) Zhangsan$_i$ gaosu wo$_j$ Wangwu$_k$
     Zhangsan tell   I   Wangwu
     piping-le   ziji$_{*i/*j/k}$.
     criticize-ASP self

     'Zhangsan told me that Wangwu criticized self.'

Recall that (4) indicated that the non-subject is not a possible antecedent, but having *ziji* bound by *Zhangsan* was still possible. (6) has the same structure, but replaces the indirect object with a first person pronoun. Note that even though it is not considered a viable antecedent, it still induces a blocking effect. The partial derivation tree for (4) and (6) is as in Figure 8. Again, with three potential antecedents, and two clauses, there are six possible derivations to consider. Table 5 presents only the isomorphic families for (6).

In this case, the lowest antecedent is correctly predicted to be fine, and the first person indirect object is ruled out because in $\delta3$ βziji$_{DP*}$ will c-command βziji$_{T'*}$ with mismatched φ-features.

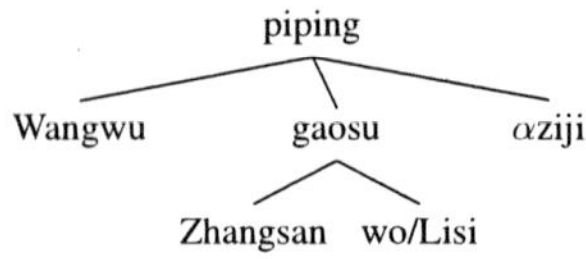

Figure 8: Partial Derivation Tree for (4) and (6)

Table 5: Isomorphic Derivations for (6)

T'* at:	piping	gaosu
DP* at: Wangwu	$\delta1$: $l=2$	
Wo	$\delta3$: $l=2$	$\delta4$: $l=2$
Zhangsan	$\delta5$: $l=2$	$\delta6$: $l=2$

With one derivation ruled out, FFF will block all derivations in the same family. What is not immediately obvious is how $\delta5$ and $\delta6$ are also ruled out. To fully lay out the issue, I also present the derivations for (4) in Table 6. In this case, the data conform with the prediction for *Zhangsan*, who is a viable antecedent, but there is no obvious reason that *Lisi* is ruled out. Given that $\delta3$ is well-formed and satisfies the c-command requirement for feature checking, $\delta4$ should be examined for the cause of the unacceptability. The intuition here is that as (4) most clearly shows the subject orientation of *ziji*, that effect should fall out from the one derivation where βziji$_{T'*}$ ends up in a position to dominate βziji$_{DP*}$. However, fully ruling out this relationship would block exactly the configuration in the unexpectedly grammatical $\delta1$ from (3). So, just the right constraint which predicts the grammaticality of (3) and (4) with the reported readings, and possibly offer some insight into the so-far unexplained blocking effect in (6) needs to be found.

Looking at (3) and (4), the most obvious difference is that the first case dealt with a singleton family, while the unavailable *Lisi* reading of (4) has two isomorphic derivations. An additional structural constraint on the two degenerate nodes of the syntactic *ziji* set obtains the correct result: βziji$_{T'*}$ may only dominate βziji$_{DP*}$ if there is no other isomorphic derivation where the c-command relationship which enables feature checking obtains. Framing the constraint in this way allows an escape hatch for *ziji* to have different properties in the most local domain, as the lowest clause attachment of βziji$_{T'*}$ will always reduce any derivation with local binding of *ziji* to a singleton derivation family, and any higher antecedent will always have

Table 6: Isomorphic Derivations for (4)

T* at:	piping	gaosu
DP* at: Wangwu	$\delta1$: $l=2$	
Lisi	$\delta3$: $l=2$	$\delta4$: $l=2$
Zhangsan	$\delta5$: $l=2$	$\delta6$: $l=2$

a larger family of isomorphic derivations. This constraint isolates exactly the derivations where subject orientation and blocking appear to be suspended. Applying this constraint to the derivations in Table 6, $\delta4$ will be ruled out, which in turn eliminates the derivational family associated with the antecedent *Lisi*, following the FFF.

There is an additional consequence for (6). Following this new well-formedness constraint on the combination of the βziji components, $\delta4$ in Table 5 is also blocked. This leads to another situation which has so far not been seen: one in which all members of an isomorphic family of derivations are separately ill-formed. My final proposal is that this triggers another constraint between derivations: the Poisoned Path Principle, or PPP.

(7)　　POISONED PATH PRINCIPLE: If one isomorphic family consists entirely of ill-formed derivations, no other family of the same or greater l value is licit.

This principle captures the distinction between (4) and (6) where the same derivations are licit in one case but not the other. The distinction lies not in those derivations, but in the status of another family of derivations with the same l value. In (4), it is actually the well-formedness of $\delta3$ which allows the $\delta5/\delta6$ family to survive.

This set of constraints yields the desirable result of capturing the distinction between (4) and (6), but other analytic options are available. Indeed, (Huang et al., 2009) describe the distinctions between local and long-distance *ziji* as so intractable that they suggest treating the two as distinct forms with different properties. A reviewer points out that following such a path would allow for a simpler characterization of subject orientation in the long distance domain as falling out from a requirement that βziji$_{DP*}$ must c-command βziji$_{T'*}$. It is also suggested that the blocking effect in (6) can be captured by adding another component to the *ziji* MCS which will check for agreement at some position in the predicate tree where the indirect object's φ features are checked. While this certainly

has a precedent in the literature (Kallmeyer and Romero use a similar device to check for agreement with an indirect object), its use in this context would be hard to stipulate. Assuming that all three of βziji$_{DP*}$, βziji$_{T'*}$, and the proposed βziji$_{V'*}$ would have to match in φ features, then a clash would result if both βziji$_{T'*}$ and βziji$_{V'*}$ adjoined at the highest clause in the derivation of the ungrammatical matrix subject reading of (6). Recalling that Storoshenko and Han (2015) uses a minimum l value to force long distance binding, then a dedicated tree set for long distance *ziji* would need a minimum l based on the distance between βziji$_{DP*}$ and αziji in the derivation tree, but the position of βziji$_{V'*}$ does not change the l value. As such, there is no way to force βziji$_{V'*}$ to attach to the higher clause rather than the lower one (which could potentially avoid the clash) short of writing in a stipulation that βziji$_{V'*}$ and βziji$_{T'*}$ must have a relative l of zero with respect to each other (tree local) and a relative l of one with respect to βziji$_{DP*}$ (in the same clause as the subject), all within an overall l of two for the whole MCS (the anaphor is in an embedded clause). This is just to say that no treatment of these data will be devoid of stipulations somewhere in the account; it is left to further debate which are more likely. Furthermore, the local domain is no less complex, as (3) has a close counterpart in which subject orientation *does* obtain in the local domain:

(8)　　Wangwu$_i$ shuo Zhangsan$_j$ zengsong gei
　　　　Wangwu say　Zhangsan　give　　to
　　　　Lisi$_k$ yipian guanyu ziji$_{i/j/*k}$ de wenzhang.
　　　　Lisi one　about　self　DE article
　　　　'Wangwu says that Zhangsan gave an article about self to Lisi.'

Unlike in (3), the lower clause indirect object of (8) cannot be an antecedent. So, just as a distinct long-distance account would require some derivational stipulations, a dedicated local treatment of *ziji* would need to be sensitive to the distinction between a "true" ditransitive as in (8) and the so-called *ba*-construction of (3).

In closing this discussion of the core analysis, it's worth pointing out that all of the cases discussed under the initially proposed analysis do scale to longer sentences than those used here. Looking at the core blocking example (2), it's clear to see how any reading where the antecedent c-commands a φ-feature mismatched element will incur a feature mismatch in one of its isomorphic derivations. Similarly, even though the constraints obviate blocking in the lowest clause, any clause higher with a mismatched antecedent will be blocked. In the case of (6), a mismatched non-subject at any embedding level will have no viable derivations: all attachments of βziji$_{T'}$ in lower clauses will incur feature mismatches because they are c-commanded by the antecedent, while attachments to the local clause or higher will all be ruled out because βziji$_{T'}$ will c-command its own antecedent DP within a family where other isomorphic derivations are available. By the PPP, this will block all antecedents in the same or higher clauses. Conversely, in (4), only derivations where βziji$_{T'}$ attaches to a position c-commanding a matched non-subject in an embedding clause will be ruled out, while the lower attachments will be felicitous derivations. While the FFF is triggered to rule out the non-subject antecedent, the existence of some well-formed derivations will obviate application of the PPP, allowing other longer derivation families to go through.

4 Interaction with Other Forms

When blocking occurs, and a bound variable use of *ziji* is impossible, Mandarin is similar to English in that it allows third person pronouns to act as bound variables:

(9) Mei-ge   ren$_i$ dou renwei [wo$_j$ piping-le
     every-CL man all think   I   criticize-ASP
     ta$_{i/*j}$.]
     he
     'Every man thought that I criticized him.'

I assume that bound variable *ta* will have tree sets similar to English. Lacking the extra T$'$* component, no blocking effect obtains, and the derivation goes through. However, in the local domain, *ta* may not be used:

(10) * Mei-ge   ren dou piping-le   ta$_i$.
        every-CL man all criticize-ASP he
        'Every man criticized himself.'

Even though there should be nothing formally constraining the use of *ta* in (10), native speakers report *ziji* to be preferable in this context[3]. *Ta* is also dispreferred in a non-blocking version of (9):

---

[3]The bimorphemic *taziji* is also acceptable, though restricted only to local uses similar to English *himself*. A reviewer correctly points out that the example could be ruled out by Condition B of the standard binding theory; the same does not however apply to the bound *ta* in (11), which suggests more than just Condition B would be at play. Furthermore, the only implementations of Condition B for TAG that

(11) Mei-ge   ren$_i$ dou renwei ta$_j$ piping-le
     every-CL man all think   she criticize-ASP
     ta.$_{?i/*j/k}$
     he
     'Every man thought that she criticized him.'

For the long distance bound variable reading in (11), *ziji* is the clear choice, even though it would be ambiguous between a local or long distance reading. While it would be simple to characterize *ta* as an anti-local bound variable, examining the full set of data suggests this to be an overstatement. It is not merely that *ta* cannot be used as a bound variable locally, the facts are that *ta* is only ever used when no other form is available. One could make the same claim about bound variable uses of the English third person pronouns, which are not used in local reflexive contexts. Keeping in mind that TAG accounts of English reflexive pronouns have treated them as tree-local derivations (see for example Kallmeyer and Romero (2007) and and Frank (2008), among others), one could imagine a derivational economy account restricting uses of *her*: a derivation that yields the same meaning without resorting to delayed locality is available. Similarly, while isomorphic derivations using either *ta* or *ziji* will have identical l values in (10) and (11), the ambiguity introduced by the fact *ta* also has a non-bound referential use may block its use: the obligatorily bound *ziji* wins out. Given that this paper argues for constraints over sets of derivations, it is not unreasonable to propose that the same types of comparisons come into play when selecting the optimal expression of a desired meaning.

This reasoning calls for a re-examination the typological conclusions reached in Storoshenko and Han (2015), where three types of bound variable are defined: ones similar to *ziji* or *caki* which can be used locally or long distance, ones restricted to non-local uses formalized as an l value greater than one, and finally ones restricted only to the most local use where $l=1$. Firstly, that the present paper explains the nonexistence of any bound variables with minimum l values of two or greater. These would be hyper-anti-local bound variables whose antecedents need to be two or more clauses

---

I am aware of (Champollion, 2008; Nesson, 2009) each make different assumptions about the semantics of binding than are made in this paper. Defining the full set of Chomskyan binding conditions in this particular version of STAG remains a matter for further research, though see Storoshenko et al. (2008) for discussion of Condition A as epiphenomenal.

removed. As seen here, this would amount to ruling out entire families of derivations with smaller l values, which would trigger the PPP. The account for why non-subjects are not antecedents and yet induce blocking with a feature mismatch is captured by exactly the derivational constraint which would rule out such a bound variable. However, one may wonder whether the anti-local category exists at all, or should rather just be re-cast as an epiphenomenon falling out from the fact that better local derivations are available?

Still, there is no compelling reason to eliminate the category of bound variable where l=1. While it could be the case that apparent local bound variables may warrant closer examination to see whether a tree-local derivation is available, there may be other cases where a certain MCS is forced to make use of delayed locality, but is constrained to using only as much as possible for a felicitous composition. One possibility for such a case outside the realm of binding would be subextraction in *wh*-movement:

(12)   What$_i$ did you take a picture of t$_i$?

While it has been compellingly argued that *wh*-extraction should be treated as tree-local movement (Frank, 2002), such an analysis is untenable for (12), as the trace is in a different lexical projection than the *wh*-word's landing site. Treating this *wh*-movement as a MCS consisting of the *wh*-word and its trace would need a derivation with an l value of one, but the use of such a MCS would need to be held to that value, or else numerous subjacency violations would become possible. This analysis is held over for future work.

5   On Trans-Derivational Constraints

The analysis presented in this paper relies crucially on a set of trans-derivational constraints (TDCs) which run the risk of extending the generative capacity of the grammar. Here, I address this concern by comparing the present analysis with that presented in Freedman (2012). In that paper, two constraints are presented, along with a proof that a TAG with restricted TDCs is no more expressive than one without those constraints. The first constraint Freedman proposes is the DERIVATIONAL COMPLEXITY CONSTRAINT ON SEMANTIC INTERPRETATION or DCCSI: "A derivation d producing meaning m is ruled out if another shorter derivation d' also produces m."

The maximal isomorphism constraint I have assumed to act as an initial filter on possible derivations has essentially this effect, militating against derivations with identical semantic outputs but larger l values in the syntactic derivation. This seems to be a reasonable comparison class for derivations where an uneven syntactic and semantic MCS pairing is allowed to combine using delayed locality. The FFF proposed above uses a subset of the same comparison class, the family of maximally isomorphic derivations. The second constraint Freedman proposes is a means of limiting the comparison class for TDCs. His LOCALITY CONSTRAINT ON COMPETITION dictates that any two derivation trees may only be compared if the are identical save for the daughters of one node, which may be either excised or replaced. The comparisons within families required by the FFF are similarly restricted in that they are identical in all measures save for the position in the tree of the βziji$_{T'}$ component. Applying the constraint symmetrically to the pair $\delta4$ and $\delta5$ in Table 2, each derivation differs from the other by the daughters of one node. Moving on to the PPP, there is a similar constraint on comparison classes when looking at the whole families being compared. Examining the relevant derivations in Table 5, the $\delta3/\delta5$ and $\delta4/\delta6$ pairs differ only by the positions of αziji. While TDCs are definitely tools to be used sparingly, restricting these constraints to applying within families or at most between adjacent families (allowing the PPP to apply transitively) provides similar restrictions as those discussed by Freedman.

6   Conclusion

In this paper I have presented a model of the behaviour of the Mandarin long distance anaphor *ziji*. By combining two well-formedness constraints on the relationship between elements in the *ziji* MCS with two more global constraints on derivation families, the blocking effect and certain asymmetries between local and long distance domains are captured. Furthermore, while the more global constraints provide motivation for the existing claim that hyper-anti-local bound variables should not exist, the existence of trans-derivational constraints poses a new question of whether anti-local bound variables are a *bona fide* category, or merely epiphenomenal.

75

Acknowledgments

I would like to the TAG+ reviewers for their comments and suggestions, all which have improved the quality of this paper, and also the audiences at Yale University and the University of Delaware who heard preliminary versions of the work contained here. This work was started at Yale under SSHRC Postdoc Fellowship 756-2010-067, and has been completed under a Faculty Start-Up Grant from the University of Calgary. My thanks also to Peng Han for providing some new data and confirming judgements. All errors are my own.

References

Daniel Büring. 2005. *Binding Theory*. Cambridge, UK: Cambridge University Press.

Lucas Champollion. 2008. Binding theory in LTAG. In Claire Gardent and Anoop Sarkar, editors, *Proceedings of the 9th International Workshop on Tree Adjoining Grammars and Related Formalisms*, pages 1–8.

David Chiang and Tatjana Scheffler. 2008. Flexible composition and delayed tree-locality. In Claire Gardent and Anoop Sarkar, editors, *Proceedings of the 9th International Workshop on Tree Adjoining Grammars and Related Formalisms*, pages 17–24.

Peter Cole, Gabriella Hermon, and Li-May Sung. 1990. Principles and parameters of long-distance reflexives. *Linguistic Inquiry*, 21(1):1–22.

Robert Frank. 2002. *Phrase Structure Composition and Syntactic Dependencies*. Cambridge, MA: MIT Press.

Robert Frank. 2008. Reflexives and TAG semantics. In Claire Gardent and Anoop Sarkar, editors, *Proceedings of the 9th International Workshop on Tree Adjoining Grammars and Related Formalisms*, pages 97–104.

Michael Freedman. 2012. Scope economy and TAG locality. In *Proceedings of the 11th International Workshop on Tree Adjoining Grammars and Related Formalisms*, pages 223–231.

James C.T. Huang, Yen-hui Audrey Li, and Yafei Li. 2009. *The Syntax of Chinese*. Cambridge University Press.

Laura Kallmeyer and Maribel Romero. 2007. Reflexives and reciprocals in LTAG. In Jeroen Geertzen, Elias Thijsse, Harry Bunt, and Amanda Schiffrin, editors, *Proceedings of the Seventh International Workshop on Computational Semantics*, pages 271–282.

Rebecca Nesson. 2009. *Synchronous and Multicomponent Tree-Adjoining Grammars: Complexity, Algorithms, and Linguistic Applications*. Ph.D. thesis, Harvard University.

Hong-Ki Sohng. 2004. A minimalist analysis of X^0 reflexivization in Chinese and Korean. *Studies in Generative Grammar*, 14(3):375–396.

Dennis Ryan Storoshenko and Chung-hye Han. 2015. Using Synchronous Tree Adjoining Grammar to derive the typology of bound variable pronouns. *Journal of Logic and Computation*, 25(2):371–403.

Dennis Ryan Storoshenko, Chung-hye Han, and David Potter. 2008. Reflexivity in English: An STAG analysis. In Claire Gardent and Anoop Sarkar, editors, *Proceedings of the 9th International Workshop on Tree Adjoining Grammars and Related Formalisms*, pages 149–157.

Node-Based Induction of Tree-Substitution Grammars

Rose Sloan

Yale University

`rose.sloan@yale.edu`

Abstract

Because PCFGs are, as their name suggests, context-free, they cannot encode many dependencies that occur in natural language, such as the dependencies between determiners and nouns, allowing them to overgenerate phrases like *those cat*. One formalism that is able to capture many dependencies that PCFGs cannot is that of probabilistic tree-substitution grammars (PTSGs). Because PTSGs allow larger subtrees to be used as grammar rules, they can better model natural language but are also more difficult to induce from a corpus. In this paper, I will show how PTSGs can be used to represent dependencies between determiners and nouns and present a novel method for inducing a PTSG from a parsed corpus.

1 Introduction

PCFGs are ill equipped to handle the case of simple noun phrases consisting of a determiner followed by a noun, as the grammaticality of these phrases is dependent on what types of nouns the determiner in question can precede. For example, while *the* can precede any noun, determiners like *a* and *another* can only occur with singular count nouns, while *those* can only precede plural nouns, and determiners like *more* can precede either plural nouns or mass nouns but not singular count nouns. Thus, the noun phrases *a book*, *more coffee*, and *those cards* are grammatical, whereas *a cards*, *more book*, and *those coffee* are not.

Representing these sorts of noun phrases with a PCFG is difficult. Consider the following toy corpus:

(1)   a. 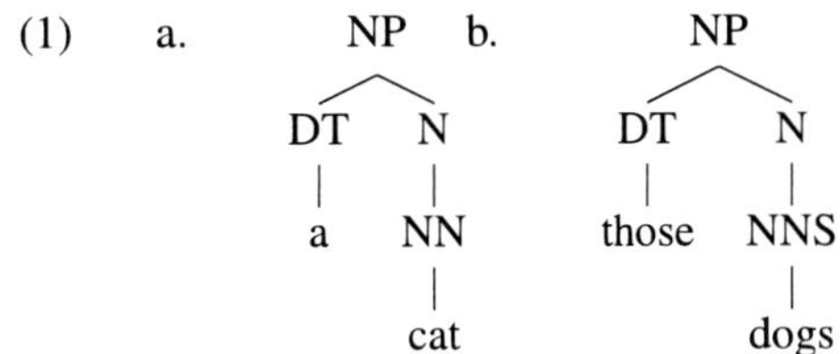   b.

A CFG representing this corpus would need to contain the rules NP → DT N, DT → those, N → NN, and NN → cat. While these are all reasonable rules, combining them gives us the following tree:

(2) 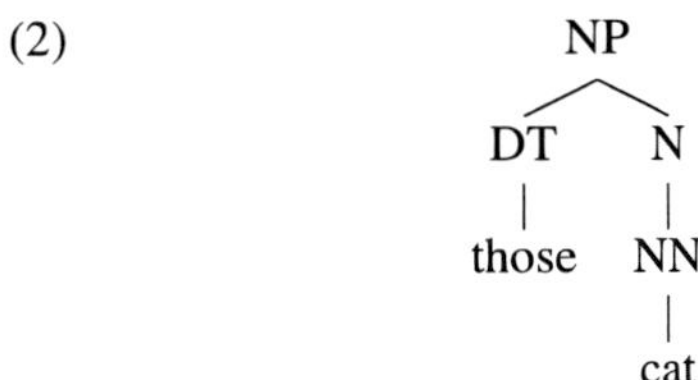

Thus, such a grammar would generate the blatantly ungrammatical noun phrase *those cat*. Furthermore, even to assign it a low probability, we would need a low probability for at least one of the rules that generated it, which would reduce the probability of at least one of the trees in (1). While we could perhaps mitigate this problem by removing the nodes labeled N and splitting the DT label into a set of labels corresponding to specific types of DTs, such a solution would overlook some generalizations (including, say, that *the* could precede any noun). Instead, we look for a formalism that represents these dependencies more naturally.

One such formalism is tree-substitution grammars (TSGs). Whereas CFG rules can be seen as one-level subtrees of the parse trees they generate, TSG rules can be any subtrees of these parse trees. A leaf node of a TSG rule whose label is not a lexical item is known as a substitution node, and parse trees can be built by replacing a substitution

Proceedings of the 12th International Workshop on Tree Adjoining Grammars and Related Formalisms (TAG+12), pages 77–84,
Düsseldorf, Germany, June 29 - July 1, 2016.

node with a rule whose root has the same label as the substitution node.

Because TSGs allow for larger rules than CFGs, they can handle dependencies that CFGs do not. Consider, once again, the toy corpus presented in (1). While it is impossible to represent it using a CFG that does not overgenerate ungrammatical noun phrases, we could represent it with a TSG containing the following rules:

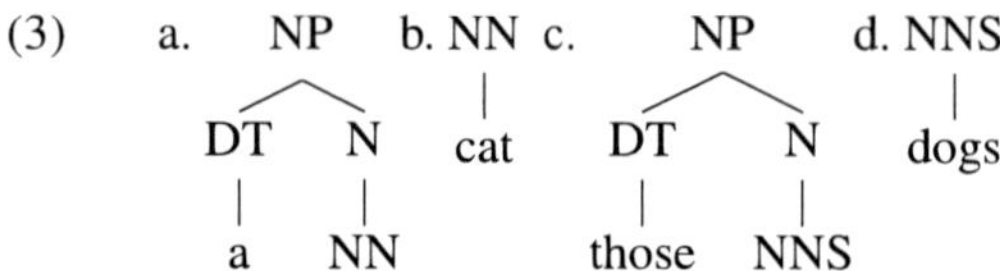

(3a) and (3b) can be combined to get (1a), and (3c) and (3d) can be combined to get (1b). It is no longer possible to generate (2), as the rule that produces *those* has a substitution node labeled NNS and thus can only accept plural nouns. (Similarly, the rule that produces *a* requires a singular count noun). Thus, TSGs allow us to accurately capture the dependencies between noun types and determiners.

While PTSGs present a more accurate model of natural language than PCFGs, they are also harder to induce from a corpus. Given a parse tree for a sentence, one can determine what CFG rules must have generated it simply by looking at each non-terminal node and its children. Then, given an entire treebank of parse trees, one can simply extract all the necessary CFG rules to produce that treebank and then get a PCFG by estimating the probability of each rule using one of a variety of techniques, the simplest of which involve simply counting the number of times each rule is used in producing the context. However, given a parse tree generated from a PTSG, it is less clear which rules formed it, as it is unknown which of the tree's internal nodes were substitution nodes in its derivation and which ones were already internal nodes in elementary trees. Furthermore, while some of the subtrees of the completed parse trees, such as the rules presented in (3), contain linguistically relevant information, others, such as many CFG rules or rules that simply memorize each full tree in the corpus, are not specific enough or overly specific and, as such, should have low probability or not be present in a PTSG at all.

In this paper, I will present a novel approach for inducing a PTSG from a parsed corpus, focusing specifically on PTSGs that model noun phrases such as the one in (3). This approach focuses on determining which nodes in the training set are substitution nodes. It does so by repeatedly sampling grammars from the training set. It then parses the data set with these grammars and uses the results of the parses to update the probability of trees' internal nodes being substitution nodes. This approach is simpler to understand and implement than other node-based approaches and does not require complex prior distributions.

2 Previous Approaches

Many previous approaches to TSG induction are data-oriented parsing (DOP) approaches that attempt to create grammars that include every possible rule that could have generated a corpus (Bod and Scha, 1996). In the most straightforward case, this means that the rules that comprise the tree-substitution grammar are simply all subtrees of all the trees in the training set. Unsurprisingly, these approaches lead to very large grammars, and in many cases, it is even necessary to transform each tree into some implicit representation (such as representing larger rules in terms of smaller rules instead of fully storing the trees) in order to store the grammar or at least to use it for parsing. Other approaches to data-oriented parsing try to limit the size of the grammar to some extent. For example, one approach, known as double-DOP, creates a grammar by taking every pair of parse trees from the training set and adding the largest subtree included in both trees (Sangati and Zuidema, 2011). This grammar is then interpolated with a CFG to create a grammar that can fully represent the training set and that includes all larger "productive" rules.

A number of more recent approaches, including the one presented in this paper, attempt not to find all TSG rules that could represent a corpus but to represent the corpus using the optimal distribution of TSG rules. One such approach called fragment grammars looks at TSGs from a generative perspective as a Bayesian model of the relative probability of productivity (forming novel phrases) and reuse (reusing previously constructed fragments) (O'Donnell et al., 2009). The mathematical model used to generate the grammar is a generalization of a Pitman-Yor Adaptor Grammar, a PCFG-based model that weakens the independence assumptions by introducing a vector of adaptor functions that map one probability distribution over trees to another (Johnson et al., 2006). In Pitman-Yor Adaptor Grammars specifically (as opposed to adaptor grammars in general), these adaptor functions are based loosely on a Chinese restaurant process so that the distribution generated by the grammar reflects the outputs of a "rich get richer"-based process. Fragment grammars use these mathematical underpinnings within the PTSG framework, incorporating a "grow-child-or-not" term into the generative model, allowing it to assign and optimize the weights of elementary trees.

Similarly, approaches presented by Cohn et al. and by Post and Gildea use priors based on a Dirichlet process to obtain a grammar (Cohn et al., 2009; Post and Gildea, 2009). These approaches use Gibbs sampling to induce the grammar, and, like my approach, they focus on determining which nodes are substitution nodes, although the sampling methods I present are different.

3 Algorithm

3.1 Concept

Like the fragment grammars approach, my algorithm of node-based induction for inducing a PTSG attempts to find an optimal subset of subtrees. However, instead of explicitly representing probability distributions over grammars, I instead assign a probability to each internal node of each parse tree in the corpus, corresponding to the probability that the node is a substitution node. (For simplicity of notation, throughout this section, I will refer to this probability for node n as $p(n)$ or simply as node n's probability.) It is these probabilities that are optimized over the course of many iterations of training. Specifically, during each iteration, an intermediate PTSG is used to parse the training set, and the probability of each node is recalculated based on the probabilities of the different parses it generates.

Initially, the probability is set to the same value for every node in the training set. After trying values in the range [0.35, 0.9], I experimentally determined an initial probability of 0.55 for each node is most likely to result in a grammar that performs well on the test set. This is likely because this value imposes a slight prior against simply memorizing the training set. However, because the weighting of the different parses later in the algorithm tends to mitigate most of the bias introduced

from the initial node probabilities, small changes in this initialization parameter have little effect on the final result.

3.2 Sampling and Parsing

To complete one iteration of training, we start by inducing a PTSG by randomly sampling from the parsed training set. Specifically, we decompose each tree, randomly choosing whether or not each internal node is a substitution node based on its probability at the start of the iteration (so that node n has probability $p(n)$ of being a substitution node in the decomposed tree). The set of trees resulting from this decomposition become our set of elementary trees, and we set the probability of each elementary tree using a relative frequency estimate (that is, simply letting the probability be the number of times that tree appears in the set of decomposed trees divided by the total number of trees with the same root node).

Once we have induced this PTSG, we then use it to parse each tree in the training set. In order to make parsing more efficient, any rules containing lexical items that do not appear in the phrase being parsed are removed before parsing with a standard CKY algorithm (Schabes et al., 1988). Doing so, we get all possible parses for the tree with our grammar, and we can then get an intermediate probability (p_{int}) for each node by examining the probabilities of the parses in which node n is a substitution node. This intermediate probability corresponds to the probability that the node is a substitution node when using this particular intermediate grammar. Furthermore, we assign a weight to each parse to prioritize parses in which some but not all of the nodes are substitution nodes (to discourage the model from doing something similar to simply inducing a PCFG or from memorizing entire trees). Specifically, in order to weight a parse more favorably the closer it is to having about half the internal nodes be substitution nodes, the weight of a parse is $\binom{t}{s}$ (t choose s) where s is the number of substitution nodes in a parse and t is the total number of internal nodes (i.e. the number of potential substitution nodes). Then, if $p(x)$ is the probability of a parse, $w(x)$ is the weight of a parse, S is the set of all parses in which n is a substitution node, and T is the set of all parses for the tree that n appears in, we can compute p_{int} using the following formula:

$$p_{int}(n) = \frac{\sum_{x \in S} w(x)p(x)}{\sum_{x \in T} w(x)p(x)}$$

3.3 An Example

Consider the following tree from a hypothetical training set:

(4)

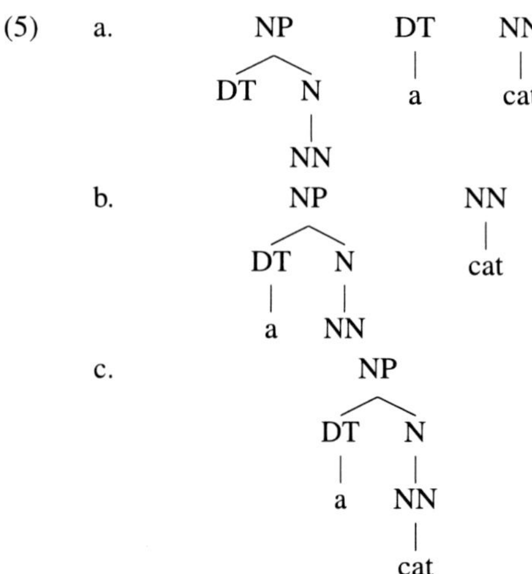

Let us assume that our intermediate grammar produced parses with the following three sets of elementary trees with probabilities p_1, p_2, and p_3 respectively:

(5)   a.

b.

c.

The parses in (2a) and (2b) both have weights of $\binom{3}{1} = \binom{3}{2} = 3$, as (5a) has 2 substitution nodes and (5b) has 1. However, the parse in (5c) only has weight $\binom{3}{0} = 1$, as it has no substitution nodes. Then, we can compute p_{int} for the node labeled DT, which is only a substitution node in (5a), as:

$$p_{int} = \frac{3p_1}{3p_1 + 3p_2 + p_3}$$

3.4 Updating Probabilities

Once we have calculated $p_{int}(n)$, we adjust the probability of node n by taking a weighted average of this intermediate probability and the probability from the start of the round, using the following formula:

$$p_{new}(n) = 0.6p_{old}(n) + 0.4p_{int}(n)$$

The higher p_{int} is weighted, the faster the node probabilities converge, but when p_{int} is weighted higher, each randomly selected grammar has a larger impact on the final grammar and thus could result in a final grammar that performs poorly on the test set. The precise weighting above was determined experimentally by running the algorithm a number of times with different weights to provide an optimal balance between allowing each round to significantly affect the node probabilities while still weighting p_{int} little enough so that a round in which the intermediate PTSG is chosen suboptimally will not derail the training process.

3.5 Getting the Final Grammar

We compute a convergence metric by examining how close our intermediate probabilities are to the node probabilities at the start of a round. We can say that node n has "converged" if the difference between $p_{old}(n)$ and $p_{int}(n)$ is less than 0.05. The convergence metric then is the number of "converged" nodes divided by the total number of internal nodes in all trees in the training set. If this number is over 0.95, training comes to an end and the node probabilities set at the end of the last round of training are used to sample the final grammar.

Once the node probabilities have been finalized, we decompose the training set 100 times using the same method we used in training. Then, the set of decomposed trees becomes the set of rules of our final PTSG, and, as before, probabilities are set using relative frequency estimates. Then, once we have determined the rules and probabilities for the final PTSG, we parse each rule in this PTSG using the other rules of the PTSG. If there is a parse for the rule made up of smaller rules and if the probability of this parse is greater than the probability of the larger rule, the rule is determined to be superfluous. Superfluous rules are removed from the grammar, and the probabilities are renormalized.

Finally, in order to account for unknown words, for each part of speech appearing in the training set, a tree with height 1 with a root labeled with the part of speech tag and with one leaf node labeled "unk" (short for "unknown") is added to the grammar. The probability of these rules is set according to the number of types and tokens for the part of speech so that a part of speech with many distinct lexical items, such as count nouns, has a relatively high probability of unknown words compared to a part of speech with relatively few distinct lexical items, such as determiners. Specifically, the probability of the rule $POS \rightarrow unk$ was set to:

$$\frac{types(POS)}{types(POS) + tokens(POS)}$$

After adding these rules, the probabilities of all other rules whose roots are part of speech tags are renormalized.

4 Methods

4.1 Data Selection

The trees used for training and test sets are taken from the Adam portion of the Pearl-Sprouse corpus, a parsed version of the child-directed portions of the Brown subcorpus from CHILDES (Pearl and Sprouse, 2012; Brown, 1973; MacWhinney, 2000). Only noun phrases are examined, as they can be parsed quickly and are a structure for which a PTSG should be able provide an accurate model. Additionally, in order to allow the algorithm to distinguish between mass and count nouns, the NN label (the POS tag for singular nouns) corresponding to any mass noun is manually replaced by an NNM label. Similarly, to allow the algorithm to have rules applicable to all nouns, a node labeled simply N is inserted immediately above any node labeled NN, NNM, or NNS (the POS tag for plural nouns).

Furthermore, as the algorithm makes use of a CKY parser, any tree in the corpus which is not binary branching is modified to become right-branching. If an inserted node's children are both labeled N, it is labeled with N, so that the algorithm would treat compound nouns the same way as other nouns, and similarly, if the first child is labeled JJ (the POS tag for adjectives) and the second is labeled N, the inserted node is labeled N, as adjective-noun pairs distribute similarly to nouns in this dataset. All other inserted nodes are labeled by concatenating the labels of their children.

4000 noun phrases are then extracted from this modified corpus. None of these noun phrases include smaller internal noun phrases, so as to allow the algorithm to focus on dependencies between determiners and nouns, and all of them include at least one node labeled N (so as to eliminate single pronouns from the data set). They are also selected

so that at least 30% of them contain mass nouns. 3200 of these nouns are randomly chosen to be the training set. The remaining 800 become the test set. Furthermore, every lexical item in the test set that does not appear in the training set was replaced with the word "unk" so that it can be properly parsed by the induced grammar.

4.2 Tests Run

The first baseline the induced grammar is tested against was a PCFG. The rules of the grammar are taken from all the PCFG productions in the training, and the probabilities are set using relative frequency estimates. Furthermore, rules going from each part of speech to "unk" are added with probabilities set the same way as they were in the PTSG so that trees with unseen lexical items can be parsed.

The second baseline is a PTSG whose rules are simply the full trees in the training set. The probability of each rule is set using a relative frequency estimate, so the probability of a given tree is simply the number of times the tree appears in the training set divided by the total number of trees in the training set.

The third baseline is a PTSG obtained by randomly sampling from the training set, specifically by decomposing each tree 100 times and setting the probabilities using relative frequency estimates, just as at the end of the induction algorithm. However, instead of using the trained probabilities, while sampling, the probability of each node being a substitution node is simply set to its initial probability of 0.55. To make this more comparable to the induced grammar, rules going from each POS tag to "unk" are added with their probabilities equal to their probabilities in the induced PTSG, and all other rules' probabilities are renormalized.

Lastly, Sangati and Zuidema's code for double-DOP is run on the training set to obtain their set of fragments and CFG rules with counts. Using these counts, probabilities for each rule are obtained using relative frequency estimates. Then the same rules for unknown lexical items with the same probabilities as in the induced grammar were added, and the probabilities are renormalized. Other previous approaches were not tested because of the difficulty of finding a working implementation of them.

Finally, to avoid zero probabilities, especially

Method	Training	Test	Grammar Size
Node-Based	-25263	-6770	1359
PCFG	-30905	-7091	990
Full Trees	-22280	-6814	1572
Sampling	-30135	-7266	1721
Double-DOP	-28882	-7032	2404

Table 1: Log probabilities of training and test sets on different grammars

for the full trees baseline, when computing the probability of a tree in the test set with the PTSGs obtained through node-based induction, sampling, and taking full trees, we also parse it with the PCFG induced for the first baseline. (This is not necessary for double-DOP, as the algorithm for double-DOP already incorporates all possible CFG rules.) The probability of the tree is then calculated to be a weighted average of the two probabilities, with the PCFG weighted at 0.05, while the PTSG is weighted at 0.95. Any trees in the test set that cannot be parsed with the PCFG are removed from the test set and ignored.

5   Results

Table 1 shows the results for how node-based induction compares to the baselines with a training set of size 3200 and a test set of size 793. (Initially, the test set was of size 800, but 9 noun phrases were removed because they contained structures unseen in the training set and thus could not be parsed by any of the grammars.) The numbers provided here are obtained by summing the log probabilities of the best parses for each tree in the data set. (In every case except for the PCFG baseline, these probabilities are also computed by taking a weighted average of the probability of the best parse with the chosen model and the best parse with a PCFG, as explained in the methods section). Thus, larger (i.e. less negative) numbers correspond to higher probabilities and therefore better results.

These results demonstrate that, apart from simply memorizing the training set (and grossly overfitting), the PTSG induced by node-based induction assigns the highest probability to the training set. Additionally, when tested on an unseen test set, node-based induction outperforms each of the baselines. It is also worth noting that when sampling randomly without first training the substitution node probabilities, the resulting grammar

performs nearly as badly as a PCFG on the training set and worse than all other grammars on the test, thus demonstrating that the optimization of the substitution node probabilities is in fact what allows node-based induction to produce a well-performing grammar. It is also worth noting that node-based induction produces the smallest grammar except for the PCFG, making it faster to parse with.

In order to determine how well the induce PTSG models the distribution of nouns and determiners, all 1442 noun phrases of the format "determiner noun" were extracted from the training set and, for each determiner that appeared more than 5 times, the probability distribution over different types of nouns occurring with that determiner was computed. These distributions are shown in table 2. Then, 1442 noun phrases of the form "determiner noun" were generated using the PTSG induced with node-based induction, and the same distributions were computed, shown in table 3. The same was done for the PCFG. Then, the Kullback-Leibler divergence was computed between the distributions generated from each of the PTSG induced through node-based induction and the PCFG and the true distribution from the training corpus, using add-one smoothing to avoid zero probabilities. These values are shown in table 4.

Determiner	Count Noun	Mass Noun	Plural Noun
a	0.983	0.015	0.002
an	0.952	0.048	0.000
another	0.714	0.286	0.000
any	0.048	0.714	0.238
no	0.571	0.286	0.143
some	0.000	0.913	0.087
that	0.857	0.143	0.000
the	0.712	0.230	0.058
this	0.960	0.040	0.000

Table 2: Probability distributions of noun types cooccurring with common determiners in the training set

These results show that, while the distributions produced by the node-based PTSG are not as strongly skewed as the empirical distributions, where many of the probabilities are over 0.9, they do reflect dependencies between determiners and noun types. (This may also reflect that, even in the empirical distributions, none of the probabilities are 1, reflecting the presence of noun phrases like

Determiner	Count	Mass	Plural
a	0.82	0.15	0.03
an	0.71	0.18	0.11
any	0.32	0.53	0.16
some	0.18	0.79	0.03
that	0.85	0.10	0.05
the	0.74	0.21	0.05
this	0.86	0.03	0.10

Table 3: Probability distributions of noun types cooccurring with common determiners in noun phrases generated by the PTSG

Determiner	Node-Based	PCFG
a	0.13	0.40
an	0.11	0.80
any	0.16	0.52
some	0.18	1.03
that	0.03	0.09
the	0.00	0.03
this	0.05	0.33

Table 4: K-L divergences of noun phrases generated by the node-based PTSG and the PCFG compared to the empirical distribution

another coffee where a noun that would normally be a mass noun serves as a coffee.) Furthermore, the K-L divergences are much smaller than those generated by the PCFG, a formalism that cannot encode these dependencies.

Furthermore, qualitatively speaking, many of the elementary trees that appear in the grammar induced by node-based induction make linguistic sense, such as those below:

(6) a. NP b. NP c. NP
         DT N   CD N   DT N
         | | | | | |
         a   NN   two NNS some NNM

(6a) represents that *a* only appears before count nouns. (6b) represents that *two* appears before plural nouns. (6c) represents that *some* generally appears before mass nouns. Furthermore, to account for the fact that *some* can also appear before plural nouns (which are rarer in the data set than mass nouns) and even count nouns in limited grammatical contexts (as in sentences like *some person will like this*), there is another elementary tree in the grammar identical to (6c) but without the NNM

node (so that N is a substitution node). However, this tree's probability is an order of magnitude lower than the tree in (6c), indicating that *some* appears primarily but not exclusively before mass nouns. Other rules indicate that the induced grammar learns several common compound nouns, including *cookie dough*, *rubber band*, and *trash can*, as single rules (instead of requiring each of the nouns to individually be substituted into a N $\rightarrow$ N N rule, as would be the case in a CFG).

6 Conclusion

In this paper, I have presented a novel approach for induction of probabilistic tree substitution grammars, which represents the probability distribution over possible tree-substitution grammars by assigning probabilities to potential substitution nodes and determines the optimal probabilities through repeated sampling and parsing. This approach is able to produce grammars that accurately represent dependencies between determiners and nouns, including, for example, elementary trees that require *a* to appear before a count noun. Furthermore, these grammars produce higher probability parses than standard PCFGs when tested on an unseen test set and also outperform a purely sampling-based approach where the probabilities assigned to the substitution nodes are not optimized.

Here, I have shown that tree-substitution grammars induced through node-based induction can more accurately represent the probabilities of potential parses for non-recursive noun phrases than traditional PCFG-based approaches or grammars induced from DOP-based approaches. We have not yet run experiments testing this algorithm on structures beyond noun phrases, but future work could adapt this algorithm to work with larger grammatical structures, including full sentences, and it could then be used to induce grammars that more accurately model language and generate more accurate parses.

References

Rens Bod and Remko Scha. 1996. Data-oriented language processing: An overview. *Computing Research Repository*.

Roger Brown. 1973. *A first language: The early stages*. Harvard U. Press.

Trevor Cohn, Sharon Goldwater, and Phil Blunsom. 2009. Inducing compact but accurate tree-substitution grammars. In *Proceedings of Human Language Technologies: The 2009 Annual Conference of the North American Chapter of the Association for Computational Linguistics*, pages 548–556. Association for Computational Linguistics.

Mark Johnson, Thomas L. Griffiths, and Sharon Goldwater. 2006. Adaptor grammars: A framework for specifying compositional nonparametric bayesian models. In *Advances in neural information processing systems*, pages 641–648.

Brian MacWhinney. 2000. *The CHILDES project: The database*, volume 2. Psychology Press.

Timothy J. O'Donnell, Noah D. Goodman, and Joshua B. Tenenbaum. 2009. Fragment grammars: Exploring computation and reuse in language. Technical Report MIT-CSAIL-TR-2009-013, Massachusetts Institute of Technology.

Lisa Pearl and Jon Sprouse. 2012. Computational models of acquisition for islands. *Experimental syntax and island effects*, pages 109–131.

Matt Post and Daniel Gildea. 2009. Bayesian learning of a tree substitution grammar. In *Proceedings of the ACL-IJCNLP 2009 Conference Short Papers*, pages 45–48.

Federico Sangati and Willem Zuidema. 2011. Accurate parsing with compact tree-substitution grammars: Double-DOP. In *Proceedings of the Conference on Empirical Methods in Natural Language Processing*, pages 84–95. Association for Computational Linguistics.

Yves Schabes, Anne Abeille, and Aravind K. Joshi. 1988. Parsing strategies with 'lexicalized' grammars: Application to tree adjoining grammars. In *Proceedings of the 12th Conference on Computational Linguistics - Volume 2*, pages 578–583.

Revisiting Supertagging and Parsing: How to Use Supertags in Transition-Based Parsing

Wonchang Chung
Dept. of Computer Science
Columbia University
New York, NY, USA
wc2550@columbia.edu

Siddhesh Suhas Mhatre
Dept. of Computer Science
Columbia University
New York, NY, USA
sm4083@columbia.edu

Alexis Nasr
LIF
Université Aix Marseille
Marseille, France
Alexis.Nasr@lif.univ-mrs.fr

Owen Rambow
CCLS
Columbia University
New York, NY, USA
rambow@ccls.columbia.edu

Srinivas Bangalore
Interactions, Inc.
New Providence, NJ, USA
sbangalore@interactions.com

Abstract

We discuss the use of supertags derived from a TAG in transition-based parsing. We show some initial experimental results which suggest that using a representation of a supertag in terms of its structural and linguistic dimensions outperforms the use of atomic supertags.

1 Introduction

The notion of supertagging was introduced by Bangalore and Joshi (1999). A supertag is the name of an elementary tree assigned to a word in a TAG derivation of the sentence. A supertag therefore encodes not only the part of speech, but also the syntactic properties of the word. They proposed a two-step approach to parsing: a supertagger determines the supertag for each word in a sentence, and a deterministic and rule-based "lightweight dependency analyzer" then derives the structure from the supertags.

The MICA parser (Bangalore et al., 2009) uses a supertagger and a subsequent chart parser which takes the 10-best supertags for each word as input. MICA uses a probabilistic context free grammar which is lexicalized on the supertags, but not on words. The MICA parser is fast, and has good performance. Nasr and Rambow (2006) showed that the MICA approach outperforms the lightweight dependency analyzer of Bangalore and Joshi (1999). To our knowledge, MICA is the only TAG parser trained on the Penn Treebank that uses supertagging; it is freely available.[1]

The MICA parser has several drawbacks: while it is fast, the time complexity is $O(n^3)$. Further-

more, the system is complex as the chart parser itself is compiled using the SYNTAX system (Boullier and Deschamp, 1988), making further development difficult. Finally, it is unclear how to include recent advances in lexical representation (word embeddings) and machine learning (deep learning).

This paper presents a new parser based on TAG, which uses supertagging and a distinct parsing step. Unlike MICA, the parsing is based on the transition-based parser of Nivre et al. (2004). While there has been some work using supertags with transition-based parsing (Ouchi et al., 2014), this is the only work (to our knowledge) which specifically refers to TAG grammar.

Bangalore et al. (2009) train a version of MALT with gold and predicted supertags. MALT can exploit the gold supertags, but not the predicted supertags (they do not improve over not using them). The problem with using supertags in transition-based parsing is that exploiting n-best supertag input is difficult, and given the large number of supertags, supertagging is hard and the 1-best supertag is not good enough to allow for a good parse to be constructed. In this paper, we present initial investigations to address this problem. We decompose the supertag into linguistic dimensions, which provides for a generalization of the notion of supertag.

2 Corpus and Grammar

We use the grammar and the corpus extracted by Chen (2001). This grammar was engineered in such a way that the derivation trees are meaningful deep-syntactic representations. This grammar was also used in the MICA parser (Bangalore et al., 2009). It has 4725 elementary trees extracted from

---

[1] urlhttp://mica.lif.univ-mrs.fr

Proceedings of the 12th International Workshop on Tree Adjoining Grammars and Related Formalisms (TAG+12), pages 85–92,
Düsseldorf, Germany, June 29 - July 1, 2016.

the training set of the WSJ portion of the Penn Treebank (Sections 01-22). Every sentence in the corpus is given a derivation. Sentences in the development set (Section 00) and the test set (Section 23) may contain elementary trees that have not been seen in the training corpus.

We automatically analyzed the elementary trees that make up the extracted TAG, assigning each tree a vector of 20 dimensions. These dimensions fall into three categories:

- Dimensions that describe the phrase structure of the elementary tree. We concentrate on aspects that we think will be important for parsing.

- Interpretations of the tree. These are linguistic dimensions which abstract from the phrase structure of the tree.

- Linguistic transformations on the tree. These are syntactic variations that the tree encodes, such as *wh*-movement.

This approach of breaking down a supertag into components is inspired by the hypertags of Kinyon (2000). Our set of dimensions is shown in Figure 1.

3   Supertagging

The supertagger architecture is very simple: supertags are predicted independently of each other. The prediction is performed using an on-line passive-agressive algorithm (Crammer et al., 2006). We used the implementation of the Python Scikit-Learn library.[2]

The classifier uses a total of 26 features: the word to be supertagged, its part-of-speech tag as well as the 6 preceding and following words and part-of-speech tags. To vectorize the feature data, the one-hot encoding method was used.

Training was performed on the training set of the WSJ portion of the Penn Treebank (950,028 tokens) and the evaluation on the development set (40,461 tokens). In order to reduce the amount of memory used for training, the sparse matrix constructor was used. The peak amount of memory used for training task was less than 50GB, and the processing time was less than 1 hour in wall-clock time on our machines.

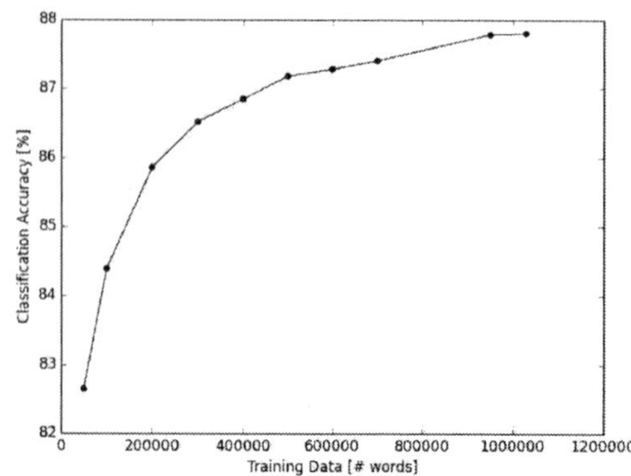

Figure 2: Learning curve of the supertagger

The supertagger accuracy is 87.88% on the development set, a bit lower than the results obtained on this data by Bangalore et al. (2005), which was 88.53%. The learning curve is shown in Figure 2.

4   Parsing

4.1   Background

The parser used in this study, named SUTRA (for Supertag- and Transition-based Parser), is a standard transition based parser (Nivre et al., 2004). Giving a thorough descriptions of transition based parsers is not the aim of this paper; we will just briefly describe below the basic ideas behind transition based parsing to allow the reader to follow the rest of the paper.

Transition-based parsers are based on two fundamental objects: configurations and transitions

A configuration (s, b, D) describes the state of the parsing process at a given time. b is a buffer that contains the words of the sentence to parse not yet processed. The leftmost word of the buffer is noted b_0. b_0 can be taken from the buffer and pushed on the stack s. D is a set containing dependencies that have been built to this point by the parser. The parser tries to build a dependency between the word that is on the top of the stack (s_0) and the next word in the buffer (b_0). Two types of attachements are considered, left attachements that have as a governor word b_0 and as a dependent s_0 and right attachements that have s_0 as governor and b_0 as dependent. The initial configuration of the parser is $([], [w_1 \ldots w_n], \emptyset)$: the stack is empty, the buffer contains all the words of the sentence to parse and the dependency set is empty. A fi-

Dimension	Description
	Dimensions describing the phrase structure of the elementary tree
root	The label of the root node of the tree
lfront	A list of substitution nodes to the left of the lexical anchor; each node is listed with its category, its node type (substitution or co-head), and its deep-syntactic argument label
rfront	Same as lfront, but for the substitution nodes to the right of the lexical anchor
adjnodes	A list of nodes at which adjunction can occur
substnodes	A list of all substitution nodes of the tree
coanc	Does this tree have a co-anchor?
modif	For modifier auxiliary trees, the cateory of its root node (and thus of its foot node)
dir	The direction in which a modifier auxiliary tree adjoins
	Dimensions interpreting the elementary tree
predaux	Is the tree a predicative auxiliary tree (i.e., a tree used for matrix clauses)?
pred	Is this tree a nominal, adjectival, or prepositional tree which projects a predicative structure, i.e., takes a subject (even if not realized)?
appo	Is this tree an apposition?
comp	Does this tree have a complementizer (which is a co-head in this grammar), and if yes, on what side of the anchor?
dsubcat	Deep subcategorization frame for the anchor, listed in order of argument number (i.e., not necessarily surface order), with substitution node category and strongly governed category, if any
ssubcat	Surface subcategorization frame for the anchor, listed in order of argument number (i.e., not necessarily surface order), with substitution node category and strongly governed category, if any
particle	Does this tree contain a particle (POS tag RP)?
	Dimensions describing linguistic transformations on the elementary tree
voice	Voice for verbal trees
wh	Is there a *wh*-moved dependent?
rel	Is the tree a relative clause?
esubj	Is the subject of the tree empty?
datshift	For ditransitive trees, did dative shift happen?

Figure 1: Description of tree dimensions

nal configuration is a configuration for which the buffer is empty.

A transition operates on a configuration c_i to produce a configuration c_{i+1}. In our implementation, three types of transitions are defined:

Left Arc builds a dependency (b_0, l, s_0) (a transition that has b_0 as a governor, s_0 as a dependent and l as a label). This transition adds the new dependency to D and pops the stack.

Right Arc builds a dependency (s_0, l, b_0). This transition adds the new dependency to D and replaces b_0 with s_0.

Shift does not create a new dependency, it just remove b_0 from the buffer and pushes it on the stack.

The parser is a greedy deterministic parser. Given a configuration, it predicts the most likely transition to make. A new configuration is produced and the process iterates until a final configuration is reached. The dependency structure produced is the set D.

The heart of the parser is the classifier that predicts which transition to make given a configuration. The number of possible configurations being very large, we decompose a configuration into a feature vector. During training, the classifier associates a score to each feature. At decoding time, the classifier adds the scores of the features corresponding to the current configuration in order to select the most likely transition. The classifier used in this work is a simple averaged perceptron (Freund and Schapire, 1999).

The feature templates used by the classifier are of three sorts:

Word features describe different aspects of the words that are present either on the stack of the parser or in the buffer. They are of the form (s|b)(0|1|2|3)(f|l|c|p|m) where:

- s|b indicates whether the word described is in the stack or the buffer

- 0|1|2|3 indicates the position of the word in the stack or the buffer (s0 is the top stack word and b0 is the first word in the buffer).

- f|l|c|p|m indicates whether we are referring to the form of the word (f), its lemma (l), its coarse part of speech (c), its part of speech (p) or its morphological features (m).

Distance features indicate the distance in the string between two words. They are of the form d_X_Y where X and Y correspond to words either on the stack or in the buffer. The only feature of this category that is used is d_s0_b0.

Structural features describe some aspects of the dependency structure built so far by the parser. They are of three sorts:

- l_X which indicate the syntactic function (role label) of the leftmost dependent (if any) of word X. Two features of this category are defined: r_s0r and r_b0r.

- r_X which indicate the syntactic function (role label) of the rightmost dependent (if any) of word X. Two features of this category are defined: l_s0r and l_b0r.

- n_X which indicate the number of dependents of word X. Two features of this category are defined: n_s0 and n_b0.

Configuration features describe some aspects of the current configuration of the parser. They are of four sorts:

- sh indicates the height of the stack

- bh indicates the number of elements in the buffer

- dh indicates the number of dependencies built so far

- tn with n=1, 2, 3, 4, indicates the nth preceding transition that led to the current configuration

Each feature template can be used independently or in combination with others, in which case a weight is computed for a combination of their values.

4.2 Parser 1: Baseline Parser without Supertags

We start by describing our baseline parser, which is SUTRA without any supertag features at all.

Table 4 shows the set of feature templates (called a feature model) used for our baseline parser. (All of the tables related to the machine learning features are at the end of the paper.) Feature templates 1 to 18 are simple feature templates, those ranging from 19 to 29 are combination of two simple feature templates.

The performance of the baseline parser is shown in Table 1 in the first row, with separate results for labeled attachment score (LAS) and unlabeled attachment score (UAS). Since we are not using supertags in this experiment, the results are the same for gold and predicted supertags.

For the sake of comparison, we also give results for a MALT parser trained on our corpus (2nd line in Table 1; the results are taken from (Bangalore et al., 2009)). Our baseline results are directly comparable to those for MALT without supertags, as both are transition-based parsers which do not use supertags. We see that our results are a little worse, which we attribute to differences in the machine learning, and differences in the feature set used. However, for the sake of the experiments in this paper, we take our results as meaning that we have replicated the previous results.

4.3 Parser 2: Using Supertags

We now use supertags. In the first experiment, we simply add the supertags as labels in our parser by means of the following word feature templates: (s|b)(0|1|2|3)(s), where the first two components of the templates (s|b) and (0|1|2|3) keep the same meaning as before and s refers to the supertag of the word. The feature model of Parser 2 adds to the feature model of the baseline Parser the feature templates shown in Table 5. These templates correspond to templates of the baseline parser in which part of speech tags are remplaced by supertag tags.

Parser		Gold Stags		Predicted Stags		
		UAS	LAS	Stag acc.	UAS	LAS
Baseline	Words, POS tags	—	—	—	87.65	85.23
MALT	Words, POS tags	—	—	—	88.9	86.9
P2	Words, POS tags, stags	97.02	96.00	87.88	89.83	87.75
MALT-Stag	Words, POS tags, stags	97.20	96.90	88.52	88.50	86.80
MICA	Stags only	97.60	97.30	88.52	87.60	85.80
P3	Words, POS tags, stags, stag dimensions	97.46	96.51	87.88	89.96	87.86

Table 1: Results for different configurations.

The results of P2 are displayed in Table 1 in row 3. As one can see, when feeding the parser with gold supertags, the results accuracy of the parser jumps to 96.97 UAS and 95.99 LAS. Supertags carry much more syntactic information than just POS tags that the parser can make use of in order to predict the syntactic structure of the sentence. When supertags are predicted with the supertagger of section 3, the accuracy dips to 89.86 UAS and 87.75 LAS, respectively. This represents an absolute increase of 2.24 points of UAS and 2.52 points of LAS with respect to the baseline parser. We also compare P2 to MALT using supertags, shown in row 4. We see that our parser outperforms MALT with stags by a small margin when using predicted supertags (but not gold supertags). Part of the difference in the predicted supertags is due to the use of gold POS tags in our experiments, so we conclude that we are again replicating the previous result.

We also provide the results for MICA (row 5). We see that for gold supertags, MICA provides the best overall results, but not for predicted supertags. This is because MICA in fact *only* uses supertags.

4.4 Parser 3: Using Dimensions of Supertags

We now perform experiments to see whether the individual dimensions of the supertags can help in parsing. The motivation is that if a supertag is incorrectly predicted, some of the dimensions may still be correct (for example, the predicted supertag has a transitive verb instead of an intransitive verb, but the subject is empty in both supertags).

In order to be able to exploit the supertag dimensions in the parser, we add the following word feature templates: (s|b) (0|1|2|3) (A|B|...|T|U) where, as before, the first two components of the template (s|b) and (0|1|2|3) keep the same signification and the letters A to U refer to one dimension of the vector representation of supertags. The correspondence is given in Table 3. The feature model of parser 3 is the union of the feature model of P2 and the features of Table 6.

We observe that we cannot use all dimensions of the linguistic vector representation of the supertag, because the combinations would result in a combinatorial explosion in the number of features for machine learning. In order to gain a better understanding of which dimensions of the decomposed supertags are useful for parsing, we performed ablation studies, first on the dimensions, and then on the machine learning features. We discuss them in turn.

In the first study we removed each dimension of the supertag (eg. dsubcat, ssubcat, ...) in turn and computed the parsing accuracy. For this ablation study, we use a feature model that comprises simple features derived from supertags and non-supertags. Specifically, this model comprises the following features: features 1 through 18 from Table 4, plus s0x, s1x, b0x, and b1x, where x is a variable denoting the dimensions (represented as in Table 3). We use this model because it is a simple model. The results are shown for gold and predicted stags in Table 2.

For the gold experiments (first two columns), we see that mainly the dimensions that describe the phrase structure are useful for parsing: all of these dimensions except for coanc help, and all the most useful dimensions are of this type. This is because in a TAG grammar, the phrase structure encodes exactly how trees can combine in the parse, so that this is the information needed for a correct parse. In addition, we have several of the dimensions relating to transformations that help a bit. When we look at the predicted supertags, we see that seven of the eleven dimensions that are useful for the gold condition are still useful, most of them structural. However, we also expect to see a shift, as some dimensions are harder to predict with sufficient accuracy. In particular, we see that rfront no longer helps. We hypothesize that this is because there is a large number of possible values for this dimension (more than for lfront, because of the syntax of English), and that an error immediately reduces the usefulness of this dimension. Perhaps as a result, the dsubcat dimension is useful in the predicted condition. The dsubcat dimension abstracts over actual phrase structure, and therefore has a smaller set of possible values, while still providing some of the same information that the dsubcat dimension provides (what dependents this head expects).

Now we turn to the second ablation study, in which we concentrate on specific features rather than dimensions. To pick out those individual features (eg. s0A, s1B, ...) in the feature model of the remaining supertag dimensions (eg. dsubcat, ssubcat, ...) that cause a decrease in performance, we performed another level of feature ablation. We use the same feature model we used in the first ablation study. For each supertag dimension that remained after the first ablation study, we removed each corresponding machine learning feature one by one in and computed the parsing accuracy. For example, if we consider supertag dimension dsubcat (represented as A), then we performed experiments where we removed the feature s0A in the feature model, followed by s1A and so on, every time observing the effects on the parsing accuracy. This was done for every remaining supertag dimension. Again, at the end of this set of experiments we eliminated those features from our feature model that cause a decrease in parsing performance when included. Because of the large number of results, we do not present them in detail.

Till now we had considered only the supertag dimensions in our model independently. Our last set of experiments comprises combining some of these features from the feature model. Here, we used our intuition to propose certain combinations. One set of features we combined were the ones corresponding to the dimensions 'lfront' and 'rfront'. These correspond to ordered list of frontier nodes to the left and right of the main lexical anchor respectively. We merge both lfront or rfront with the root of the elements on top of the stack and buffer. These features were then combined with the 'dir' dimension which gave encouraging results. We tried 8 different combinations in this manner and got the best results for the following feature model which is shown in Table 6. This set of features also includes those features that correspond to non-supertag features that gave us the best performance.

The results of P3 are displayed in the last line of Table 1. As one can see the decomposed representation of the supertag has a beneficial impact for both the gold and predicted supertag conditions. The error reduction for gold supertags (UAS) is 15%; for predicted, the error reduction is much smaller (1%). We think this smaller error reduction may be due to the fact that in our feature engineering, which was guided by our intuition, we did not take into account the accuracy of different dimensions, assuming implicitly the case in which the dimensions are correctly predicted. Our new results are better than the best published parsing results so far on this corpus, as far as we know.

5 Conclusion

We have presented work in progress, that shows that supertagging can be useful for transition-based parsing. Our initial experiments suggest that considering the dimensions of the supertag can help further.

A major problem is devising machine learning features for the parser from the dimensions, given the very large number of possibilities due to the combinatorics of the combined features. In future work, we plan to use deep learning to obviate the need for feature engineering. This will also entail using word embeddings, which we will also use for supertagging. We will look to the rich literature on supertagging and parsing in CCG for guidance. In addition, we will also start using predicted POS tags in our experiments.

References

Srinivas Bangalore and Aravind Joshi. 1999. Supertagging: An approach to almost parsing. *Computational Linguistics*, 25(2):237–266.

Srinivas Bangalore, Patrick Haffner, and Gaël Emami. 2005. Factoring global inference by enriching local representations. Technical report, AT&T Labs – Reserach.

	Gold		Predicted	
Dim.	LAS	UAS	LAS	UAS
predaux	+.07	+.05	+.04	0
rel	+.07	+.06	**-.06**	**-.05**
particle	+.05	+.05	**0**	**-.05**
coanc	+.04	+.02	**0**	**-.07**
ssubcat	+.04	+.03	0	-.01
wh	+.02	+.02	+.05	+.02
comp	+.01	+.01	**-.01**	**-.05**
dsubcat	+.01	+.02	**-.07**	**-.09**
pred	0	0	+.06	+.03
none	94.87	95.83	83.15	85.43
datshift	**-.01**	**-.01**	+.07	+.03
voice	**-.02**	**-.02**	**-.03**	**-.07**
esubj	**-.03**	**-.02**	**-.03**	**-.06**
appo	**-.04**	**-.04**	+.02	0
substnodes	**-.04**	**-.02**	0	-.01
adjnodes	**-.04**	**-.04**	**-.17**	**-.19**
modif	**-.07**	**-.10**	**-.09**	**-.11**
lfront	**-.07**	**-.06**	**-.05**	**-.07**
rfront	**-.16**	**-.15**	+.02	-.02
root	**-.32**	**-.32**	**-.09**	**-.12**
dir	**-.90**	**-.88**	**-.40**	**-.43**

Table 2: Ablation study for supertag linguistic features, with gold standard supertags and predicted supertags. Each row lists one feature which was removed in turn. The resulting difference in performance is shown (labeled and unlabeled dependency accuracy without punctuation), first for gold supertags, then for predicted supertags. If a result gets worse upon removal of a feature (negative value), then that dimension is important. We show the retained dimensions by boldfacing their resulting change in accuracy.

Srinivas Bangalore, Pierre Boullier, Alexis Nasr, Owen Rambow, and Benoît Sagot. 2009. MICA: A probabilistic dependency parser based on tree insertion grammars. In *NAACL HLT 2009 (Short Papers)*.

Pierre Boullier and Philippe Deschamp. 1988. Le système SYNTAX[TM] – manuel d'utilisation et de mise en œuvre sous UNIX[TM]. http://syntax.gforge.inria.fr/syntax3.8-manual.pdf.

John Chen. 2001. *Towards Efficient Statistical Parsing Using Lexicalized Grammatical Information*. Ph.D. thesis, University of Delaware.

Koby Crammer, Ofer Dekel, Joseph Keshet, Shai Shalev-Shwartz, and Yoram Singer. 2006. On-line Passive-Aggressive Algorithms. *Journal of Machine Learning Research*, 7:551–585.

Yoav Freund and Robert E Schapire. 1999. Large margin classification using the perceptron algorithm. *Machine learning*, 37(3):277–296.

Alexandra Kinyon. 2000. Hypertags. In *Proceedings of the 18th International Conference on Computational Linguistics (COLING 2000)*.

Alexis Nasr and Owen Rambow. 2006. Parsing with lexicalized probabilistic recursive transition networks. In *Finite-State Methods and Natural Language Processing*, Springer Verlag Lecture Notes in Commputer Science.

Joakim Nivre, Johan Hall, and Jens Nilsson. 2004. Memory-based dependency parsing. In *HLT-NAACL 2004 Workshop: Eighth Conference on Computational Natural Language Learning (CoNLL-2004)*, pages 49–56, Boston, Massachusetts, USA.

Hiroki Ouchi, Kevin Duh, and Yuji Matsumoto. 2014. Improving dependency parsers with supertags. In *Proceedings of the 14th Conference of the European Chapter of the Association for Computational Linguistics, volume 2: Short Papers*, pages 154–158, Gothenburg, Sweden, April. Association for Computational Linguistics.

A	dsubcat	B	ssubcat	C	voice
D	comp	E	datshift	F	root
G	lfront	H	rfront		
J	adjnodes	K	substnodes	L	rel
M	particle	N	coanc	O	modif
P	dir	Q	pred	R	esubj
S	wh	T	appo	U	predaux

Table 3: List of supertag dimensions used, with short name used in the tables of machine learning features

45	s0s			
46	s1s			
47	b0s			
48	b1s			
49	b2s			
50	b3s			
51	b0s	b0f		
52	b0s	l_b0r		
53	b1s	b2s		
54	s0s	b0s		
55	s1s	b1s		
56	s0s	b0s	b0f	
57	s0s	b0s	b1s	
58	s0s	b0s	d_s0_b0	
59	s0s	l_s0r	r_s0r	
60	s0s	s0f	b0s	
61	s0s	s1s	b0s	
62	b0s	b1s	b2s	
63	b1s	b2s	b3s	
64	b1s	b1f	b2s	b3s
65	b1s	b1f	b2s	b2f	b3s

Table 5: Parser 2 feature model (in addition to the features shown in Table 4).

1	s0c		15	l_b0r	
2	s0f		16	r_b0r	
3	s0p		17	n_s0	
4	s1p		18	n_b0	
5	b0c		19	s0c	b0c
6	b0f		20	s0f	b0f
7	b0p		21	s0p	b0p
8	b1c		22	b0c	b0f
9	b1f		23	b0p	b0f
10	b1p		24	b0p	l_b0r
11	b2p		25	s1c	b1c
12	b3p		26	s1p	b1p
13	l_s0r		27	b1c	b2c
14	r_s0r		28	b1p	b2p

29	s0c	b0c	b0f	
30	s0c	s0f	b0c	
31	s0p	b0p	b0f	
32	s0p	b0p	b1p	
33	s0p	l_s0r	r_s0r	
34	s0p	s0f	b0p	
35	s0c	b0c	d_s0_b0	
36	s0p	b0p	d_s0_b0	
37	s1p	s0p	b0p	
38	b0p	b1p	b2p	
39	b1c	b2c	b3c	
40	b1p	b2p	b3p	
41	b1c	b1f	b2c	b3c
42	b1p	b1f	b2p	b3p
43	b1c	b1f	b2c	b2f	b3c
44	b1p	b1f	b2p	b2f	b3p

Table 4: Baseline feature model

38	s0A	47	b0F	57	s0J	66	s1P
39	b1A	48	b1F	58	b0J	67	b0P
40	s0B	49	b0G	59	s0K	68	b1P
41	b1B	50	s0H	60	b1K	69	s0Q
42	s0C	51	s1H	61	s0M	70	s1Q
43	b0C	52	b0H	62	b0M	71	b0R
44	b0D	53	b1H	63	s0O	72	b0S
45	s1E	55	b0I	64	b1O	73	s0U
46	s1F	56	b1I	65	s0P		

72	s0H	b0F	
73	s0F	b0G	
74	b0H	b1F	
75	b0F	b1G	
76	s0H	s1F	
77	s0F	s1G	
78	s0H	b0F	s0P
79	s0F	b0G	b0P
80	b0H	b1F	b0P
81	b0F	b1G	b1P
82	s0H	s1F	s0P
83	s0F	s1G	b1P
84	s1H	s0F	b0G
85	s0H	b0F	b1F
86	s0H	b0F	d_s0_b0
87	s0F	b0G	d_s0_b0
88	s0H	b0F	s0P	d_s0_b0
89	s0F	b0G	b0P	d_s0_b0

Table 6: Parser 3 feature model (in addition to the features shown in Table 4 and Table 5).

An Alternate View on Strong Lexicalization in TAG

Aniello De Santo[1]   **Alëna Aksënova**[1]   **Thomas Graf**[2]

Department of Linguistics
Stony Brook University
[1]`{aniello.desanto,alena.aksenova}@stonybrook.edu`
[2]`mail@thomasgraf.net`

Abstract

TAGs were recently shown not to be closed under strong lexicalization but to be strongly lexicalizable by context-free tree grammars of rank 2. This paper presents an alternative lexicalization procedure that builds on an earlier generalization of TAGs to multi-dimensional trees. A previous theorem that every Tree Substitution grammar is strongly lexicalized by a corresponding TAG is lifted to higher dimensions to show that for every d-dimensional TAG there exists a $(d + 1)$-dimensional TAG that strongly lexicalizes it. A similar lifting reveals that d-dimensional TAGs are not closed under strong lexicalization, so for arbitrary TAGs an increase in dimensionality is an unavoidable consequence of strong lexicalization.

1 Introduction

The lexicalization properties of different grammar formalisms have been a topic of interest for a long time. A grammar is lexicalized if the atoms from which compound structures are assembled each contain a pronounced lexical item. In the case of TAGs, this means that no elementary trees may contain only non-terminal symbols or the empty string. Lexicalized grammars have the advantage of being *finitely ambiguous* — no string of finite length can have an infinite number of possible analyses. Not only does this guarantee that recognition is decidable, parsing is also simplified in practice (Schabes et al., 1988): the hypothesis space of the parser at any given point is significantly reduced because elementary trees that cannot be introduced by one of the symbols in the input string never need to be considered. As a result, many parsing algorithms assume that the grammar is lexicalized or at least can be lexicalized in an automatic fashion (cf. Kallmeyer (2010)).

In particular for parsing, though, the issue is not just whether a grammar can be lexicalized but whether the lexicalization procedure preserves essential properties of the grammar. While a recognizer only needs to determine the well-formedness of strings, a parser has to assign them structures licensed by the grammar. One thus has to distinguish between two types of lexicalization: *weak* lexicalization produces a weakly equivalent lexicalized grammar, whereas *strong lexicalization* yields a lexicalized grammars that also generates the same structural descriptions. Recent work showed that TAGs I) can be weakly lexicalized (Fujiyoshi, 2004), II) are not closed under strong lexicalization (Kuhlmann and Satta, 2012) and III) are strongly lexicalized by context-free tree grammars of rank 2 (Maletti and Engelfriet, 2012).

This paper offers a different perspective on strong lexicalization of TAGs that stays close to the basic intuition of TAGs as a mechanism for rewriting nodes by objects that are more complex than strings. The main advantage is that this allows us to preserve the basic insights of previous proofs on TAG lexicalization. We adopt Roger's formalism of multi-dimensional trees (Sec. 2.2 and 2.3), with TAGs as the special case where trees are limited to 3 dimensions (Rogers, 1998a; Rogers, 1998b; Rogers, 2003a; Rogers, 2003b). With TAGs lifted to arbitrary dimensions, we establish three central results:

1. Every d-dimensional TAG is a $(d + 1)$-dimensional Tree Substitution Grammar (TSG; Sec. 3.1)

2. Every d-dimensional TSG is strongly lexicalized by some d-dimensional TAG (Sec. 3.2; cf. Schabes (1990)).

Proceedings of the 12th International Workshop on Tree Adjoining Grammars and Related Formalisms (TAG+12), pages 93–102,
Düsseldorf, Germany, June 29 - July 1, 2016.

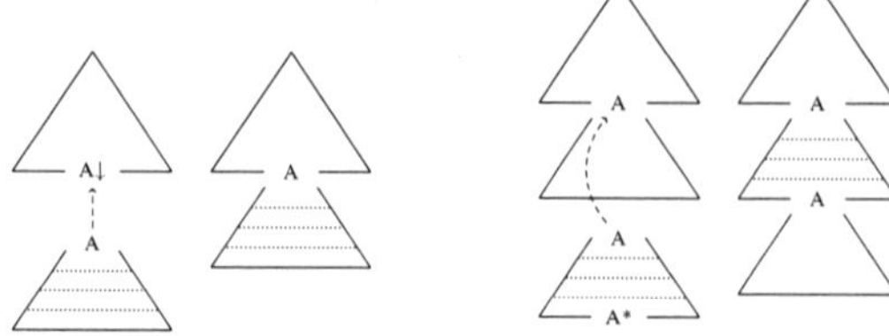

Figure 1: Substitution and adjunction

3. The class of d-dimensional TAGs is not closed under strong lexicalization (Sec. 3.3; cf. Kuhlmann and Satta (2012)).

This entails as a corollary that an increase in dimensionality is unavoidable in the strong lexicalization of (at least some) d-dimensional TAGs.

2 Preliminaries

In order to appreciate the results of Sec. 3.1–3.3, the reader has to be familiar with a few core concepts: the relation between adjunction and substitution (2.1), the view of TAGs as a formalism over 3-dimensional trees (2.2), and their generalization to trees of higher dimensionality (2.3).

2.1 Adjunction and Substitution

We assume familiarity on the reader's part with the TAG formalism as defined in Joshi (1985). A TAG is specified by two finite sets I and A of *initial* and *auxiliary* trees, respectively. Their union is the set E of *elementary* trees. Every auxiliary tree contains exactly one node that is marked as a foot node (indicated by * in our figures). Initial trees must not contain any foot nodes. Elementary trees are then combined by the operations of adjunction and substitution, illustrated in Fig. 1.

The distinction between adjunction and substitution plays an important role in this paper. Both operations replace nodes by trees. *Tree substitution* can only replace leaf nodes, and the tree being substituted may not contain a foot node. *Tree adjunction*, on the other hand, may rewrite any nonterminal node by any tree that contains exactly one foot node (i.e. by an auxiliary tree). Usually, it is also required that the label of the rewritten node is identical to the labels of the root (and the foot node, if it exists) of the substituted tree. Nodes are furthermore annotated with features to indicate whether adjunction and substitution are mandatory or optional as well as which trees may rewrite a given node.

Substitution can be regarded as adjunction of a foot-less tree at a leaf node. We thus use a more general definition of adjunction. Given a tree t, let $t \upharpoonright r$ be the subtree of t rooted in node r. Furthermore, $t[n \leftarrow u]$ replaces a node n of t with tree u. If n does not exist, then $t[n \leftarrow u] = t$. Now adjunction of u into t at node n is defined as $t \overset{n}{\Leftarrow} u :=$ $t[n \leftarrow u[f \leftarrow t \upharpoonright n]]$, where f is the foot node of u. Substitution is the special case where f does not exist so that $t[n \leftarrow u[f \leftarrow t \upharpoonright n]] = t[n \leftarrow u]$. As long as nodes are correctly annotated with features to ensure that n is a leaf iff u does not contain a foot node and that labels are correctly matched, this generalized notion of adjunction behaves exactly as the combination of standard adjunction and substitution. We can now define a *tree substitution grammar* as a restricted TAG where all licit instances of adjunction only rewrite leaf nodes — this characterization will play an essential role in Sec. 3.1.

2.2 TAGs as 3-Dimensional Grammar Formalisms

The history of how a TAG G generates a specific tree can be recorded as a derivation tree. Each node in the derivation tree is labeled with the name of an elementary tree and an edge $\langle t, a, u \rangle$ from t to u with label a indicates $t \overset{a}{\Leftarrow} u$. The label of the root node must be the name of an initial tree. Now suppose that each node in the derivation tree is replaced by the tree it denotes, and each edge $\langle t, a, u \rangle$ is instead replaced by a collection of unlabeled edges that go from each node of u to the node in t at address a. The result can be regarded as a 3-dimensional tree such as the one in Fig. 2, with the first dimension corresponding to precedence, the second one to dominance, and the third one to adjunction.

Rogers (1998b) shows that TAGs are equivalent to context-free grammars over such 3-dimensional trees. Each elementary tree is no longer a standard 2-dimensional tree but instead has a 3-dimensional root node that is the mother of all nodes in the 2-dimensional tree. Just like a context-free grammar may combine 2-dimensional trees t and u if t contains a leaf with the same label as the root node of u, a TAG may combine 3-dimensional trees t and u if t contains a leaf in the third dimension whose label matches the 3-dimensional root of u. (Note that the feature annotations regulating adjunction are not considered part of node labels here.)

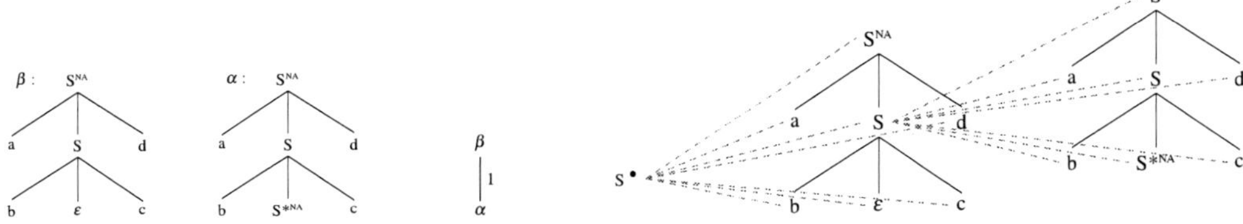

Figure 2: A standard TAG, one of its derivations, and the corresponding 3-dimensional tree

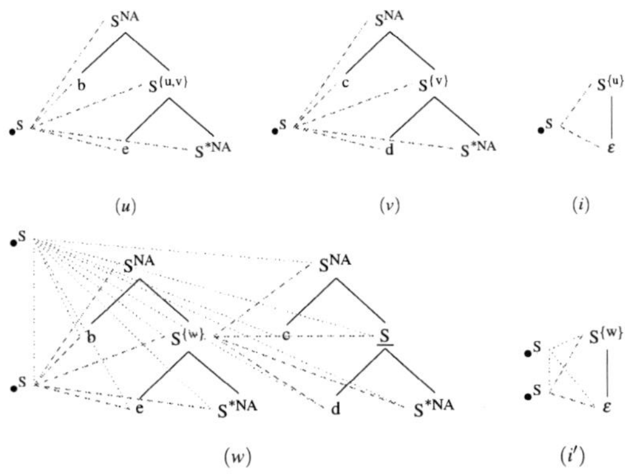

Figure 3: Example of 3- and 4-dimensional TAGs

2.3 Generalization to Multi-Dimensional Trees

Rogers (2003a; 2003b) explores how TAGs can be made more powerful by increasing the dimensionality of elementary trees. Let us illustrate the idea with a simple example first, which is also depicted in Fig. 3.

Consider a TAG with $I := \{i\}$ and $A := \{u, v\}$ such that the only valid adjunction steps are $i \overset{a_i}{\Leftarrow} u$, $u \overset{a_u}{\Leftarrow} u$, $u \overset{a_u}{\Leftarrow} v$, and $v \overset{a_v}{\Leftarrow} v$ for some fixed addresses a_i, a_u, a_v. In Fig. 3, the node at a_i is labeled $S^{\{u\}}$, the one at a_u has label $S^{\{u,v\}}$, and a_v refers to the node with label $S^{\{v\}}$.

This TAG allows derivations of the form iu^*v^*. It is impossible for any TAG to allow only derivations of the form iu^nv^n ($n \geq 0$) so that the number of u-trees matches the number of v-trees. However, a TAG with 4-dimensional trees has sufficient power to generate exactly those derivations.

First we lift i to the 4-dimensional tree i' by adding a single node in the fourth dimension that is the mother of all nodes in the 3-dimensional tree. Then we build a 4-dimensional auxiliary tree w that contains both u and v. Consider the complex 3-dimensional tree t obtained from u and v by identifying the 3-dimensional root of v with the

node at address a_u in u. Just as was done for i we add a new root to t in the fourth dimension that is the 4-dimensional mother of all nodes in t, thus creating the 4-dimensional tree w. We also make the node at address a_v the 3-dimensional foot node of w (indicated by underlining) and add features so that w can optionally adjoin into another instance of w at address a_u. The result is a 4-dimensional TAG that only licenses derivations of the form iw^*, which produce standard TAG derivations of the form iu^nv^n, $n \geq 1$ (see Fig. 4). This example can be lifted to arbitrary dimensions to show that each new dimension adds more power to TAGs.

With the general intuition well-established, we now turn to the formal definition of higher-dimensional TAGs. A detailed axiomatization of multi-dimensional trees has already been provided by Rogers (2003a), so we limit the discussion to the bare essentials.

Let Σ be some fixed alphabet. For the sake of simplicity, we assume that Σ directly encodes adjunction constraints. A 2-dimensional tree is an ordered tree as usually defined, with nodes labeled by symbols drawn from Σ. The tree is *footed* iff it contains a foot node in the second dimension. A *d-dimensional local structure l* over Σ ($d \geq 3$) consists of a Σ-labeled *d-root* r and a $(d-1)$-dimensional tree t over Σ such that r immediately dominates every node n of t along the d-th dimension. The notion of $(d-1)$-dimensional tree will be clarified in the next paragraph. We also call $t := \mathrm{yd}^{d-1}(l)$ the $(d-1)$-*yield* of the local structure, and we say that r is a *d-dimensional mother* of a $(d-1)$-dimensional tree. Lower-dimensional yields are obtained by iterated application of the yield operator: $\mathrm{yd}^n(l) = \mathrm{yd}^n(\mathrm{yd}^{n+1}(\cdots \mathrm{yd}^d(l)))$, $2 \leq n < d$. We sometimes omit the dimension of the yield if it is clear from context.

The set of d-dimensional trees ($d \geq 3$) is defined in a recursive fashion. First, every d-dimensional local structure is a d-dimensional tree. Then t is a d-dimensional tree iff I) its root r and all

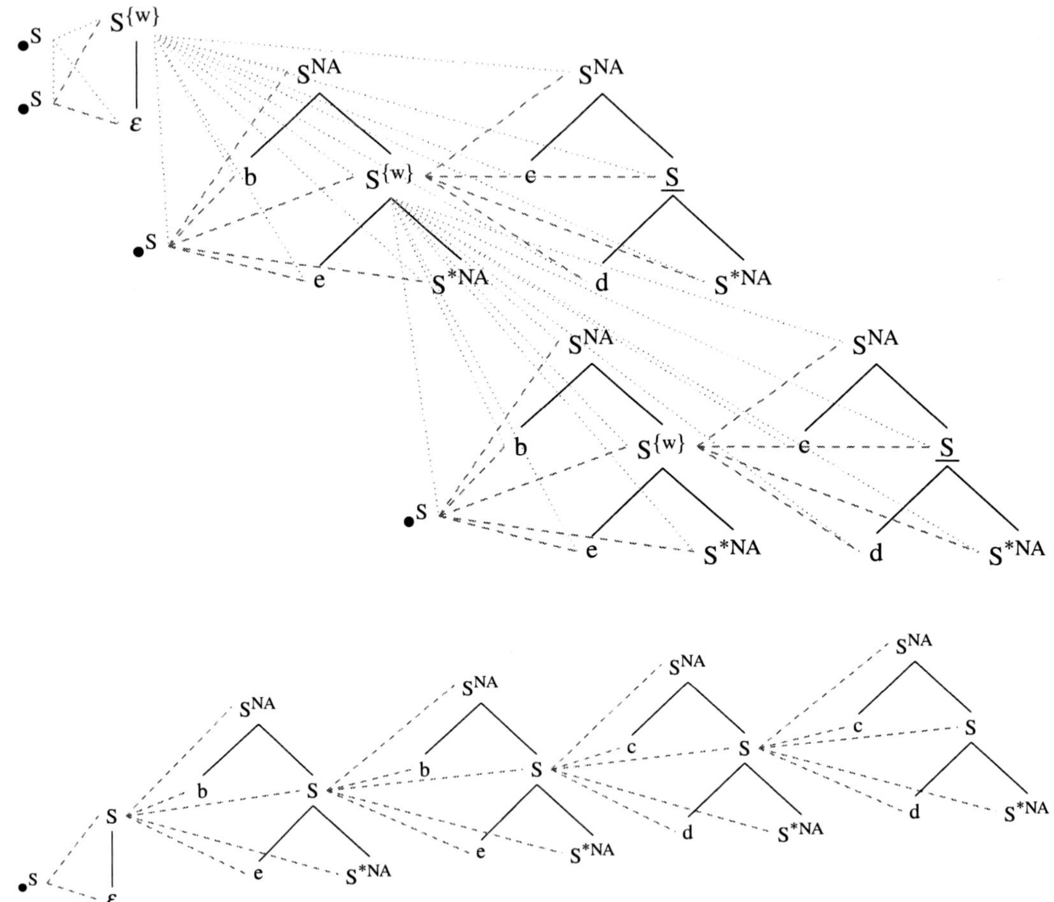

Figure 4: A complex 4-dimensional tree and the 3-dimensional tree obtained from it

the nodes immediately dominated by r along the d-th dimension jointly form a d-dimensional local structure, and II) every node that is immediately dominated by r in the d-th dimension and that is itself a d-dimensional mother must be the root of a d-dimensional tree. A d-dimensional tree is *footed* iff one of its nodes is marked as a $(d-1)$-dimensional foot node. Note that no d-dimensional tree may contain more than one foot node for dimension $(d-1)$. Starting out with the standard definition of 2-dimensional trees it is thus possible to construct 3-dimensional local structures, which can be combined into 3-dimensional trees, from which one can build 4-dimensional local structures, and so on. The examples in Fig. 2 and 4 highlight that d-dimensional trees are indeed trees in the sense that every point is reachable from the d-dimensional root by exactly one path along dimension d.

Whenever the $(d-1)$-dimensional yield of some local d-dimensional structure contains a node that is a mother along the d-th dimension of some $(d-1)$-dimensional tree, this encodes an instance of d-dimensional adjunction (in the generalized sense of Sec. 2.1 with substitution as a special case of adjunction). Consider a d-dimensional tree in which some node n is a d-dimensional mother of a $(d-1)$-dimensional tree u. Then the output of this d-dimensional adjunction is computed as follows. First, n becomes the $(d-1)$-dimensional mother of the $(d-2)$-dimensional v tree whose mother is the root of u. Note that if some nodes of v are $(d-1)$-dimensional mothers, this relation is preserved. Second, if n is already a $(d-1)$-dimensional mother of some $(d-2)$-dimensional tree w and u contains a $(d-1)$-dimensional foot node f, then f becomes the new mother of w. In all other cases, adjunction is undefined. The reader may consult Fig. 4 for a concrete example of 4-dimensional adjunction.

We are now in a position to fully define d-dimensional TAGs. An *elementary d-dimensional tree* (d-tree) is a d-dimensional local structure. It is an *initial d-tree* if it is not footed, and an *auxiliary d-tree* otherwise. Given two elementary d-dimensional trees u and v, we write $u \overset{d\,a}{\Leftarrow} v$ to indicate that v may adjoin into u at node address a. This is tantamount to stating that the grammar allows for d-dimensional trees where the node at address a in $\mathrm{yd}^{d-1}(u)$ is the d-dimensional mother of $\mathrm{yd}^{d-1}(v)$. A *d-dimensional TAG* (d-TAG) G^d

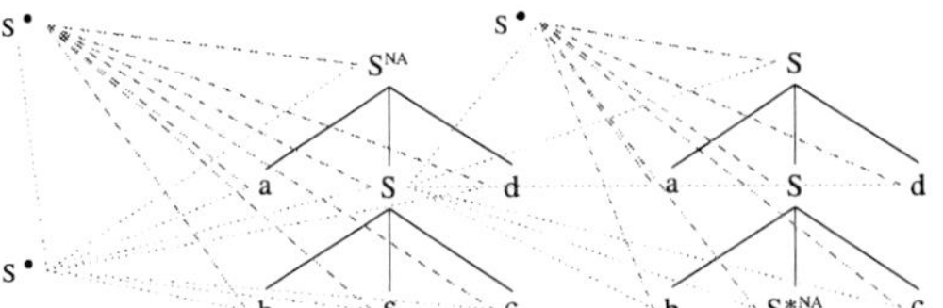

Figure 5: The 3-dimensional adjunction from Fig. 2 is replaced by 4-dimensional substitution

consists of a finite set of *elementary d-trees*. A *d-dimensional TSG* (d-TSG) is the special case of a d-TAG where it holds for every tree that a node is a d-dimensional mother iff it is not a $(d-1)$-dimensional mother.

3 Strong Lexicalization of d-TAGs

3.1 d-TAGs are $(d+1)$-TSGs

The advantage of d-TAGs is that proofs for standard TAGs can be generalized to arbitrary dimension with little modification. The proof that TSGs are strongly lexicalized by TAGs will be suitably modified in the next section, thereby establishing that d-TSGs are strongly lexicalized by d-TAGs. This directly implies that $(d+1)$-TAGs strongly lexicalize d-TAGs thanks to a basic fact we show now: every d-TAG is a $(d+1)$-TSG.

We first observe that a given d-TAG G^d can be easily converted to a $(d+1)$-TAG G^{d+1}. Let e be some elementary d-tree of G^d. We construct an equivalent $(d+1)$-tree e' such that $\mathrm{yd}^d(e') = e$. To this end, let e' be a $(d+1)$-dimensional local structure with root r and yield e such that the label of r is identical to the root label of e. Each node in $\mathrm{yd}^{d-1}(e')$ may (or must) be adjoined to in dimension $d+1$ iff the corresponding node in $\mathrm{yd}^{d-1}(e)$ may (or must) be adjoined to in dimension d.

An example of the construction was already shown in Fig. 3: the 3-dimensional tree i is converted into a 4-dimensional structure i' by adding a new root node S and edges linking the new root to the nodes in i. Since there is a direct link between the 4-dimensional root node and each node in the 3-dimensional tree, every node that was part of i is now a leaf node in i'.

The conversion of interior nodes to leaves is the essential aspect of the construction: all nodes of e' that can be adjoined to are d-dimensional leaves. This holds because e is a d-dimensional local structure, so the only node of e that is not a leaf in dimension d is its root r, which cannot be adjoined to. Clearly every node of e that can be a mother in dimension $(d+1)$ must be a node that can be adjoined to, and consequently it is necessarily a leaf in dimension d. By definition, then, G^{d+1} is a $(d+1)$-TSG.

A concrete example is given in Fig. 5, where the 3-dimensional trees α and β from Fig. 2 have been lifted to 4-dimensional structures via the addition of 4-dimensional root nodes. As a result, the node of 3-dimensional β that α was adjoined to in Fig. 5 is now a leaf node of 4-dimensional β, and the instance of adjunction in the third dimension is replaced by substitution in the fourth dimension.

Proposition 1. For every d-TAG G^d there exists a $(d+1)$-TSG G^{d+1} such that the d-tree language generated by G is the d-yield of the $(d+1)$-tree language generated by G^{d+1}.

3.2 d-TAGs Strongly Lexicalize d-TSGs

It has been known for a long time that TAGs strongly lexicalize TSGs (Schabes, 1990; Joshi and Schabes, 1997; Kuhlmann and Satta, 2012). In this section we show that the corresponding proof can be lifted to multidimensional structures.

Proposition 2. For each finitely ambiguous d-dimensional TSG that does not generate the empty string and contains only useful trees, there is a strongly equivalent d-dimensional Lexicalized TAG.

Let us first consider the general idea behind the construction from Schabes (1990) for normal TSGs, i.e. 3-TAGs where adjunction is only allowed at leaf nodes. Given such a 3-TSG G, we can build a lexicalized 3-TAG G_l that generates the same tree language as G. The basic idea is that G can be bifurcated into a recursive part and a non-recursive part. The recursive part contains all elementary trees u such that there is at least one 3-dimensional tree generated by G in which a node of u dominates another instance of u in the third dimension. The non-recursive part consists of all other elementary 3-trees, which form the set I_l of

initial trees of the lexicalized 3-TAG G_l. The set A_l of auxiliary trees of G_l is then created by taking the recursive part of G and computing its closure under 3-dimensional adjunction of trees from I_l (which is only allowed to target leaf nodes since no $t \in I_l$ contains a foot node). Both I_l and A_l are guaranteed to be finite, so G_l is indeed a 3-TAG. Schabes proves, in our generalized terminology, that G and G_l generate 3-dimensional tree languages with the same 2-dimensional yield.

We now show that Schabes' lexicalization algorithm can be directly lifted to work on d-TAGs such that every d-TSG is strongly lexicalized by some d-TAG. As an illustrative example, we refer to the 3-TSG depicted in Fig. 6 and the equivalent, lexicalized 3-TAG in Fig. 7.

We start out with some well-known concepts from graph theory that are needed in the construction of the graph from which the auxiliary trees are computed. Given a Σ-labeled graph $\mathscr{G} := \langle N, B \rangle$ with set N of nodes and set $B \subseteq N \times \Sigma \times N$ of branches, a *path* on $\mathscr{G}$ is a sequence $\langle n_1, \ldots, n_k \rangle \in N^k$ such that for all $1 \leq i < k$, $\langle n_i, \sigma, n_{i+1} \rangle \in B$ for some $\sigma \in \Sigma$ (we use the term branches instead of the more common "edges" to avoid confusion between E as the set of edges and E as the set of elementary trees of some TAG). If furthermore $n_1 = n_k$, then the path is a *cycle*. A subgraph of $\mathscr{G}$ is a graph $\mathscr{H} = (N', B')$ such that $N' \subseteq N$, $B' \subseteq B$, and $\langle n_1, \sigma, n_2 \rangle \in B'$ implies $n_1, n_2 \in N'$. The *graph composition* (also, *lexicographic product* (Harary, 1972)) $\mathscr{G}_1 \cdot \mathscr{G}_2$ of graphs $\mathscr{G}_1 := \langle N_1, B_1 \rangle$ and $\mathscr{G}_2 := \langle N_2, B_2 \rangle$ is a graph such that: I) the node set of $\mathscr{G}_1 \cdot \mathscr{G}_2$ is the cartesian product $N_1 \times N_2$, and II) any two nodes (u, v) and (x, y) are connected by a σ-labeled edge in $\mathscr{G}_1 \cdot \mathscr{G}_2$ iff either $\langle u, \sigma, x \rangle \in B_1$ or $u = x$ and $\langle u, \sigma, y \rangle \in B_2$.

Now let us consider a d-dimensional finitely ambiguous d-TSG G^d with set I of initial trees such that the string yield of the language generated by G^d does not include the empty string. We also assume that for every initial tree $i \in I$ there is at least one well-formed derivation that contains i. Recall that a d-TSG does not have any auxiliary trees by definition, wherefore all elementary trees of G^d are useful initial trees. A lexicalized d-TAG G_{lex}^d is then built from the d-TSG G^d in four steps.

Step 1: Determine Recursion. In order to distinguish between recursive and non-recursive trees, we build a directed graph $\mathscr{G} = (N, B)$ where N is the set of nodes labeled by the names of the

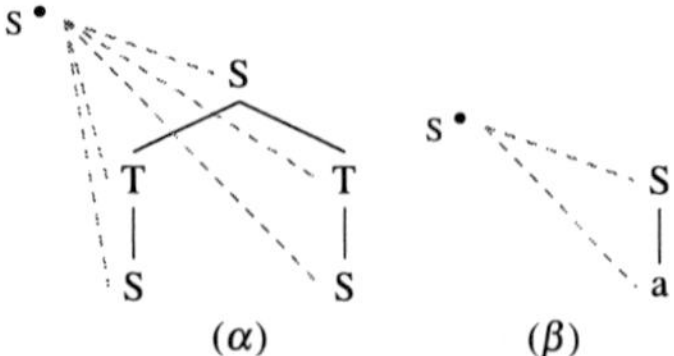

Figure 6: Non-lexicalized 3-dimensional TSG

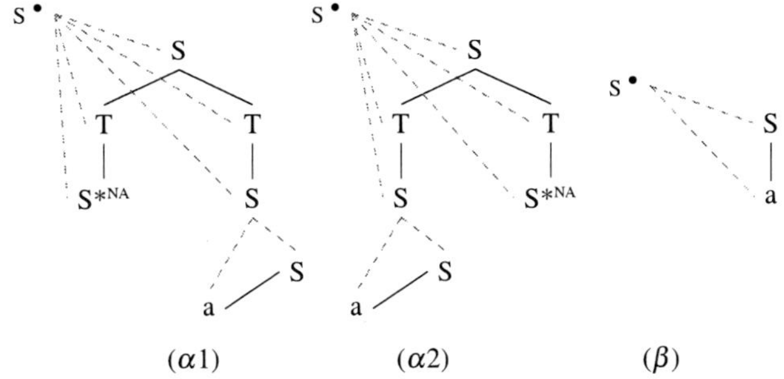

Figure 7: The lexicalized 3-dimensional TAG

trees in I, and $B \subseteq N \times Add \times N$ is a set of branches labeled by tree addresses $a \in Add$. Let us consider $t_1, t_2 \in I$, and let u be the node at address a in $\mathrm{yd}^{d-1}(t_1)$. Then B contains an edge $\langle t_1, a, t_2 \rangle$ iff $t_1 \stackrel{d\,u}{\Longleftarrow} t_2$ is licensed by the grammar. A tree $t \in I$ is *recursive* iff t in G^d belongs to a cycle of $\mathcal{G}$. We use R to denote the set of all recursive initial trees, whereas $NR := I - R$ is the set of non-recursive trees.

Step 2: Construct the set I_{lex} of initial trees. We use $T(NR)$ to denote the closure of NR under adjunction. Since all members of NR are non-recursive, $T(NR)$ is finite. The set I_{lex} of initial trees for the lexicalized d-TAG G_{lex} is the maximal subset of $T(NR)$ that only contains d-trees whose root is labeled by the start category S. As the empty string is not generated by G^d, the initial trees of G_{lex} have at least one terminal symbol on the frontier. In the example in Fig. 6, β is the only initial tree of the new grammar.

Step 3: Compute Cycles. A cycle of $\mathcal{G}$ is *minimal* iff it contains no proper subgraph that is also a cycle. Let C be a set of minimal cycles of $\mathcal{G}$ such that the closure of C under graph composition is the set of all cycles in $\mathcal{G}$. The members of C are referred to as *base cycles*.

Step 4: Construct the set of auxiliary trees. Each base cycle $c_i \in C$ is decomposed as a tree as follows: I) every node of the cycle is expanded as the tree whose name labels the node; II) substitution of a tree into another is performed at the addresses labeling the edge connecting the corresponding nodes; III) the edge leading to recursion is *cut* from the graph and the tree node whose address labeled that edge is labeled as the foot node. A null adjunction constraint (NA) is also put on the foot nodes to disallow recursive adjunction within the auxiliary trees. The set of auxiliary trees for G_{lex}^d is initialized to the empty set A. Then, substitution is exhaustively applied to the nodes in the yield of any of the base cycle trees — except for the unique node marked as a foot node — through the elements of the set of initial trees. The resulting set of trees is the set of auxiliary trees of the lexicalized d-dimensional TAG G_{lex}^d. This concludes the construction of G_{lex}^d.

Figure 7 shows the final lexicalized 3-dimensional grammar. The set of initial trees contains tree β, whereas $\alpha 1$ and $\alpha 2$ belong to the set of auxiliary trees. The resulting d-TAG G_{lex}^d generates exactly the same set of trees as the original, finitely ambiguous d-TSG G^d.

We can now see how previous results directly imply that d-dimensional TAGs strongly lexicalize d-dimensional TSGs. Furthermore, in the previous section we discussed how d-TAGs are equivalent to $(d+1)$-TSGs. This jointly implies that $(d+1)$-TAGs strongly lexicalize d-TAGs.

Proposition 3. For each finitely ambiguous d-dimensional TAG that does not generate the empty string and contains only useful trees, there is a strongly equivalent $(d+1)$-dimensional Lexicalized TAG.

3.3 d-TAGs are Not Closed Under Strong Lexicalization

In the previous sections we have shown that each d-TSG has a strongly equivalent $d+1$-TAG, and that d-TAGs are strongly lexicalized by $(d+1)$-TAGs. These results have been obtained by lifting previous proofs for TAGs to d-dimensional TAGs. However, one might wonder if the extension of TAGs to multidimensional structures is enough to assure lexicalization. In other words, are d-dimensional TAGs closed under strong lexicalization?

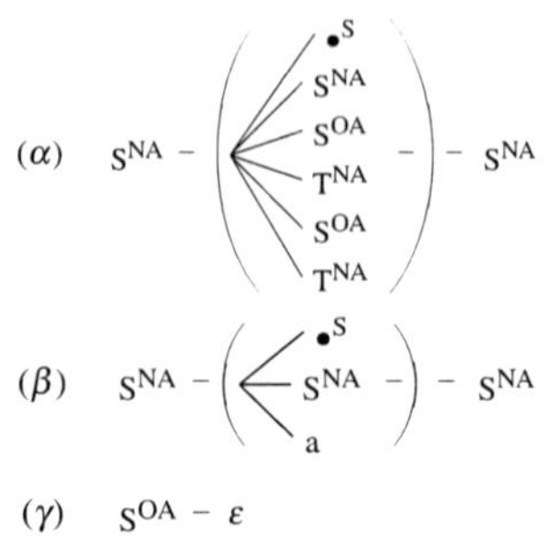

(α) S^{NA} — $\begin{pmatrix} \bullet S \\ S^{NA} \\ S^{OA} \\ T^{NA} \\ S^{OA} \\ T^{NA} \end{pmatrix}$ — S^{NA}

(β) S^{NA} — $\left(\begin{array}{c} \bullet S \\ S^{NA} \; - \\ a \end{array} \right)$ — S^{NA}

(γ) S^{OA} — ε

Figure 8: Parenthetical encoding for the 4-dimensional version of the non lexicalized grammar in Fig. 6

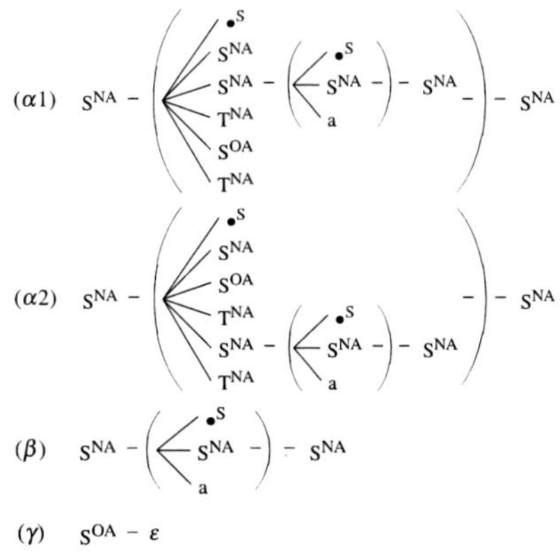

$(\alpha1)$ S^{NA} — $\begin{pmatrix} \bullet S \\ S^{NA} \\ S^{NA} - \left(\begin{array}{c} \bullet S \\ S^{NA} - \\ a \end{array} \right) - S^{NA} \\ T^{NA} \\ S^{OA} \\ T^{NA} \end{pmatrix}$ — S^{NA}

$(\alpha2)$ S^{NA} — $\begin{pmatrix} \bullet S \\ S^{NA} \\ S^{OA} \\ T^{NA} \\ S^{NA} - \left(\begin{array}{c} \bullet S \\ S^{NA} - \\ a \end{array} \right) - S^{NA} \\ T^{NA} \end{pmatrix}$ — S^{NA}

(β) S^{NA} — $\left(\begin{array}{c} \bullet S \\ S^{NA} \; - \\ a \end{array} \right)$ — S^{NA}

(γ) S^{OA} — ε

Figure 9: Parenthetical encoding for a 4-dimensional lexicalized grammar

Diligent readers may have already anticipated that the answer is negative. As before, it suffices to lift an existing proof from the literature to higher dimensions, in this case Kuhlmann and Satta's (2012) result that TAGs are not closed under strong lexicalization. This entails that the increase in dimensionality from d to $d + 1$ brought about by the strong lexicalization procedure cannot be avoided in the general case.

Kuhlmann and Satta start out with the observation that adjunction may be regarded as context-free rewriting on the path of trees. They build a counterexample grammar to show that a lexicalized TAG cannot generate the same trees as the non-lexicalized, original TAG. They then provide a proof based on the intuition that, while a non-lexicalized grammar can potentially extend the length of the shortest path from the tree root node to any terminal node *ad infinitum*, the length of such paths is finitely bounded for the corresponding lexicalized grammar. This property also holds for d-TAGs, where recursive adjunction of d-trees that do not contain any lexical nodes can increase the length of paths without bounds.

Kuhlmann and Satta's proof rests on two basic concepts. The first one is their *parenthetical* notation, which represents trees as string paths and thus highlights how adjunction operates on the path from the root node to a foot node (the *spine* of a tree). The second is a function called *excess*, which is used to measure the distance between a root node and a terminal node on a tree path.

The *parenthetical* encoding of TAGs can be adopted for multidimensional trees without problems. Consider some arbitrary d-dimensional tree T^d. Every leaf node of T^d is reachable from its d-dimensional root following the branches encoding the d-dimensional dominance relation. This unique path from the root node to a frontier node along the d-th dimension is the *spine* of the d-dimensional structure (cf. Rogers (2003a)). The parenthetical notation simply encodes the d-dimensional spine of d-trees: every internal node n along the d-th dimension is represented by a pair of matching brackets, e.g. "S– (" and ") –S"). These brackets surround the parenthetical encoding of the d-dimensional subtree rooted in n. A tree encoded in this notation is called a *spinal tree*. Examples are given in Fig. 8 and 9.

Since d-dimensional trees can be described in the same fashion as 2-dimensional ones via the parenthetical notation, the notion of *excess* remains untouched. For every terminal node v, the excess of v is the mismatch of left parentheses over right parentheses in the sequence of nodes in the path from the d-dimensional root node to v. This is done by subtracting the number of all right parenthesis from the number of all left parenthesis that occur along the path from the root to v. For example, the excess of a in $\alpha2$ of Fig. 9 is 2. The *excess* of the whole spinal tree is always 0.

Let us now return to the 3-TAG given in Fig. 6. It can be lifted to a 4-dimensional TSG as described in the Sec. 2.3. Figure 8 shows a parenthetical rewriting of the 4-dimensional trees in the grammar, while Fig. 9 shows the rewriting of a possible lexicalized d-dimensional grammar, obtained via the procedure in Schabes (1990). Let us call the non-lexicalized parenthetical encoding G_1, and the hypothetical lexicalized version G_1^{lex}. If G_1^{lex} is a correct lexicalization of G_1, it should generate exactly the same 4-dimensional trees. But

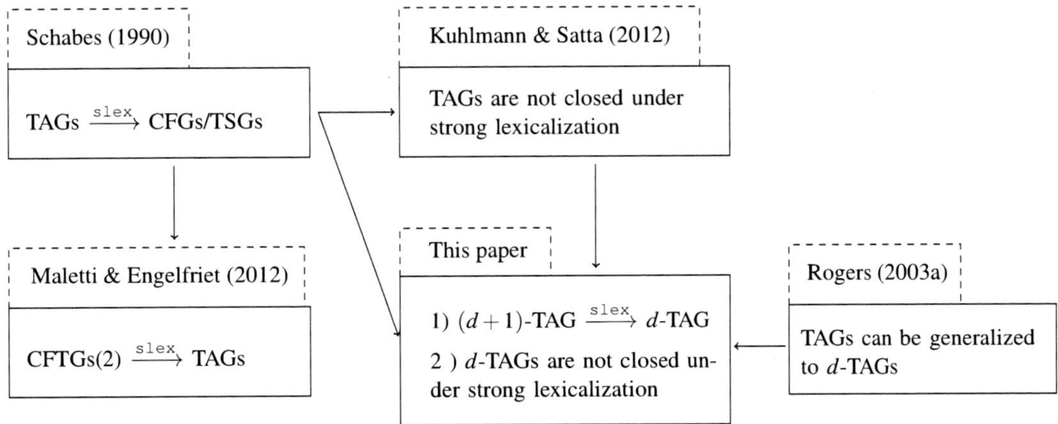

Figure 10: Summary of relevant existing results

the notion of *excess* reveals that this is not the case. In G_1, adjunction of α into another instance of α can take place an arbitrary number of times. As a result, when β finally adjoins into α, an unbounded number of left brackets may occur between the root of the tree and leaf node a of β, wherefore there is no upper bound on the excess of trees generated by G_1. For G_1^{lex}, on the other hand, every tree must contain a lexical node with excess at most 2. Hence G_1 and G_1^{lex} cannot generate the same language of d-trees.

While this simple example does not preclude that some other grammar strongly lexicalizes G_1, this is in fact impossible. Kuhlmann and Satta prove that the potential variation in the excess of a lexical node in an elementary tree is bounded by a constant tied to the grammar, while the excess of a lexical node in a non-lexicalized grammar is potentially infinite. Like so many other facts about 3-TAGs, this one carries over to d-TAGs, too, and consequently d-TAGs turn out not to be closed under strong lexicalization either.

4   Conclusion

The generalization of TAGs to higher-dimensional trees first proposed in Rogers (2003a) is very useful in increasing the power of TAGs while preserving the mechanics of their structure-building operations. This paper has exploited this fact to lift a variety of previously known results about TAGs to higher dimensions, culminating in the realization that TAGs are strongly lexicalized by 4-dimensional TAGs and, more generally, that every d-TAG is strongly lexicalized by some $(d+1)$-TAG. A major advantage of lexicalization is

that it simplifies the parsing problem. At the same time, increasing the dimensionality of TAGs makes parsing harder, which can be gleaned from the fact that 4-dimensional TAGs can generate the 8-language $a^n b^n c^n d^n e^n f^n g^n h^n$, whereas standard (3-dimensional) TAGs are restricted to the 4-language $a^n b^n c^n d^n$. An interesting question for future research will be whether the simplifications of lexicalization can offset the parsing disadvantages of higher dimensions.

Acknowledgments

We are very grateful to the three anonymous reviewers, whose comments led to several improvements in the presentation of the material.

References

Akio Fujiyoshi. 2004. Epsilon-free grammars and lexicalized grammars that generate the class of the mildly contextsensitive languages. In *Proceedings of the 7th International Workshop on Tree Adjoining Grammar and Related Formalisms*, pages 16–23.

Frank Harary. 1972. *Graph Theory*. Addison-Wesley, Reading, MA.

Aravind K. Joshi and Y. Schabes. 1997. Tree-adjoining grammars. In Grzegorz Rosenberg and Arto Salomaa, editors, *Handbook of Formal Languages*, pages 69–123. Springer, Berlin.

Aravind K. Joshi. 1985. Tree-adjoining grammars: How much context sensitivity is required to provide reasonable structural descriptions? In David Dowty, Lauri Karttunen, and Arnold Zwicky, editors, *Natural Language Parsing*, pages 206–250. Cambridge University Press, Cambridge.

Laura Kallmeyer. 2010. *Parsing Beyond Context-Free Grammars*. Springer, Berlin.

Marco Kuhlmann and Giorgio Satta. 2012. Tree-adjoining grammars are not closed under strong lexicalization. *Computational Linguistics*, 38:617–629.

Andreas Maletti and Joost Engelfriet. 2012. Strong lexicalization of tree adjoining grammars. In *Proceedings of the 50th Annual Meeting of the Association for Computational Linguistics: Long Papers - Volume 1*, ACL '12, pages 506–515.

James Rogers. 1998a. A descriptive characterization of tree-adjoining languages. In *Proceedings of the 17th International Conference on Computational Linguistics (COLING'98) and the 36th Annual Meeting of the Association for Computational Linguistics (ACL'98)*, pages 1117–1121.

James Rogers. 1998b. On defining TALs with logical constraints. In Anne Abeillé, Tilman Becker, Owen Rambow, Giorgio Satta, and K. Vijay-Shanker, editors, *Fourth International Workshop on Tree Adjoining Grammars and Related Frameworks (TAG+4)*, pages 151–154.

James Rogers. 2003a. Syntactic structures as multi-dimensional trees. *Research on Language and Computation*, 1:265–305.

James Rogers. 2003b. wMSO theories as grammar formalisms. *Theoretical Computer Science*, 293:291–320.

Yves Schabes, Anne Abeillé, and Aravind K. Joshi. 1988. Parsing strategies with 'lexicalized' grammars: Application to tree adjoining grammars. Technical Report MS-CIS-88-65, Department of Computer & Information Science, University of Pennsylvania, Philadelphia, PA.

Yves Schabes. 1990. *Mathematical and Computational Aspects of Lexicalized Grammars*. Ph.D. thesis, Philadelphia, PA, USA.

Hyperedge Replacement and Nonprojective Dependency Structures

Daniel Bauer and **Owen Rambow**
Columbia University
New York, NY 10027, USA
{bauer,rambow}@cs.columbia.edu

Abstract

Synchronous Hyperedge Replacement Graph Grammars (SHRG) can be used to translate between strings and graphs. In this paper, we study the capacity of these grammars to create non-projective dependency graphs. As an example, we use languages that contain cross serial dependencies. Lexicalized hyperedge replacement grammars can derive string languages (as path graphs) that contain an arbitrary number of these dependencies so that their derivation trees reflect the correct dependency graphs. We find that, in contrast, string-to-graph SHRG that derive dependency structures on the graph side are limited to derivations permitted by the string side. We show that, as a result, string-to-graph SHRG cannot capture languages with an unlimited degree of crossing dependencies. This observation has practical implications for the use of SHRG in semantic parsing.

1 Introduction

Hyperedge Replacement Grammars (HRG) are a type of context free graph grammar. Their derived objects are hypergraphs instead of strings. A synchronous extension, Synchronous Hyperedge Replacement Grammars (SHRG) can be used to translate between strings and graphs. To construct a graph for a sentence, one simply parses the input using the string side of the grammar and then interprets the derivations with the graph side to assemble a derived graph.

SHRG has recently drawn attention in Natural Language Processing as a tool for semantic construction. For example, Jones et al. (2012) propose to use SHRG for semantics based machine translation, and Peng et al. (2015) describe an approach to learning SHRG rules that translate sentences into Abstract Meaning Representation (Banarescu et al., 2013).

Not much work has been done, however, on understanding the limits of syntactic and semantic structures that can be modeled using HRG and SHRG. In this paper, we examine syntactic dependency structures generated by these formalisms, specifially whether they can create correct dependency trees for non-projective phenomena. We focus on non-projectivity caused by copy language like constructions, specifically cross-serial dependencies in Dutch. Figure 1 shows a (classical) example sentence containing such dependencies and a dependency graph.

This paper looks at dependency structures from two perspectives. We first review HRGs that derive string languages as path graphs. The set of these languages is known to be the same as the languages generated by linear context free rewriting systems (Weir, 1992). We consider HRG grammars of this type that are lexicalized (each rule contains exactly one terminal edge), so we can view their *derivation trees* as dependency structures. We provide an example string-generating HRG that can analyze the sentence in Figure 1 with the correct dependency structure and can generate strings with an unlimited number of crossing dependencies of the same type.

Under the second perspective, we view the *derived graphs* of synchronous string-to-HRG grammars as dependency structures. These grammars can generate labeled dependency graphs in a more flexible way, including labeled dependency edges, local reordering of dependencies (allowing a more semantically oriented analysis of prepositional phrases and conjunctions), structures with arbitrary node degree, and reentrancies. We present a grammar to analyze the string/graph pair in Fig-

Proceedings of the 12th International Workshop on Tree Adjoining Grammars and Related Formalisms (TAG+12), pages 103–111,
Düsseldorf, Germany, June 29 - July 1, 2016.

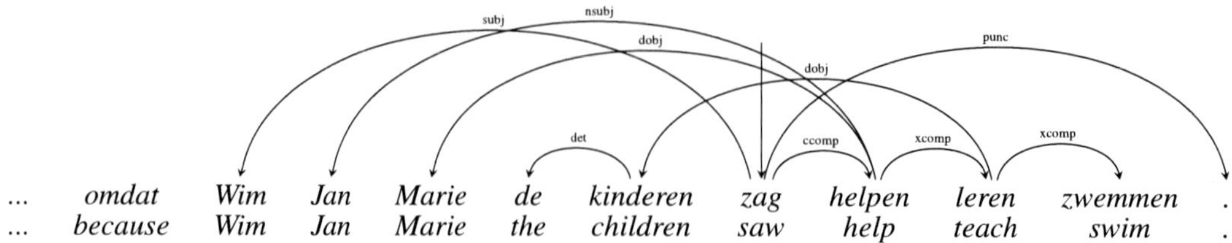

Figure 1: Example sentence illustrating cross-serial dependencies in Dutch. English translation: *"because Wim saw Jan help Marie teach the children to swim."*

ure 1, that derives the correct labeled dependency structure, but whose derivation does not resemble syntactic dependencies. Using this example, we observe an important limitation of string-to-graph SHRG: With nonterminal hyperedges of bounded type (number of incident vertices), we cannot analyze cross-serial dependencies with an unlimited number of crossing edges. Specifically, for a given dependency edge covering a span of words, the number of nodes outside the span that can have a dependent or parent inside the span is limited. This is because, on the input side, the grammar is a plain string CFG. In a string CFG derivation, each node must correspond to a connected subspan of the input. Because of this constraint on the derivation, the dependency subgraphs constructed by the HRG must maintain a reference to all words that have a long distance dependent elsewhere in the string. These references are passed on through the derivation in the external nodes of each graph rhs of the SHRG rules. External nodes are special vertices at which graph fragments are connected to the surrounding graph.

To avoid this problem, instead of a plain string CFG one can use other formalisms that produce context free derivation trees, such as the string-generating HRGs we discuss in this paper or LTAG.

Semantic representations, such as Abstract Meaning Representation, resemble dependency structures. Therefore, while we do not discuss semantic graphs to skirt the issue of reentrancy, non-projective linguistic phenomena that appear in syntactic dependency structure are also relevant when translating strings into semantic representations. We believe that our observations are not only of theoretical interest, but affect practical applications of SHRG in semantic parsing.

The paper proceeds as follows: Section 2 pro-

vides a formalization of Hyperedge Replacement Grammars and introduces necessary terminology. In section 3, we discuss string generating HRGs and illustrate how they can be used to correctly analyze cross-serial dependencies in an example. Section 4 examines string-to-graph SHRGs and observes their limitations in generating cross-serial dependencies. In section 5, we analyze this limitation in more detail, demonstrating a relationship between the *order* of a grammar (the maximum hyperedge type) and the maximum number of edges crossing another edge. Section 6 provides an overview of related work. Finally, we conclude and summarize our findings in section 7.

2 Hyperedge Replacement Graph Grammars

A *directed, edge-labeled hypergraph* is a tuple $H = \langle V, E, \ell \rangle$, where V is a finite set of vertices, $E \subseteq V^+$ is a finite set of hyperedges, each of which connects a number of vertices, and ℓ is a labeling function with domain E. The number of vertices connected by a hyperedge is called its *type*.

A *hyperedge replacement grammar* (HRG, Drewes et al. (1997)) is a tuple $\mathcal{G} = \langle N, \Sigma, P, S \rangle$ where N is a ranked, finite set of nonterminal labels, Σ is a finite set of terminal labels such that $\Sigma \cap N = \emptyset$, $S \in N$ is the designated start symbol, and P is a finite set of rules. Each rule $r \in P$ is of the form $(A \rightarrow R, X)$, where $A \in N$, $R = \langle V, E, \ell \rangle$ is a hypergraph with $\ell \colon E \rightarrow N \cup T$, and $X \in V^*$ is a list of *external nodes*. We call the number of vertices $|V|$ in a rule rhs the *width* of the rule. The maximum type of any nonterminal hyperedge in the grammar is called the *order* of the grammar.[1]

---

[1] We choose the term *order* instead of *rank*. Both terms

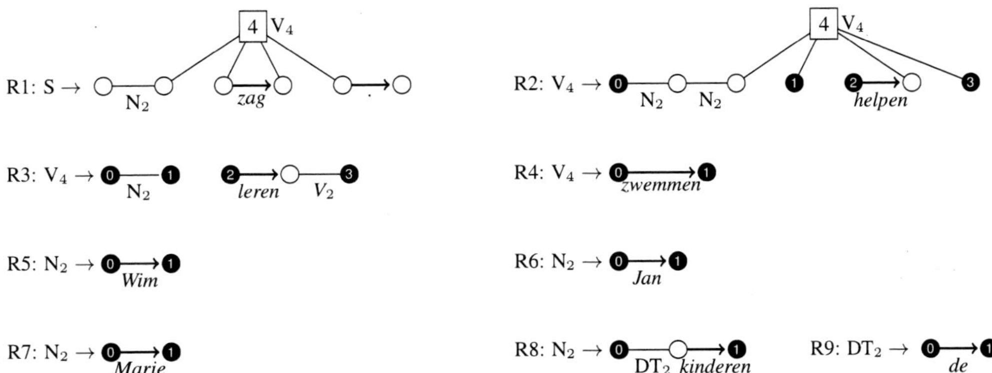

Figure 2: A 'string-generating' lexicalized hyperedge replacement grammar for Dutch cross serial dependencies. The grammar can derive the sentence in figure 1. The derivation tree for this sentence represents the correct dependency structure.

Given a partially derived graph H we can use a rule $(A \rightarrow R, X)$ to rewrite a hyperedge $e = (v_1, \cdots, v_k)$ if e has label A and $k = length(X)$. In this operation, e is removed from H, a copy of R is inserted into H and the external nodes $X = (u_1, \cdots, u_k)$ of the copy of R are *fused* with the nodes connected by e, such that u_i is identified with v_i for $i = 1, \ldots, k$.

When showing rules in diagrams, such as Figure 2, we draw external nodes as black circles and number them with an index to make their order explicit. Nonterminal hyperedges are drawn as undirected edges whose incident vertices are ordered left-to-right.

The relation $H \Rightarrow_{\mathcal{G}} H'$ holds if hypergraph H' can be derived from hypergraph H in a single step using the rules in $\mathcal{G}$. Similarly $H \Rightarrow_{\mathcal{G}}^* H'$ holds if H' can be derived from H in a finite number of steps. The *hypergraph language* of a grammar $\mathcal{G}$ is the (possibly infinite) set of hypergraphs that can be derived from the start symbol S. $L(\mathcal{G}) =$

$$\bigcup_{(S \rightarrow H, \langle \rangle) \in P} \{H \Rightarrow_{\mathcal{G}}^* H' | H' \text{ has only terminals }\}$$

We will show examples for HRG derivations below.

HRG derivations are context-free in the sense that the applicability of each production depends on the nonterminal label and type of the replaced edge only. We can therefore represent derivations as trees, as for other context free formalisms. Context freeness also allows us to extend the formalism to a synchronous formalism, for example to

translate strings into trees, as we do in section 4. We can view the resulting string and graph languages as two interpretations of the same set of possible derivation trees described by a regular tree grammar (Koller and Kuhlmann, 2011).

3 HRG Derivations as Dependency Structures

We first discuss the case in which HRG is used to derive a sentence and examine the dependency structure induced by the derivation tree. Hyperedge Replacement Grammars can derive string languages as path graphs in which edges are labeled with tokens. For example, consider the path graph for the sentence in Figure 1.

Wim   Jan Marie de kinderen zag   helpen leren zwemmen

Engelfriet and Heyker (1991) show that the string languages generated by HRG in this way are equivalent to the output languages of Deterministic Tree Walking Transducers (DTWT). Weir (1992) shows that these languages are equivalent to the languages generated by linear context free rewriting systems (LCFRS) and that the LCFRS languages with fan-out k are the same as the HRG string languages with order $2k$.

The analysis of cross-serial dependencies has been studied in a number of 'mildly context sensitive' grammar formalisms. For example, Rambow and Joshi (1997) show an analysis in LTAG. Because the string languages generated by these formalisms are equivalent to languages of LCFRS with fan-out 2, we know that we must be able to write an HRG of order 4 that can capture cross-

---

are used in the literature. We use the word *rank* to refer to the maximum number of nonterminals in a rule right hand side.

serial dependencies.

Figure 2 shows such a string generating HRG that can derive the example in Figure 1. Each rule rhs consists of one or more internally connected spans of strings paths of labeled edges. The external nodes of each rhs graph mark the beginning and end of each span. The nonterminal labels of other rules specify how these spans are combined and connected to the surrounding string. For illustration, consider the first two steps of a derivation in this grammar. Rule 1 introduces the verb '*zag*' and its subject. Rule 2 inserts '*helpen*' to the right of '*zag*' and its subject and direct object to the right of the subject of '*zag*'. This creates crossing dependencies between the subjects and their predicates in the derivation.

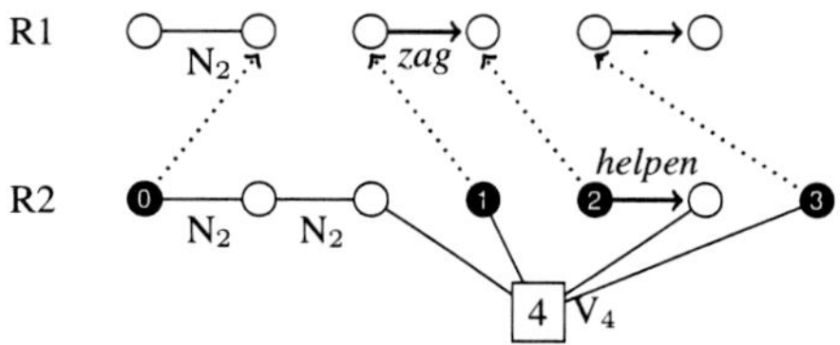

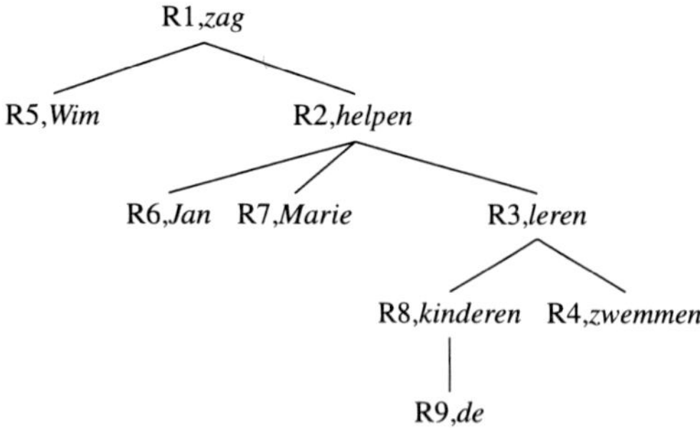

The partially derived graph now contains a span of nouns and a span of verbs. The nonterminal hyperedge labeled V_4 indicates where to append new nouns and where to add new verbs. Note that rule 2 (or an identical rule for a different verb) can be re-applied to generate cross-serial dependencies with an arbitrary number of crossings. It is easy to see that grammars of this type correspond to LCFRS almost directly.

Using the grammar in Figure 2, there is a single derivation tree for the example sentence in Figure 1.

This derivation tree represents the correct syntactic dependency structure for the sentence. This is not the case for all lexicalized 'mildly context sensitive' grammar formalisms, even if it is possible to write grammars for languages that contain cross-serial dependencies. In TAG, long distance dependencies are achieved using adjunction.

Both dependents are introduced by the same auxiliary tree, stretching the host tree apart. An LTAG derivation for the example sentence would start with an elementary tree for '*zwemmen*' and then adjoin '*leren*'. The resulting dependency structure is therefore inverted.

4 Deriving Dependency Graphs with Synchronous String-to-Graph Grammars

We now consider grammars whose *derived* graphs represent the dependency structure of a sentence. The goal is to write a synchronous context-free string-to-graph grammar that translates sentences into their dependency graphs. If the string side of the grammar is a plain string CFG, as we assume here, the derivation cannot reflect non-projective dependencies directly. Instead, we must use the graph side of the grammar to assemble a dependency structure.

This approach has several potential advantages in applications. In the string-generating HRG discussed in the previous section, the degree of a node in the dependency structure is limited by the rank of the grammar. Using a graph grammar to derive the graph, we can add an arbitrary number of dependents to a node, even if the rules contributing these dependency edges are nested in the derivation. This is especially important for more semantically inspired representations where all semantic arguments should become direct dependents of a node (for example, deep subjects). We can also make the resulting graphs reentrant. In addition, because HRGs produce labeled graphs, we can add dependency labels. Finally, even though the example grammar in Figure 3 is lexicalized on the string side, lexicalization is no longer required to build a dependency structure. Unfortunately, 'decoupling' the derivation from the dependency structure in this way can be problematic, as we will see.

Figure 3 shows a synchronous hyperedge replacement grammar that can translate the sentence from Figure 1 into its dependency graph. A *synchronous hyperedge replacement grammar* (SHRG) is a synchronous context free grammar in which at least one of the right hand sides uses hypergraph fragments. The two sides of the grammar are synchronized in a strong sense. Both rhs of each grammar rule contain exactly the same instances of nonterminals and the instances

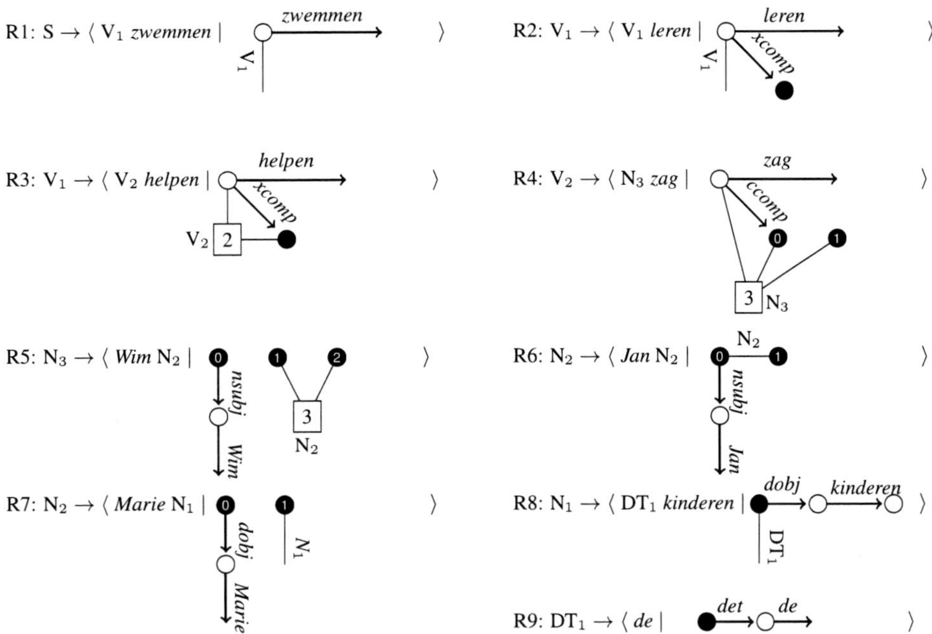

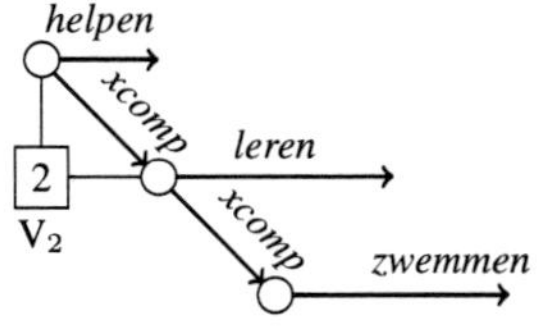

Figure 3: A synchronous string-to-graph grammar for Dutch cross-serial dependencies. The grammar can derive the sentence/dependency graph pair in in Figure 1, but the derivation tree does not reflect syntactic dependencies.

are related by a bijective synchronization relation (in case of ambiguity we make the bijection explicit by indexing nonterminals when representing grammars). In a SHRG, each nonterminal label can only be used to label hyperedges of the same type. For example, V_2 is only used for hyperedges of type 2. As a result, all derivations for the string side of the grammar are also valid derivations for graphs.

In the grammar in Figure 3, vertices represent nodes in the dependency structure (words). Because HRGs derive edge labeled graphs but no vertex labels, we use a unary hyperedge (a hyperedge with one incident vertex) to label each node. For example, the only node in the rhs of rule 1 has the label 'zwemmen'.

Nonterminal hyperedges are used to 'pass on' vertices that we need to attach a dependent to at a later point in the derivation. External nodes define how these nodes are connected to the surrounding derived graph. To illustrate this, a derivation using the grammar in Figure 3 could start with rule 1, then replace the nonterminal V_1 with the rhs of rule 2. We then substitute the new nonterminal V_1 introduced by rule 2 with rule 3. At this point, the partially derived string

is 'V_2 helpen leren zwemmen' and the partially derived graph is

The nonterminal V_2 passes on a reference to two nodes in the graph, one for 'helpen' and one for 'leren'. This allows subsequent rules in the derivation to attach subjects and objects to these nodes, as well as the parent node ('zag') to 'helpen'.

To derive the string/graph pair in Figure 1, the rules of this grammar are simply applied in order (rule 1 $\Rightarrow$ rule 2 $\Rightarrow$ $\cdots$ $\Rightarrow$ rule 9). Clearly, the resulting derivation is just a chain and bears no resemblance to the syntactic dependency structure.

While the grammar can derive our example sentence, it does not permit us to derive dependency structures with an arbitrary number of crossing dependencies. This is because the nonterminal edges need to keep track of all possible sites at which long distance dependents can be attached at a later point in the derivation. To add more crossing

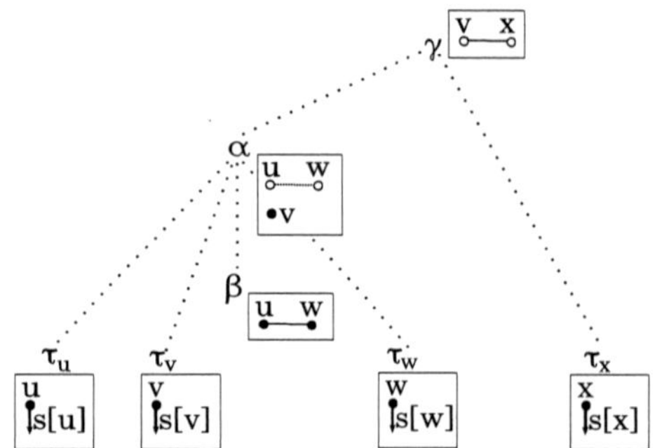

Figure 4: Sketch of the derivation tree of a synchronous hyperedge replacement grammar, showing two dependency edges (u, w) and (v, x), and $u < v < w < x$. The graph fragment associated with the rule at node α needs to contain nodes u, w and v. v must be an external node.

dependencies we therefore need to create special rules with nonterminal hyperedges of a larger type, as well as the corresponding rules with a larger number of external nodes. Because any grammar has a finite number of rules and a fixed order, we cannot use this type of SHRG grammar to model languages that permit an arbitrary degree of crossing edges in a graph. While the graph grammar can keep track of long-distance dependencies, the string grammar is still context free, so any non-local information needs to be encoded in the nonterminals. The penalty we pay for being able to remember a limited set of dependents through the derivation is that we need a refined alphabet of nonterminals (V_1, V_2, V_3, $\cdots$; instead of just V).

5 Edge Degree and Hyperedge Type

In section 4 we demonstrate that we need an ever-increasing hyperedge type if we want to model languages in which a dependency edge can be crossed by an arbitrary number of other dependency edges. So far, we have only illustrated this point with an example. In this section we will demonstrate that no such grammar can exist.

It is clear that the problem is not with generating the tree language itself. We could easily extend the string-generating grammar from section 3, whose derivation trees reflect the correct dependency structure, by adding a second graph rhs that derives an image of the derivation tree (potentially with dependency labels). Instead, the problem appears to be that we force grammar rules to be applied according to the string derivation.

Specifically, the partially derived string associated with each node in the derivation needs to be a contiguous subspan. This prevents us from assembling dependencies locally.

To make this intuition more formal, we demonstrate that there is a relationship between number of crossing dependencies and the the minimum hyperedge type required in the SHRG. We first look at a single pair of crossing dependency edges and then generalize the argument to multiple edges crossing into the span of an edge. For illustration, we provide a sketch of a SHRG derivation tree in Figure 4.

Assume we are given a sentence $s = (w_0, w_1, \cdots, w_{n-1})$, and a corresponding dependency graph $G = \langle V, E, \ell \rangle$ where $V = \{0, 1, \cdots, n - 1\}$. We define the range of a dependency edge (u, v) to be the interval $[u, v]$ if $v > u$ or else $[v, u]$. For each dependency edge (u, v) the number of crossing dependencies is the number of dependency nodes properly outside its range, that share a dependency edge with any node properly inside its range. The degree of crossing dependencies of a dependency graph is the maximum number of crossing dependencies for any of its edges.

Given a SHRG derivation tree for s and G, each terminal dependency edge $(u, w) \in E$ must be produced by the rule associated with some derivation node β (see Figure 4). Without loss of generality, assume that $u < w$. String token $s[u]$ is produced by the rule associated with some derivation node τ_u and $s[w]$ is produced by the rule of some derivation node τ_w. On the graph side, τ_u and τ_w must contain the nodes u and w because they generate the unary hyperedges labeling these vertices. There must be some common ancestor α of β, τ_u, and τ_w that contains both u and w. u and w must be connected in α by a nonterminal hyperedge, because otherwise there would be no way to generate the terminal edge (u, w) in β (note that it is possible that α and β are the same node in which case the rule of this node does not contain a nonterminal edge).

Now consider another pair of nodes v and x such that $u < v < w < x$ and there is a dependency edge $(v, x) \in E$ or $(x, v) \in E$. $s[v]$ is generated by τ_v and $s[x]$ is generated by τ_x. As before, there must be a common ancestor γ of τ_v and τ_x, in which v and x are connected by a nonterminal hyperedge. Because $u < v < w < x$ either

α is an ancestor of γ or γ is an ancestor of α. For illustration, we assume the second case. The case where α dominates γ is analogous.

Since the graph fragments of all derivation nodes on the path from γ to τ_v must contain a vertex that maps to v, α must contain such a vertex. This vertex needs to be an external node of the rule attached to α because otherwise v could not be introduced by γ.

We can extend the argument to an arbitrary number of crossing dependency edges. As before, let (u, w) be a dependency edge and α be the derivation node whose graph fragment first introduces the nonterminal edge between u and w. For *all* dependency edges (x, y) or (y, x) for which y is in the range of (u, w) and x is outside of the range of (u, w) (either $x < u < y < w$ or $u < y < w < x$) there must be some path in the derivation tree that leads through α. All graph fragments on this path contain a vertex mapped to y. As a result, the graph fragment in α needs to contain one external node for each x that has a dependency edge to some node y inside the range (u, w). In other words, α needs to contain as many external nodes as there are nodes outside the range (u, w) that share a dependency edge with a node inside the range (u, w).

Because every HRG has a fixed order (the maximum type of any nonterminal hyperedge), no SHRG that generates languages with an arbitrary number of cross-serial dependencies can exist. It is known that the hypergraph languages $\mathcal{HRL}_k$ that can be generated by HRGs of order k form an infinite hierarchy, i.e. $\mathcal{HRL}_1 \subsetneq \mathcal{HRL}_2 \subsetneq \cdots$ (Drewes et al., 1997). Therefore, the string-to-graph grammars required to generate cross-serial dependencies up to edge degree k are strictly more expressive than those that can only generate edge degree $k - 1$.

6 Related Work

While the theory of graph grammars dates back to the 70s (Nagl, 1979; Drewes et al., 1997), their use in Natural Language Processing is more recent. Fischer (2003) use string generating HRG to model discontinuous constituents in German. Jones et al. (2012) introduce SHRG and demonstrate an application to construct intermediate semantic representations in machine translation. Peng et al. (2015) automatically extract SHRG rules from corpora annotated with graph based

meaning representations (Abstract Meaning Representation), using Markov Chain Monte Carlo techniques. They report competitive results on string-to-graph parsing. Braune et al. (2014) empirically compare SHRG to cascades of tree transducers as devices to translate English strings into reentrant semantic graphs. In agreement with the result we show more formally in this paper, they observe that, to generate graphs that contain a larger number of long-distance dependencies, a larger grammar with more nonterminals is needed, because the derivations of the grammar are limited to string CFG derivations.

Synchronous context free string-graph grammars have also been studied in the framework of Interpreted Regular Tree Grammar (Koller and Kuhlmann, 2011) using S-Graph algebras (Koller, 2015). In the TAG community, HRGs have been discussed by Pitsch (2000), who shows a construction to convert TAGs into HRGs. Finally, Joshi and Rambow (2003) discuss a version of TAG in which the *derived* trees are dependency trees, similar to the SHRG approach we present here.

To use string-generating HRG in practice we need a HRG parser. Chiang et al. (2013) present an efficient graph parsing algorithm. However, their implementation assumes that graph fragments are connected, which is not true for the grammar in section 3. On the other hand, since string-generation HRGs are similar to LCFRS, any LCFRS parser could be used. The relationship between the two parsing problems merits further investigation. Seifert and Fischer (2004) describe a parsing algorithm specificaly for string-generating HRGs.

Formal properties of dependency structures generated by lexicalized formalisms have been studied in detail by Kuhlmann (2010). He proposes measures for different types of non-projectivity in dependency structures, including *edge degree* (which is related to the degree of crossing dependencies we use in this paper), and *block degree*. A qualitative measure of dependency structures is well nestedness, which indicates whether there is an overlap between subtrees that do not stand in a dominance relation to each other. In future work, we would like to investigate how these measures relate to dependency structures generated by HRG derivations and SHRG derived graphs.

7   Conclusion

In this paper we investigated the capability of hyperedge replacement graph grammars (HRG) and synchronous string-to-graph grammar (SHRG) to generate dependency structures for non-projective phenomena. Using Dutch cross-serial dependencies as an example, we compared two different approaches: string-generating HRGs whose derivation trees can be interpreted as dependency structures, and string-to-graph SHRGs, whose can create dependency structures as their derived graphs.

We provided an example grammar for each case. The derivation tree of the HRG adequately reflected syntactic dependencies and the example grammar could in principle generate an arbitrary number of crossing dependencies. However, these derivation trees are unlabeled and cannot be extended to represent deeper semantic relationships (e.g semantic argument structure and coreference). For the string-to-graph SHRG, we saw that the derived graph of our grammar represented the correct dependencies for the example sentence, while the derivation tree did not.

The main observation of this paper is that, unlike the string-generating HRG, the string-to-graph SHRG was only able to generate a limited number of crossing dependencies. With each additional crossing edge in the example, we needed to add a new rule with a higher hyperedge type, increasing the order of the grammar. We argued that the reason for this is that the synchronous derivation for the input string and output graph is constrained to be a valid string CFG derivation. Analyzing this observation more formally, we showed a relationship between the order of the grammar and the maximum permitted number of edges crossing into the span of another edge.

An important conclusion is that, unless the correct syntactic dependencies are already local in the derivation, HRGs cannot derive dependency graphs with an arbitrary number of cross-serial dependencies. We take this to be a strong argument for using lexicalized formalisms in synchronous grammars for syntactic and semantic analysis, that can process at least a limited degree of non-projectivity, such as LTAG.

In future work, we are aiming to develop a lexicalized, synchronous string-to-graph formalisms of this kind. We would also like to relate our results to other measures of non-projectivity discussed in the literature. Finally, we hope to expand the results of this paper to other non-projective phenomena and to semantic graphs.

References

Laura Banarescu, Claire Bonial, Shu Cai, Madalina Georgescu, Kira Griffitt, Ulf Hermjakob, Kevin Knight, Philipp Koehn, Martha Palmer, and Nathan Schneider. 2013. Abstract meaning representation for sembanking. In *Linguistic Annotation Workshop*.

Fabiene Braune, Daniel Bauer, and Kevin Knight. 2014. Mapping between english strings and reentrant semantic graphs. In *Proceedings of LREC*, Reykjavik, Iceland.

David Chiang, Jacob Andreas, Daniel Bauer, Karl-Mortiz Hermann, Bevan Jones, and Kevin Knight. 2013. Parsing graphs with hyperedge replacement grammars. In *Proceedings of ACL*, Sofia, Bulgaria.

Frank Drewes, Annegret Habel, and Hans-Jörg Kreowski. 1997. Hyperedge replacement graph grammars. In Grzegorz Rozenberg, editor, *Handbook of Graph Grammars and Computing by Graph Transformation*, pages 95–162. World Scientific.

Joost Engelfriet and Linda Heyker. 1991. The string generating power of context-free hypergraph grammars. *Journal of Computer and System Sciences*, 43(2):328–360.

Ingrid Fischer. 2003. Modeling discontinuous constituents with hypergraph grammars. In *International Workshop on Applications of Graph Transformations with Industrial Relevance (AGTIVE)*, pages 163–169.

Bevan Jones, Jacob Andreas, Daniel Bauer, Karl-Moritz Hermann, and Kevin Knight. 2012. Semantics-based machine translation with hyperedge replacement grammars. In *Proceedings of COLING*, Mumbai, India. First authorship shared.

Aravind Joshi and Owen Rambow. 2003. A formalism for dependency grammar based on tree adjoining grammar. *Proceedings of the Conference on Meaning-Text Theory*, pages 207–216.

Alexander Koller and Marco Kuhlmann. 2011. A generalized view on parsing and translation. In *Proceedings of the 12th International Conference on Parsing Technologies*, pages 2–13. Association for Computational Linguistics.

Alexander Koller. 2015. Semantic construction with graph grammars. In *Proceedings of the 11th International Conference on Computational Semantics (IWCS)*, pages 228–238.

Marco Kuhlmann. 2010. *Dependency Structures and Lexicalized Grammars: An Algebraic Approach*, volume 6270. Springer.

Manfred Nagl. 1979. A tutorial and bibliographical survey on graph grammars. In *Proceedings of the International Workshop on Graph-Grammars and Their Application to Computer Science and Biology*, pages 70–126, London, UK, UK. Springer-Verlag.

Xiaochang Peng, Linfeng Song, and Daniel Gildea. 2015. A synchronous hyperedge replacement grammar based approach for amr parsing. In *Proceedings of CONLL*.

Gisela Pitsch. 2000. Hyperedge replacement and tree adjunction. In Anne Abeillè and Owen Rambow, editors, *Tree Adjoining Grammars*. CSLI.

Owen Rambow and Aravind Joshi. 1997. A formal look at dependency grammars and phrase-structure grammars, with special consideration of word-order phenomena. In Leo Wanner, editor, *Recent Trends in Meaning-Text Theory*, pages 167–190. John Benjamins, Amsterdam and Philadelphia.

Sebastian Seifert and Ingrid Fischer. 2004. Parsing string generating hypergraph grammars. In *International Conference on Graph Transformations(ICGT)*, pages 352–367.

David J. Weir. 1992. Linear context-free rewriting systems and deterministic tree-walking transducers. In *Proceedings of ACL*, pages 136–143, Newark, Delaware, USA, June. Association for Computational Linguistics.

Parasitic Gaps and the Heterogeneity of Dependency Formation in STAG

Dennis Ryan Storoshenko
Department of Linguistics, Languages and Cultures
The University of Calgary
dstorosh@ucalgary.ca

Robert Frank
Department of Linguistics
Yale University
bob.frank@yale.edu

Abstract

This paper presents an account of parasitic gaps in Synchronous TAG, making use of the more flexible semantic derivations that derive from the proposal in Frank and Storoshenko (2012) to add separate scope components to all predicates. We model parasitic gaps as deriving from a TAG analog of sidewards movement (Nunes, 2004), where the licensing wh-phrase combines first with the domain containing the parasitic gap, which then combines with the main clause domain via tree-local multi-component combination. Such tree-local derivations are possible only because of the manipulations of scope available in the semantics. The phenomenon explored here not only shows the continued role of the syntax in constraining syntactic dependencies, but also demonstrates the potential for derivations which are syntactically well-formed, but are rendered impossible due to the improper binding of the parasitic gap variable.

1 Overt and Covert Dependencies in TAG

Frank and Storoshenko (2012) propose a new conception of the semantic side of a synchronous TAG. Following proposals beginning with Kallmeyer and Joshi (1999), where the representation of quantifiers in TAG consists of a multi-component set including both a scope component and a variable component, Frank and Storoshenko advocate a similar division for the trees headed by lexical predicates. Specifically, they propose that the semantics of each lexical head includes a predicate component, in which each of the predi-

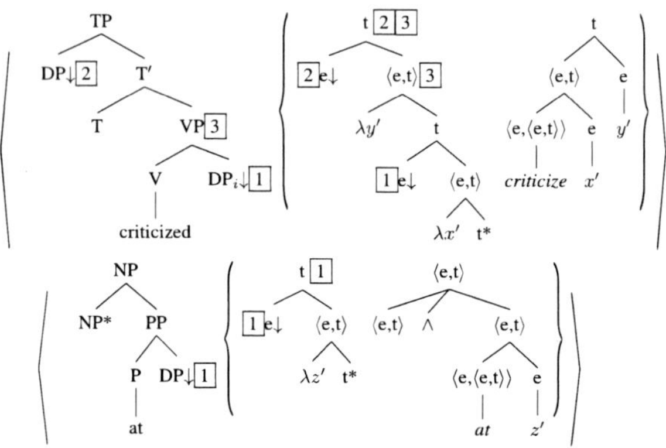

Figure 1: STAG elementary tree pairs following Frank and Storoshenko (2012).

cate's arguments is saturated by a variable, and a scope component, in which each of the variables introduced in the predicate component is lambda bound and the operator is saturated by a substitution node. It is substitution into the scope component, then, which accomplishes the saturation of the arguments of the predicate. Examples of such representations for the transitive verb *criticize* and the preposition *at* are given in Figure 1. The inclusion of a quantifier-like scope component in the elementary semantic object associated with a lexical predicate has a number of salutary consequences. It predicts, for instance, that lexical predicates can themselves introduce quantificational force over their arguments. We see this in cases of passivization, where the suppressed subject is existentially quantified. That such a subject must be present in the semantics is supported by its capacity to control into purpose clauses:

(1) The boat was sunk [PRO to collect the insurance]

In a number of languages, including ASL (Petronio, 1995), Gun-djeyhmi, and Warlpiri (Evans,

Proceedings of the 12th International Workshop on Tree Adjoining Grammars and Related Formalisms (TAG+12), pages 112–120,
Düsseldorf, Germany, June 29 - July 1, 2016.

1995), affixes on the verb can impose collective or distributive interpretations over certain arguments, suggesting the presence of a quantifier in the scope component that quantifies over that argument. In English, a similar phenomenon is found with "stubbornly distributive predicates": a plural subject of such a predicate must receive a distributive interpretation, so that (2) can only mean that each of the boxes is large, and not that the collection of boxes is large.

(2)   The boxes are large.

Again, this interpretational requirement can be represented through the presence of a universal quantifier in the scope component of predicates like *large* which takes the semantics of the subject to delimit its domain of quantification.

What motivated Frank and Storoshenko to make this proposal, however, was the fact that the scope-predicate conception of semantic tree sets allows for tree-local MCTAG derivations of cases of scopal interpretations such as (3), in which the quantifier scopes out of an adjunct.

(3)   Donald criticized three groups from every state. ($\forall > 3, 3 > \forall$)

Such examples had been taken by Nesson and Shieber (2008) to motivate the adoption of more powerful regimens of TAG derivation. Without the separate scope component, the tree local introduction of a quantifier *every state* into *from*'s elementary tree would leave the quantifier stranded inside of the modifier's semantics. With the revised representation, however, the quantifier can be tree-locally adjoined into the scope component. The two components of the preposition can then adjoin into the scope component of the quantifier *three groups*, with the location of the adjoining determining the relative scope of the two quantifiers. To complete the derivation, the two components of the object quantifier can adjoin into the scope component of *criticized*, which we assume will combine with its own predicate component.

Given the increased derivational flexibility offered by this new conception of semantic elementary trees, one might wonder whether it undermines previous work in TAG that derives locality in movement from constraints on how trees can combine. Starting with Kroch and Joshi (1985) and continuing to Frank (2002) and beyond, it has been argued that the impossibility of extraction from syntactic islands such as (4) derives from the nature of elementary trees coupled with the way in which TAG derivations proceed.

(4)   *Which state did Donald criticize the man who was from t?

Roughly speaking, this example is blocked because there is no way for the wh-phrase *which state* to end up at the front of the clause if it is inserted into the elementary tree representing the relative clause of which it is an argument. Could the flexibility afforded by scope-predicate semantic trees somehow undermine these results?

An easy, but ultimately less than satisfying, response to this question asserts that such flexibility doesn't arise for overt syntactic movement because there is no compelling motivation for the split of syntactic elementary trees on par with that which has been proposed for semantic elementary trees. Yet, even if such a split were in fact desirable for the syntax, it turns out that examples like (4) would still be blocked. To derive (4) in a massively multi-component syntax, *which state* could be inserted into an upper component associated with the relative clause. At the next step in the derivation, where the relative clause is attached to the elementary tree associated with the nominal *man*, the lower component of the relative must attach directly to the lower component of the nominal, since that is its surface position. By tree-locality, this would force the higher component of the relative, containing the wh-phrase *which state*, into the DP structure as opposed to a putative higher component of the DP, leaving it unable to reach the left peripheral position of the clause. Similar arguments can be constructed for the other "strong islands" that have been shown to derive from the TAG derivation. In short, the creation of overt syntactic dependencies are more constrained than their covert counterparts because the fact that the derivation needs to produce the correct ordering of phonological material constrains the derivation to involve the lower components.

In the remainder of this paper, we will examine another class of syntactic dependencies, involving parasitic gaps, which have not be widely explored in the TAG literature (but cf. Frank (1991)). These gaps are interesting because while they are licensed by an overt syntactic dependency, the parasitic gap does not, we claim, involve the displacement of any element in the syntax (cf. Chomsky (1982)), and is instead modulated through dependencies formed on the semantic side of the derivation. As a result, parasitic gaps permit greater derivational flexibility than the dependencies found in usual cases of overt wh-movement.

2 Parasitic Gaps

Parasitic Gap (PG) constructions are broadly defined as a set of sentences in which one trace or gap left behind by an A′ extraction is only licit when another such gap exists in the sentence (Engdahl, 1983). An example of this appears in (5):

(5) **Which papers** did Bill file ___ without Carl reading ___$_p$?

In this example, extraction from the object position of *file* is independently well-formed, though it is not possible to extract the object of *reading* in the adjunct clause on its own.

(6) *? **Which papers** did Bill file the grades without Carl reading ___$_p$?

PGs can also occur inside infinitival adjuncts, as in (7), where the arguments of the matrix and adjunct clauses are identified.

(7) **Which papers** did Carl file ___ without reading ___$_p$?

As has been widely discussed, PGs are able to be able to occur in other (strong) island contexts, such subject islands, so long as there is an additional, independently well-formed instance of extraction.

(8) a. **Which boy** did [Mary's talking to ___$_p$] bother ___?

  b. **What car** did [the attempt to repair ___$_p$] ultimately break ___?

There are three main analytical puzzles posed by PGs. First, how does a single wh-phrase bind multiple gaps? Second, how is the appearance of the PG dependent on the occurrence of another? Finally, how does the existence of one well-formed filler-gap dependency license another one that crosses an island boundary. In the following sections, we present an analysis of PG constructions in STAG, that provides an solution to both of these puzzles. We demonstrate that the distribution of well-formed parasitic gaps is determinable by a combination of syntactic factors and constraints on the semantic derivation of the PG which are only made possible once the scope trees introduced in the previous section are used. In doing so, we also show that our analysis accounts for a number of previously observed properties of PGs.

3 An Analysis of PGs

Before proceeding with the analysis of PGs, we will first sketch our assumptions concerning the analysis of of wh-movement. The elementary tree sets required are given in Figure 2. We represent local *wh*-extraction in the matrix clause as a tree-internal movement on the syntax side. We assume a syntactic constraint on the moved substitution site at the specifier of CP requiring a *wh*-phrase. However, there is no semantic consequence associated with this movement: the semantic components of the matrix clause are as expected under the split scope tree analysis: arguments are substituted into a scope component that includes lambda operators that bind variables in the argument position of the predicate.[1] The semantic effect of *wh*-extraction derives from the tree set associated with the wh-phrase, which has the same basic form as a generalized quantifier. For the proper names, we are using simple type e interpretations in the interests of space, though nothing crucially hinges on avoiding a GQ analysis of these nominals as well. To derive a simple case of clause-bound wh-movement, such as *Which papers did Bill file?*, on the syntax side of the derivation, the DP *Bill* will substitute into the specifier of TP subject position, and the wh-phrase *which papers* will substitute into the specifier of CP. The semantic side will proceed as is standard for sentences involving quantifiers: the wh-phrase's tree set will substitute and adjoin into the scope component of the *file* set, while the e-type tree associated with *Bill* will substitute into the higher substitution site. This will yield a two part derived tree set, which combines together at the conclusion of the derivation.

To derive a PG-containing sentence, such as (5), we will make use of a synchronous multi-component tree set for the adjunct clause shown on the bottom of Figure 2. This tree set has two complications relative to the split-scope adjunct represented shown above in Figure 1. On the syntax side, because this sentence involves extraction, the object position of the verb in the adjunct clause is filled by a trace. However, because the antecedent for this trace is not within this elementary tree, we represent the antecedent via a "degenerate" DP tree, into which the filler of this gap will ultimately

---

[1]Note that the VP-adjoined adverbial modifier is constrained via link $\boxed{3}$ to take a scope position above the abstractor for the object, but below the subject. We return to the reason for this assumption below.

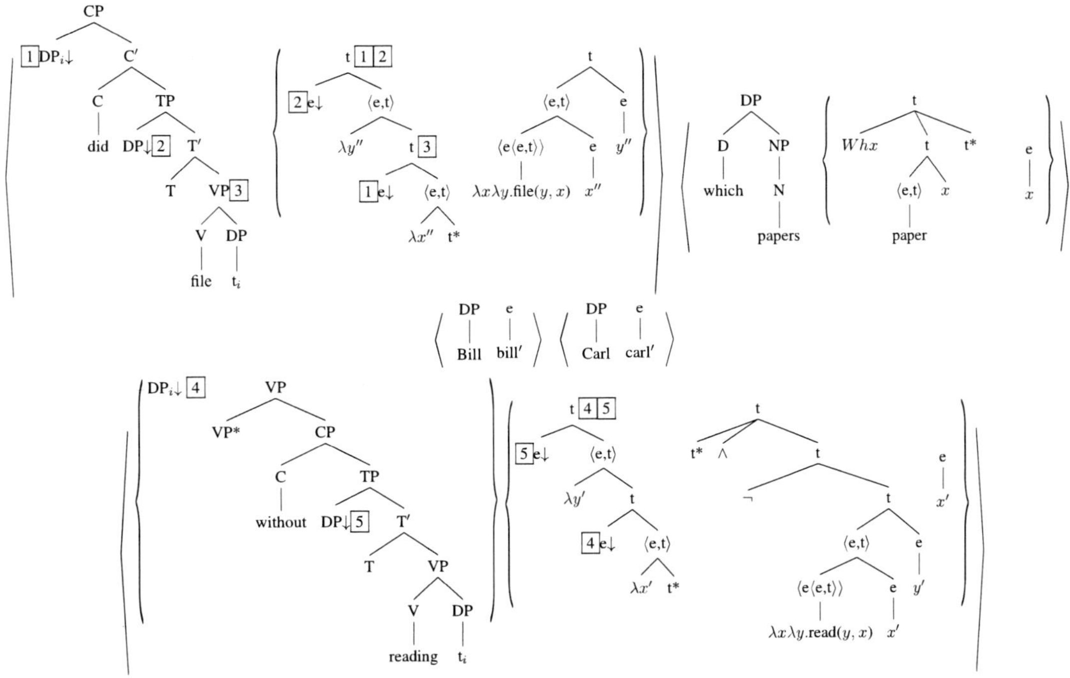

Figure 2: Elementary trees for (5)

substitute. On the semantic side, we follow the assumption made in the previous paragraph concerning the semantics of wh-movement, namely that it is not encoded in the tree of the predicate taking the wh-argument. In this case, however, the antecedent of the gap is not present in the same syntactic elementary tree, and consequently is not syntactically local. We take this to be an indication that this extraction can only be licensed in the context of another licensing gap. We encode that requirement semantically, by introducing an additional e-type variable in the semantic tree set, which will need to combine in the same domain as the adjunct.

To derive (5), we follow an analysis that is reminiscent of the sideward movement analysis in Hornstein and Nunes (2002) and Nunes (2004). Under this analysis, the *wh*-phrase originates in the adjunct (island) clause, moves to the argument position of the matrix predicate, and then on to the canonical position for wh-phrases, specifier of CP. This analysis directly accounts for the first of the PG puzzles mentioned above: a single wh-phrase can bind multiple gaps, since that phrase moves through both gap positions. Under the TAG version of this idea, we begin by combining the *without reading* adjunct tree set with both of its ar-

guments: the *Carl* DP, which substitutes into the subject position, and the wh-phrase *which papers*, which substitutes into the degenerate DP component. In the semantics, the unique e component of *Carl* will substitute into the higher substitution site of the scope tree; the components of the *wh*-phrase will combine tree-locally into the same adjunct scope tree, the scope component adjoining to the root of the adjunct's scope tree, and the e component substituting into the lower substitution position. The derived tree set is shown in Figure 3.

This derived MCS now combines tree-locally with the matrix predicate's elementary tree, not only modifying the predicate, but also filling the argument position of the moved DP in the syntax, and saturating its e-type substitution node in the semantics. This semantic combination is fully tree-local with all components of the adjunct combining into the scope tree for the matrix predicate, bringing along the binder of the *wh*-variable. Following the constraint that the two t-recursive components of the adjunct MCS must combine at the interior t node of the matrix clause scope tree, there is only one possible result where all variables are properly bound, shown in Figure 4.

As noted above, our analysis is similar to the sideward movement analysis in Minimalism, treat-

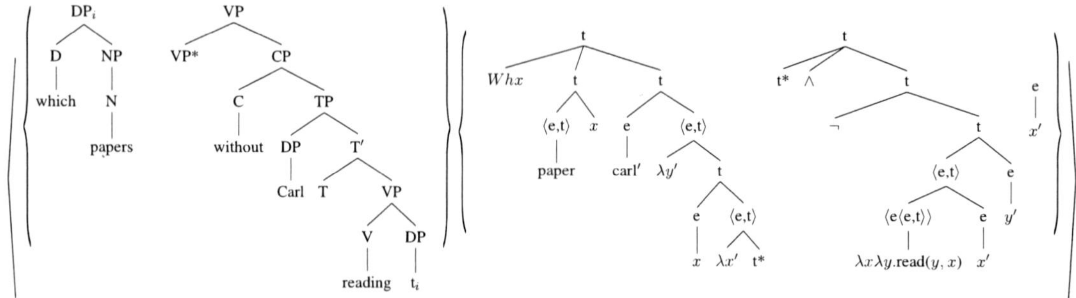

Figure 3: Derived tree set for adjunct clause in (5)

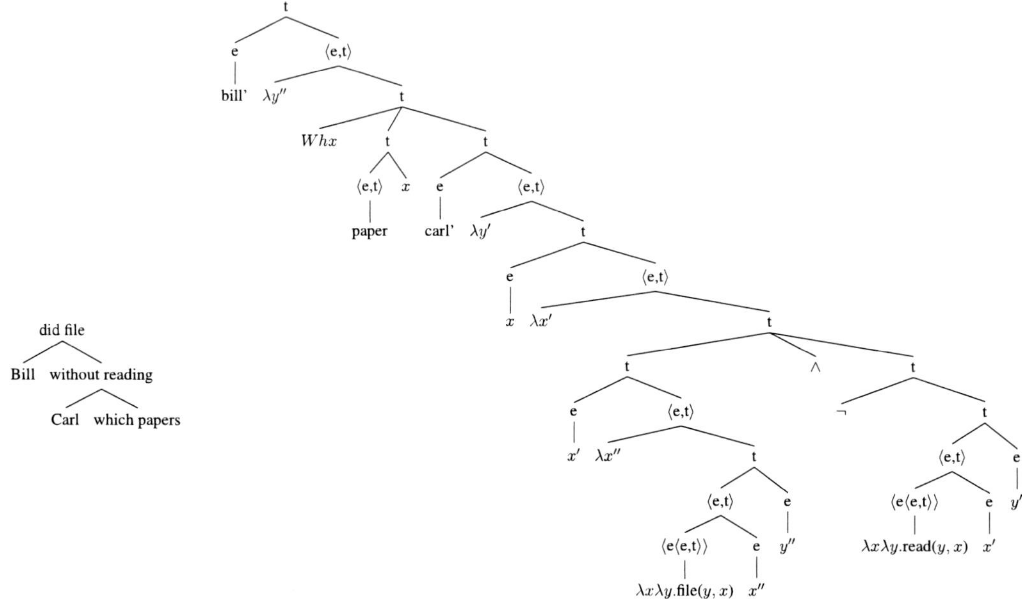

Figure 4: Derivation tree and derived semantic tree for (5)

ing the *wh*-phrase as combining directly with the adjunct, with the degenerate DP node in our syntactic MCS for the adjunct simulating the movement. However, the semantic form is quite simple, with the extra variable going from the adjunct to the matrix clause in reminiscent of the treatment of control into embedded clauses proposed by Nesson (2009), where one clause's elementary tree provides the arguments for another. Adopting this mechanism allows us to dispense with the need to posit null operators and the operation of chain composition, as proposed in Chomsky (1986) and widely assumed in more recent work on the topic. This flexibility is derived largely from the treatment of *wh*-dependencies as inherently quantificational, with no semantic effect on the predicates within which extraction takes place.

It is interesting to note that Nesson's treatment of control, which can be thought of as the inspiration for this this treatment of PGs, does not generalize to cases of adjunct control, as in examples like (7). The problem concerns the directionality of the derivation: if the adjunct adjoins into the matrix clause, the adjunct elementary tree set can provide arguments for the matrix, as it does in our PG analysis. However, the reverse cannot happen: the matrix clause cannot provide arguments which substitute into the adjunct.[2] To analyze adjunct control, then, we are forced to depart from an analysis where the two dependencies run in opposite directions, with control from the matrix into

---

[2] This might be possible if we relax constraints on TAG derivations, to permit flexible composition (Joshi et al., 2008; Chiang and Scheffler, 2008). We put this possibility aside here.

116

the adjunct for the subject but movement of the *wh*-object from the adjunct into the matrix clause. We see two possible resolutions of this conflict. On one of these, we would treat adjunct control in a manner similar to parasitic gaps, with the putative controller forming part of the adjunct clause's tree set. This would in essence involve an adoption of sidewards movement for adjunct control, as proposed by Hornstein (1999). Alternatively, we could embrace a semantic treatment of adjunct control. By taking the adverbial modifier's interpretation to be of type $\langle e,t \rangle$, with abstraction over the subject argument, combining such a predicate with the matrix VP, also of type $\langle e,t \rangle$, via predicate modification, we get the effect of subject control, as both predicates with be asserted to hold of the same entity.[3] We will not choose among these options in the remainder of the paper.

Before closing this section, we note that the present analysis accounts for another constraint on PG constructions, specifically their limitation to argument *wh*-words:

(9)   a.   * Why did you leave ___ when Bill
       walked in ___$_p$?

   b.   ?* with whom did you drive to school
      ___ before going to the concert ___$_p$??

While the sentence in (9a) may be understood as asking for the reason leaving at the time of Bill's arrival, there is no way to interpret it as including a PG, where the same reason would also hold for Bill's walking in. The same applies in (9b), where the question can ask about companions on the way to school, but not both going to the school and the concert. The contrast here follows because the adverbial clause tree set will not have the degenerate DP node into which the adjunct wh-phrase can substitute, as the position for such an adjunct is not licensed by the thematic structure of the verb in the adverbial.

4   Locality in Parasitic Gaps

The multi-component analysis set forth in the previous section allows extraction from an adjunct in a way that is not possible with non-multi-component TAG. Indeed, the impossibility of such extraction had been used to provide support for the TAG treatment of extraction, as it derives island

constraints (Kroch, 1987; Frank, 2002). By granting ourselves this additional flexibility, we might worry that those results would fall away. Note, however, that there are substantial constraints on the use of such an island-violating derivation. First of all, the syntactic tree set containing the degenerate DP node will be constrained to substitute into an A′-position, as it is the host of a wh-phrase, meaning that it will be possible only in the presence of an instance of extraction. Furthermore, under the assumption that all multi-component combination is tree-local, we will ensure that the parasitic gap dependency is local to the licensing dependency. That is, the parasitic gap-containing adjunct must combine tree-locally with the clause inside of which the licensing extraction holds, in order for the substitution of the wh-phrase and adjunction of the modifier to take place in a tree-local fashion.

Note that this analysis does not prevent us from deriving examples in which the parasitic gap occurs within an embedded clause in the adjunct.

(10)   Which papers did Bill file ___ [without
      believing that Carl had read ___$_p$]?

To do so, we need only adjoin a C′-recursive tree headed by the verb *believe* into the adjunct tree, thereby "stretching" the PG dependency across the clausal boundary. If the PG is contained within an island (within the adjunct), no such derivation is possible. And indeed it has been known since Kayne (1983) that such instances of PGs are impossible:

(11)   a.   * Which papers did Bill file ___ without
      out Carl meeting [the guy who wrote
      ___$_p$?] (Complex NP)

   b.   * Which papers should we read ___ be-
      fore [talking about ___$_p$] becomes dif-
      ficult ? (Subject Island)

Our analysis predicts this pattern exactly.

There is however a kind of case that poses a potential difficulty for our analysis. This involves an example like (12), where an additional clause intervenes between the licensing gap and the surface position of the wh-phrase.

(12)   **Which papers** did you predict that I
      would file ___ without reading ___$_p$?

This example is ambiguous, with readings possible where *without* is modifying either *predict* or *reject*, and the PG is licensed in both cases. These

---

[3]Nissenbaum (1998) makes use of predicate modification in his semantic treatment of adjunct parasitic gaps, but uses it to ensure identity of the binders of the licensing gap and PG.

readings can be easily diagnosed by the controller of the adjunct clause: when it is *you*, attachment is high, and when it is *I*, attachment is low.[4]

Using the standard TAG analysis of successive cyclic wh-movement, the lower reading can be derived straightforwardly. As before, the adjunct-wh complex (corresponding to the lexical material *which papers* and *without reading*) is adjoined to the embedded clause's elementary tree (headed by *file*), as does the matrix clause (represented by the trees in Figure 5), at C′, thereby displacing the wh-phrase from its position at the edge of the embedded clause.

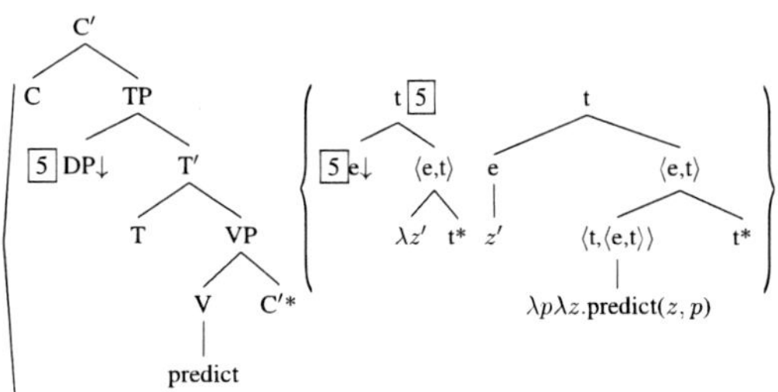

Figure 5: Elementary trees for *predict* (low attachment of adjunct)

Deriving the lower attachment of (12) is considerably less straightforward. Doing so using the same set of trees would require a non-local derivation: While the adjunct would need to be adjoined into the matrix clause's tree set, the wh-phrase, and associated variable in the semantics would need to composed into the embedded clause's tree set. In order to avoid such non-locality, we make use of the derivation of wh-extraction proposed in Kroch (1989) and Frank and Kroch (1995) to analyze cases of 'long movement' out of wh-islands. Specifically, we assume the alternative multi-component sets for the embedding predicate *predict*, shown in Figure 6. On the syntactic side, the tree is extended to a full CP (as opposed to C′), including a substitution site for the *wh*-phrase.

An immediate concern is that this substitution node appears to violate TAG version of the theta criterion (Frank, 2002), according to which all substitution nodes must be part of a chain that receives a θ-role. However, we note the exceptional nature of this position, as defined by the links in the tree. Unlike the case in Figure 2, where the ad-

junct is not required to fill the CP specifier (though it is able to do so), here the links are constructed such that it must do so (cf. the co-indexation of the specifier of CP and the VP). This means that the phrase substituting here must come from an adjunct in which it will already have received a role. Further constraints on the usage of this tree set are seen on the semantic side: the scope part of *predict* has been extended to provide a substitution site for the variable associated with the new DP, though instead of binding an argument of *predict*, the binder binds a type e tree in the new semantic MCS. On both the syntactic and semantic sides of the derivation, tree local combination into the *file* tree will complete the derivation. Because the *predict* tree set has an extra DP node and an extra variable, it will saturate an argument position in the clause it embeds, it guarantees a licensing gap for the PG it supports. As with the earlier cases, we see all variable dependencies moving in parallel through the derivation. The adjunct passes both the controlling subject and the *wh*-phrase through to the matrix clause via adjoining, and when the matrix clause adjoins into the embedded clause, it passes the *wh*-dependency on again.

As we already noted above, multi-component tree sets like the one in Figure 6 were first proposed in the analysis of extractions from (weak) wh-islands, and were taken to be the only path for such a derivation in a language like English where the lower CP could not host multiple wh-phrases in its specifier(s). If this is correct, our current analysis makes the prediction that instances of long movement will only permit the high attachment of the PG-containing adjunct. Frank and Kroch (1994) argued that this was correct for extraction out of DP, on the basis of examples like (13a), and we believe that it is also the case for extraction from (some) wh-islands:[5]

(13) a. Which building did the mayor$_i$ report on [Trump's$_j$ renovation of ___] [after

---

[4]We note that either of the treatments of control sketched above correctly capture this correlation between locus of attachment and controller.

[5]Frank (1991) reaches a different conclusion concerning extraction from wh-islands, on the basis of examples like the following:

(1) Which car$_i$ did Bill$_j$ understand how the mechanic$_k$ had fixed ___ [without PRO$_{j/k}$ dismantling ___$_p$]

This example appears to permit the lower attachment interpretation to a considerably greater degree than (13b). We do not at present have an explanation for why the presence of an argument as opposed to adjunct wh-phrase in the embedded specifier of CP should lead to this difference. We leave this for future work.

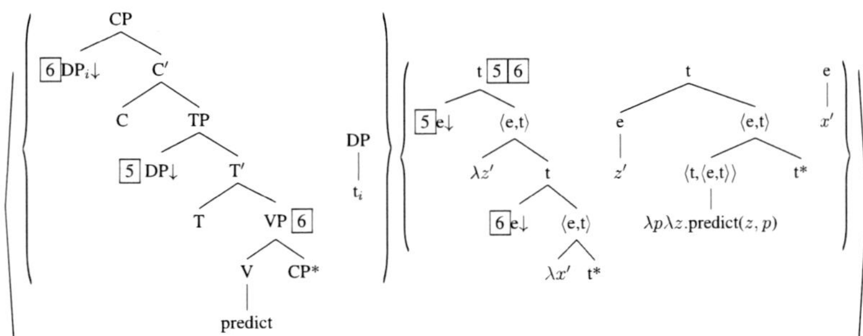

Figure 6: Elementary trees for *predict* (high attachment of adjunct)

PRO$_{i/*j}$ previously abandoning ___$_p$]?

b. Which car$_i$ did Bill$_j$ understand who$_k$ had fixed ___ [without PRO$_{j/*k}$ dismantling ___$_p$]

Such contrasts provide support for the treatment of high attachment we have provided, as well as for the analysis of PGs that we have presented.

5 Anti-C-Command and Beyond

We turn finally to another property that has been attributed to parasitic gap constructions. In the original paper on the topic, Engdahl contrasts cases like (7) with the anomalous (14).

(14) * **Which article** ___ got filed before Carl read ___$_p$?

Engdahl argues that the crucial distinction between these cases concerns the fact that the licensing gap in the well-formed case does not c-command the parasitic gap, whereas it does so in the ill-formed case. This anti-command condition has been widely assumed to be a restriction on parasitic gaps. Our present analysis captures this quite simply by forcing the adjunct's semantic content to adjoin into the matrix clause's scope tree at a position which can bind objects, but not subjects. Rather than building anti-c-command into the syntax, here we are deriving the same result from the semantics.

We also note that our approach captures another contrast relating to the use of PG constructions noted by Phillips (2006):

(15) a. **Which car** did the attempt to fix ___$_p$ ultimately destroy ___?

b. * **Which platform** did the reporter that criticized ___$_p$ ultimately endorse ___?

In neither case does the licensing gap c-command the PG, and yet there is a clear and strong contrast in judgments. While space prohibits a full analysis, the prior discussion provides the necessary insights. Though an STAG analysis of nominalizations is well outside the scope of this paper, it is plausible that *to fix* should be assimilable to the kind of infinitival adjunct present in (7). In contrast, in the case of the relative clause, our account is going to mirror the account for (4) where locality of the composition of the relative clause will be key. Of course, here we are dealing with a covert contrast not derived from overt movement, so the better analogy is to note that just as the relative clause is a scope island (versus the control case), the relative clause here remains a legitimate island for the parasitic gap.

In closing the paper with these examples, we note that parasitic gap constructions provide an ideal example of the theoretical possibilities afforded by STAG. The pairing of synchronized derivations does nothing to weaken the power of existing semantic constraints on a derivation, but does make it possible to allow semantics an equal opportunity to rule out syntactically well-formed derivations. This is a welcome result as it opens up new analyses for cases where seemingly well-formed syntactic derivations are ruled out based on a semantic contrast.

Acknowledgments

We thank Mark Steedman and the anonymous TAG+ reviewers for their helpful comments which helped us significantly in the development of this analysis.

References

Emmon Bach, Eloise Jelinek, Angelika Kratzer, and Barbara H. Partee, editors. 1995. *Quantification in Natural Languages*. Springer.

David Chiang and Tatjana Scheffler. 2008. Flexible composition and delayed tree-locality. In *Proceedings of the Ninth International Workshop on Tree Adjoining Grammars and Related Formalisms (TAG+9)*, pages 17–24, Tübingen.

Noam Chomsky. 1982. *Some Concepts and Consequences of the Theory of Government and Binding*. MIT Press, Cambridge, MA.

Noam Chomsky. 1986. *Barriers*. MIT Press, Cambridge, MA.

Elisabet Engdahl. 1983. Parasitic gaps. *Linguistics and Philosophy*, 6:5–34.

Nick Evans. 1995. A-quantifiers and scope in Mayali. In Bach et al. (Bach et al., 1995), pages 207–270.

Robert Frank and Anthony Kroch. 1994. Nominal structures and structural recursion. *Computational Intelligence*, 10(4):453–470.

Robert Frank and Anthony Kroch. 1995. Generalized transformations and the theory of grammar. *Studia Linguistica*, 49(2):103–151.

Robert Frank and Dennis Ryan Storoshenko. 2012. The shape of elementary trees and scope possibilities in STAG. In *Proceedings of the 11th International Workshop on Tree Adjoinining Grammars and Related Formalisms (TAG+11)*, Paris.

Robert Frank. 1991. Parasitic gaps and locality conditions. In *Proceedings of the 27th Regional Meeting of the Chicago Linguistics Society*, pages 167–181. University of Chicago.

Robert Frank. 2002. *Phrase Structure Composition and Syntactic Dependencies*. Cambridge, MA: MIT Press.

Norbert Hornstein and Jario Nunes. 2002. On asymmetries between parastici gap and across-the-board constructions. *Syntax*, 5(1):26–54.

Norbert Hornstein. 1999. Movement and control. *Linguistic Inquiry*, 30(1):69–96.

Aravind K. Joshi, Laura Kallmeyer, and Maribel Romero. 2008. Flexible composition in LTAG: Quantifier scope and inverse linking. In Harry Bunt and Reinhard Muskens, editors, *Computing Meaning*, volume 3, pages 233–256. Springer, Dordrecht.

Laura Kallmeyer and Aravind K. Joshi. 1999. Factoring predicate argument and scope semantics: Underspecified semantics with LTAG. In Paul Dekker, editor, *Proceedings of the 12th Amsterdam Colloquium*, pages 169–174, Amsterdam. Institute for Logic, Language and Computation.

Richard S. Kayne. 1983. Connectedness. *Linguistic Inquiry*, 14(2):223–249.

Anthony Kroch and Aravind K. Joshi. 1985. The linguistic relevance of tree adjoining grammar. Technical Report MS-CS-85-16, Department of Computer and Information Sciences, University of Pennsylvania.

Anthony Kroch. 1987. Unbounded dependencies and subjacency in a tree adjoining grammar. In Alexis Manaster-Ramer, editor, *The Mathematics of Language*, pages 143–172. John Benjamins, Amsterdam.

Anthony Kroch. 1989. Asymmetries in long distance extraction in a tree adjoining grammar. In Mark Baltin and Anthony Kroch, editors, *Alternative Conceptions of Phrase Structure*, pages 66–98. University of Chicago Press, Chicago, IL.

Rebecca Nesson and Stuart Shieber. 2008. Synchronous vector tree adjoining grammars for syntax and semantics: Control verbs, relative clauses, and inverse linking. In *Proceedings of the Ninth International Workshop on Tree Adjoining Grammars and Related Formalisms*, pages 73–80.

Rebecca Nesson. 2009. *Synchronous and Multicomponent Tree-Adjoining Grammars: Complexity, Algorithms, and Linguistic Applications*. Ph.D. thesis, Harvard University.

Jon Nissenbaum. 1998. Derived predicates and the interpretation of parasitic gaps. In Kimary Shahin, Susan Blake, and Eun-Sook Kim, editors, *Proceedings of the 17th West Coast Conference on Formal Linguistics*, pages 507–521. Stanford: CSLI.

Jairo Nunes. 2004. *Linearization of Chains and Sideward Movement*. MIT Press, Cambridge, MA.

Karen Petronio. 1995. Bare noun phrases, verbs and quantification in ASL. In Bach et al. (Bach et al., 1995), pages 603–618.

Colin Phillips. 2006. The real-time status of island phenomena. *Language*, 82(4):795–823.

Author Index

Association for Computational Linguistics
209 N. Eighth Street
Stroudsburg, Pennsylvania 18360

ISBN 978-1-5108-2683-0